Korean in Plain English

Korean
in
Plain English

Boye De Mente

Printed on recyclable paper

PASSPORT BOOKS
a division of *NTC Publishing Group*
Lincolnwood, Illinois USA

1996 Printing

Published by Passport Books, a division of
NTC Publishing Group, 4255 West Touhy Avenue,
Lincolnwood (Chicago), Illinois 60646-1975.
Manufactured in the United States of America.
Library of Congress Catalog Card Number: 86-62723

5 6 7 8 9 ML 9

Contents

Preface vii

(An English-Korean wordlist of more than 1,200 words and expressions, arranged alphabetically, with sample sentences in English and Korean)

Changing Fahrenheit to Centigrade   245

Preface

Learning a New Language

Korean is often described as a unique language, meaning that it resembles no other language spoken in the world today. It certainly does *not* resemble any of the so-called Romance languages with which most Westerners are familiar, but some similarities exist between Korean and Japanese, including their structures and a large number of words that are either the same or nearly the same. Also as in Japanese, Korean words consist of a specific number of syllables formed by combining vowel and consonant sounds.

As when learning any new language, do not compare it to your own native tongue, but accept it as it is and go on from there. The key to learning a "foreign" language is the right attitude—and avoiding the pitfall of getting "hung up" on psychological barriers.

The fastest way to develop the right attitude is to think of your new language as a mechanical device, devoid of cultural qualities. In that way, you will not be inhibited or embarrassed about using whatever words or sentences you have mastered. I know many people whose total vocabulary in a foreign language is less than 100 words. Nevertheless, they manage to communicate to an extraordinary degree and benefit tremendously from their limited knowledge.

As with so many other things, it is not *how much* Korean you know, but *how* you use what you know that counts. Just a few dozen words and sentences will greatly enhance your pleasures and options when you are in Korea or when you deal with people who speak Korean.

As in my *Japanese in Plain English*, I have taken liberties with a number of phonetic spellings, occasionally using such English words as *toe* and *way* instead of "pure" phonetics, just to make the pronunciation easier.

Boye De Mente
Seoul, Korea

Part One: The Korean Language

*K*oreans call their language *Hangugo* (Hahn-guu-go) and their writing system *Hangul* (Hahn-guul). Some scholars believe that Hangugo is distantly related to such Ural-Altaic languages as Mongolian and Finnish. The writing system was developed in relatively modern times. It was introduced in 1445 A.D. by King Sejong, who had commissioned a team of scholars to create a phonetic script for the Korean language. Prior to that time, educated Koreans (the privileged upper class) wrote with Chinese ideograms.

The new, simple Hangul script made it possible for the poor and less educated to learn how to read and write in just a few weeks. However, the upper class in Korea continued to use Chinese ideograms in their writing, and even today, Koreans often combine Chinese characters and Korean phonetic script when they write.

Many consider Hangul to be the most rational and practical of the world's writing systems, since it was deliberately devised by a team of scientific experts, as opposed to just developing. It is based on 24 phonetic symbols that are combined to make all the sounds in the Korean language. The complete alphabet consists of 140 syllables that are combinations of 10 vowel sounds and 14 consonant sounds.

The alphabet is often referred to as the *Ka-na-da* (Kah-nah-dah), after its first three syllables.

In *Korean in Plain English,* I want to help you learn to communicate quickly and easily in Korean, without having to learn a new "foreign" script.

Two challenges arise when learning to communicate in a new language: 1) acquiring the mechanical ability to pronounce the individual words so they will be understood and 2) remembering words as well as sentences so that you can say them at the proper time.

I have attempted to resolve the pronunciation problem for you by providing English phonetics for every Korean syllable and word appearing in this book. To pronounce a sound correctly, all you have to do is mimic the English phonetics.

Spoken Korean exhibits very little if any variation in pitch and has no accented syllables. When there is a pitch change, it is normally for emphasis—as in a question, a declaration, or a command.

Long vowels and short vowels exist in Korean, and, even though the Romanized spelling of two words may be the same, meanings will differ if one word has a short vowel and the other a long vowel. Consonants rather than vowels receive the primary stress, and there are frequent double consonants. But you don't have to be concerned at this time. These variations will be accounted for in the phonetics.

On numerous occasions, the pronunciation and therefore the spelling of Korean syllables change, depending on where they are in a word and what follows them. The best way to contend with this is simply to forget about it and learn each word or sentence as it is spoken, regardless of the spelling.

Honorifics also play a vital role in Korean speech, particularly when addressing someone who is older or a member of a higher social class. Some of the more important instances of honorific language are noted in the text.

Like Japanese, Korean has no particles (*the, a*). Singular and plural are usually not distinguished, and it is common to omit the subject (*you, him, they,* etc.) in a sentence when it is "understood." *Kamnikka?* (Kahm-nee-kkah?) "Are you, she, he they going? "*Kam-nida.* (Kahm-nee-dah) "I, she, they (am/is/are) going." There are no *f, v* or *z* sounds in Korean.

Consonants are pronounced very much as in English, but vowels have a more Spanish (or Japanese) sound.

In language learning it is essential that you practice out loud; that is, you must express words and sentences aloud, just as you would in actual speech. This not only attunes your hearing and understanding, it also provides the mechanical exercise you need to pronounce words correctly. By *mechanical*, I mean the way you move your tongue, lips, and mouth to make the proper sounds.

Repetition is the final secret of language learning. Repeat each word and sentence until you can say it automatically, without having to think.

The Romanization of Korean (using our familiar *ABCs* to write out Korean words) poses a special problem. There are two (or more!) ways of spelling some words, and it often seems that each Korean has his or her own way of Romanizing the language because of variations in pronunciation. I have taken considerable liberties with the more common spelling styles in an effort to make the words easier to recognize and pronounce.

In Korean script, words are commonly run together ("likethis"). This practice also carries over into Romanization, making it much more difficult for the

foreign student of the language to recognize individual words. I have also played fast and loose with this
custom (no doubt to the chagrin of traditional lin-
guists) in an effort to facilitate the task of basic communication.

Pronunciation Guide to Vowels

A	**Ya**	**Ŏ**	**Yŏ**	**O**
Ah	Yah	Ah	Yah	Oh
Yo	**U**	**Yu**	**Ŭ**	**I**
Yoh	Uu	Yuu	Oo	Ee

Pronunciation Guide to Multiple Vowels

Ae	**Yae**	**E**	**Ye**	**Oe**
Aeh	Yaeh	Eh	Yeh	Oeh
Wa	**Wŏ**	**Wae**	**We**	**Wi**
Wah	Wah	Wae	Weh	Wee

Pronunciation Guide for Syllables

Ka	**Kya**	**Kŏ**	**Kyŏ**	**Ko**
Kah	Kyah	Kah	Kyah	Koh
Kyo	**Ku**	**Kyu**	**Kŭ**	**Ki**
Kyoh	Kuu	Kyuu	Kuu	Kee
Na	**Nya**	**Nŏ**	**Nyŏ**	**No**
Nah	Nyah	Noo	Nyoe	No

Note that the third syllable in the top line (Ŏ) is pronounced
more like an "a" than an "o". For example *oje* (yesterday) is
pronounced *ah-jay*. *Odiso* (where) is pronounced *ah-dee-soe*. I
have attempted to account for this factor in the phonetics fol-
lowing each word and sentence.

Nyo Nyoh	**Nu** Nuu	**Nyu** Nyuu	**Nŭ** Nuu	**Ni** Nee
Da Dah	**Dya** Dyah	**Dŏ** Doe	**Dyŏ** Dyoe	**Do** Doe
Dyo Dyoe	**Du** Duu	**Dyu** Dyuu	**Dŭ** Due	**Di** Dee
Ra Rah	**Rya** Ryah	**Rŏ** Roe	**Ryŏ** Ryoe	**Ro** Roe
Ryo Ryoe	**Ru** Ruu	**Ryu** Ryuu	**Rŭ** Rue	**Ri** Ree
Ma Mah	**Mya** Myah	**Mŏ** Moe	**Myŏ** Myoe	**Mo** Moe
Myo Myoe	**Mu** Muu	**Muu** Myuu	**Mŭ** Mue	**Mi** Me
Ba Bah	**Bya** Byah	**Bŏ** Boe	**Byŏ** Byoe	**Bo** Boe
Byo Byoe	**Bu** Buu	**Byu** Byuu	**Bŭ** Bue	**Bi** Bee
Sa Sah	**Sya** Syah	**Sŏ** Soe	**Syŏ** Syoe	**So** Soe
Syo Syoe	**Su** Suu	**Syu** Syuu	**Sŭ** Sue	**Si** She
A Ah	**Ya** Yah	**Ŏ** Ohh	**Yŏ** Yeh	**O** Oh
Yo Yoe	**U** Yuu	**Yu** Yuu	**Ŭ** Uu	**I** Ee
Ja Jah	**Jya** Jyah	**Jŏ** Joe	**Jyŏ** Jyoe	**Jo** Joe
Jyo Jyoe	**Ju** Juu	**Jyu** Juu	**Jŭ** Juu	**Ji** Jee
Cha Chah	**Chya** Chyah	**Chŏ** Choe	**Chyŏ** Chyoe	**Cho** Choe

Chyo Chyoe	**Chu** Chuu	**Chyu** Chyuu	**Chŭ** Chuu	**Chi** Che
Ka Kah	**Kya** Kyah	**Kŏ** Koe	**Kyŏ** Kyoe	**Ko** Koe
Kyo Kyoe	**Kuu** Kuu	**Kyu** Kyuu	**Kŭ** Kuu	**Ki** Kee
Ta Tah	**Tya** Tyah	**Tŏ** Toe	**Tyŏ** Tyoe	**To** Toe
Tyo Tyoe	**Tu** Tuu	**Tyu** Tyuu	**Tŭ** Tue	**Ti** Tee
Pa Pah	**Pya** Pyah	**Po** Poe	**Pyŏ** Pyoe	**Po** Poe
Pyo Pyoe	**Pu** Puu	**Pyu** Pyuu	**Pŭ** Puu	**Pi** Pee
Ha Hah	**Hya** Hyah	**Hŏ** Hoe	**Hyŏ** Hyoe	**Ho** Hoe
Hyo Hyoe	**Hu** Huu	**Hyu** Hyuu	**Hŭ** Hue	**Hi** Hee

Some Basic Vocabulary

I
Na (Nah)

Me
Naege (Nay-gay)
Also: **Narul** (Nah-rule)

You
Tangshin [*polite*] (Tahng-sheen)
Also: **No** (Noo)

Him
Kuege (Kuu-eh-gay)
Also: **Kurul** (Kuu-rule)

Her
Kunyoege (Kuun-yo-eh-gay)
Also: **Kunnyorul** (Kuun-yoe-rule)

They
Kudul (Kuu-dule)

Yes
Ye (Yeh)
Also: **Ne** (Neh)

No
Anio (Ah-nyoh)
Also: (Ah-nee-oh)

This
Igot (Ee-gaht)

That
Jogot (Jah-gaht)

When
Onje (Ahn-jeh)

Why
Wae (Way)

What
Muot (Muu-aht)

Where
Odiso (Ah-dee-soe)

Who
Nugu (Nuu-guu)

Today
Onul (Oh-nule)

Morning
Ach'im (Ah-cheem)

Afternoon
Ohu (Oh-huu)

Tonight / This evening
Onul-chonyok / Onul-bbam
(Oh-nule-chone-yoak / Oh-nule-bahm)

Last night
Oje bbam (Oh-jay bahm)

Tomorrow
Naeil (Nay-eel)

Tomorrow morning
Naeil ach'im (Nay-eel ah-cheem)

Yesterday
Oje (Ah-jeh)

This week
I chuil (Ee chuu-eel)

Next week
Nae chuil / Ta um chuil
(Nay chuu-eel / Tah-oom chuu-eel)

Days of the Week
(**Yoil** means "day")

   Sunday **Ilyoil** (Eel-yoh-eel)
   Monday **Wolyoil** (Wole-yoh-eel)
   Tuesday **Hwayoil** (Wha-yoh-eel)
   Wednesday **Suyoil** (Suu-yoh-eel)
   Thursday **Mokyoil** (Mo-kyoh-eel)
   Friday **Kumyoil** (Kume-yoh-eel)
   Saturday **Toyoil** (Toe-yoh-eel)

Months of the Year

   January **Ilwol** (Eeel-wole)
   February **Iwol** (Ee-wole)
   March **Samwol** (Sahm-wole)

April **Sawol** (Sah-wole)
May **Owol** (Oh-wole)
June **Yuwol** (Yu-wahl)
July **Ch'ilwol** (Cheel-wahl)
August **P'alwol** (Pahl-wole)
September **Kuwol** (Kuu-wole)
October **Shiwol** (She-wahl)
November **Shibilwol** (She-beel-wahl)
December **Shibiwol** (She-bee-wahl)

Seasons

Spring **Pom** (Pome)
Summer **Yorum** (Yuh-rume)
Autumn **Kaul** (Kah-ule)
Winter **Kyoul** (Kyah-uule)

Numbers

Two sets of words exist for counting in Korean. One is native Korean, while the other derives from Chinese. The Chinese system is the most common, particularly after the number *10*. When counting things in successive order (such as days, money, mileage, and so on), the Chinese system also prevails.

The Korean numbers from one through ten are:

1 **Hana** (Hah-nah)
2 **Tul** (Tule)
3 **Set** (Sehtt)
4 **Net** (Nehtt)
5 **Tasot** (Tah-saht)
6 **Yosot** (Yoe-saht)
7 **Ilgop** (Eel-gope)
8 **Yodol** (Yah-dahl)
9 **Ahop** (Ah-hope)
10 **Yol** (Yahl)

The Chinese-derived numerals are:

1 **Il** (Eel)
2 **I** (Ee)
3 **Sam** (Sahm)
4 **Sa** (Sah)
5 **O** (Oh)
6 **Yuk** (Yuke)
7 **Ch'il** (Cheel)
8 **P'al** (Pahl)
9 **Ku** (Kuu)
10 **Sip** (Ship)
11 **Sipil** (She-beel)
12 **Sipi** (She-bee)
13 **Sipsam** (Ship-sahm)
14 **Sipsa** (Ship-sah)
15 **Sipo** (She-boh)
16 **Sipyuk** (Ship-yuke)
17 **Sipch'il** (Ship-cheel)
18 **Sipp'al** (Ship-pahl)
19 **Sipgu** (Ship-guu)
20 **Isip** (Ee-ship)
21 **Isipil** (Ee-she-beel)
22 **Isipi** (Ee-she-bee)
23 **Isipsam** (Ee-ship-sahm)
24 **Isipsa** (Ee-ship-sah)
25 **Isipo** (Ee-she-boh)
26 **Isipyruk** (Ee-ship-yuk)
27 **Isipch'il** (Ee-ship-cheel)
28 **Isipp'al** (Ee-ship-pahl)
29 **Isipgu** (Ee-ship-guu)
30 **Samsip** (Sahm-ship)
40 **Sasip** (Sah-ship)
50 **Osip** (Oh-ship)
60 **Yuksip** (Yuke-ship)
70 **Ch'ilsip** (Cheel-ship)
80 **P'alsip** (Pahl-ship)

   90 **Kusip** (Kuu-ship)
  100 **Baek** (Bake)
  101 **Baekil** (Bake-eel)
  102 **Baeki** (Bake-ee)
  200 **Ibaek** (Ee-bake)
  300 **Sambaek** (Sahm-bake)
  400 **Sabaek** (Sah-bake)
 1,000 **Chon** (Chahn)
10,000 **Man** (Mahn)
20,000 **Iman** (E-mahn)
30,000 **Samman** (Sahm-mahn)
40,000 **Saman** (Sah-mahn)
50,000 **Oman** (Oh-mahn)

Telling Time

When talking about time (minutes, hours) in Korean, it is common to use the Korean-based numbers. Time, as in "What time is it?" is *shi* (she). Time in the sense of the hour is *shigan* (she-gahn). In the sense of a period of time, it is *kigan* (kee-gahn). When used in the sense of occasion (some other time), it is *ttae* (ttay). Minute is *pun* (poon) or *bun* (boon).

 1 o'clock **Hanshi** (Hahn she)
 2 o'clock **Tu shi** (Tuu she)
 3 o'clock **Se shi** (Say she)
 4 o'clock **Ne shi** (Nay she)
 5 o'clock **Tasot shi** (Tah-saht-she)
 6 o'clock **Yosot shi** (Yoe-saht-she)
 7 o'clock **Ilgop shi** (Eel-gope she)
 8 o'clock **Yodol shi** (Yoe-doel she)
 9 o'clock **Ahop shi** (Ah-hope she)
10 o'clock **Yol shi** (Yole she)
11 o'clock **Yolhan shi** (Yahl-hahn she)

12 o'clock **Yoltu shi** (Yole-tuu-she)
A.M. **Ojon** (Oh-jahn)
P.M. **Ohu** (Oh-huu)
Night **Pam** (Pahm)

Five minutes after four.
Ne shi obun.
(Nay she oh-boon)

Fifteen minutes after five
Tasot shi shibo bun.
(Tah-soet she she-boe boon)

Six-thirty.
Yosot shi samship pun.
(Yoe-soet she sahm-ship-poon)

Six-forty.
Yoso shi saship pun.
(Yoe-so she sah-ship-poon)

What time is it?
Myot shi imnikka?
(Myaht she eem-nee-kkah?)

It is one o'clock.
Han shi imnida.
(Hahn she eem-nee-dah)

It is two-thirty.
Tu shi sam-sip pun imnida.
(Tuu she sahm-ship poon eem-nee-dah)

It is a quarter to four.
Ne shi shibobun jeon imnida.
(Nay she she-boe-boon jahn eem-nee-dah)

It is seven p.m.
Ohu ilgop shi imnida.
(Oh-huu eel-gope she eem-nee-dah)

Greetings and Farewells

One basic greeting in Korean (along with an abbreviated form) takes care of "how do you do," "how are you," "good morning," "good afternoon," "good evening," and "hello":

Annyong hashim nikka?
(Ahn-nyong hah-sheem nee-kkah?)
or
Annyong haseyo? (Ahn-nyong hah-say-yoe?)

To respond properly, repeat the same phrase to the person who greets you, but add *ne* (nay) to the beginning (*ne, annyong hashim nikka?*)

Good night.
Annyong hi chumushipshio.
(Ahn-nyong he chuu-muu-ship-she-oh)

Goodbye.
Annyonghi kashipshio.
(Ahn-nyong-he kah-ship-she-oh)
Also: **Annyong!** (Ahn-nyong!)

See you later.
Tto poepket ssumnida.
(Toe pep-kay sume-nee-dah)
Also:
Tto mannapshida.
(Toe mahn-nahp-she-dah)

See you soon
Kot poepket ssumnida.
(Kote pep-kay sume-nee-dah)

Have a good time.
Jul kopge chinaeseyo.
(Jull kop-gay chee-nay-say-yoe)

Have a nice trip./Bon Voyage.
Julgoun yohaeng-ul haseyo.
(Jull-gah-uun yah-hang-ule hah-say-yoe)

Good morning, Mr. Kim.
Kim sonsaeng nim annyong hashimnikka.
(Kim sun-sang-neem, ahn-nyong hah-sheem-nee-kkah)
Also:
Kim Kun, annyong hashimnikka.
(Kim Koon, ahn-nyong hah-sheem-nee-kah)

How do you do, Miss Kang.
Kang yang, annyong hashimnikka.
(Khang yhang, ahn-nyong hah-sheem-nee-kkah)

Hello (when answering the telephone).
Yoboseyo!
(Yoe-boe-say-yoe!)

Names

Keeping people's names straight can be confusing in Korea, because Koreans have so few family names at their disposal. It seems that well over half the people in Korea are named *Lee, Kim, Cho,* or *Park*— with various ways of spelling each of these names. (*Lee,* for example is also spelled as *Li, I, Yi,* and *Rhee*.) The paucity of names apparently goes back to the very beginnings of the Korean people, when just a few families grew into clans that eventually populated the entire peninsula.

Since that early time, the cultural importance of the family and the family name caused the names of the founding families to be carefully perpetuated from one generation to the next. In Korea today, family names are so important that women do not change them when they get married. "Miss Lee" simply becomes "Mrs. Lee," and so on.

Honorifics and titles also loom large in Korea, and custom dictates that you address people by their family name plus the title of "Mr." "Mrs." or "Miss," (or their professional or work-related title, such as "Doctor" "Professor Lee," "Purchasing Agent Lee," "Personnel Manager Lee," or "President Lee") plus the honorific *nim* or *sonsaengnim*. When addressing someone by name, the honorific *ssi* (sshe), which is the equivalent of the Japanese *san*, is usually added: i.e., *Lee-ssi*.

Address a married woman by using the last name plus *Puin* (Puu-een): i.e., *Park-Puin*. If a woman is unmarried, the proper form of address is *Yang* (Yahng): *Park-Yang*. Foreigners may use "Mr.," "Mrs.," or "Miss" when addressing Koreans. Nevertheless, using the appropriate Korean titles shows a cultural sensitivity and learning that will be appreciated. "Professor Lee," for example, would be addressed as *Lee Kyo Su-nim* (Lee Kyoh-Sue-neem), while "Dr. Choe" (which sounds very much like "Dr. Joe"), would be *Choe Paksa-nim* (Pahk-sah-neem).

Common Responses

Can you speak English?
Yongorul hashimnikka?
(Yahng-ah-rule hah-sheem-nee-kkah?)

17

Yes.
Ye.
(Yeh), often pronounced (Nay)

Yes, a little.
Ne, jom hamnida.
(Nay, jome hahm-nee-dah)
Also:
Ne, yakkan hamnida.
(Nay, yahk-kahn hahm-nee-dah)

No.
Anio.
(Ah-nyoe)

Oh, yes!
A, ne!
(Ah, nay!)

Of course.
Mullon imnida.
(Muu-lone eem-nee-dah)
Also, less formally:
Mullon ijyo.
(Muu-lone ee-joe)

Of course not!
Mullon animnida!
(Muu-lone ah-neem-nee-dah)

All right./Fine./Okay./Very well.
Chossumnida.
(Choe-sume-nee-dah)
Also:
Choayo.
(Choe-ah-yoe)

I understand.
Alket ssumnida.
(Ahl-kehtt sume-nee-dah)
Also:
Ihae hamnida.
(Ee-hay hahm-nee-dah)

I don't understand.
Moruget ssumnida.
(Moe-rue-gayt ssume-nee-dah)

I'll do it.
Kurok'e hage ssumnida.
(Kuu-rah-kay hah-gay ssume-nee-dah)

I think so.
Kurok'e saenggak hamnida.
(Kuu-rah-kay sang-gock hahm-nee-dah)

I don't think so.
Kurok'e saenggak'aji anssumnida.
(Kuu-rah-kay sang-gock ah-jee ahn-ssume-nee-dah)

Thank you.
Kamsahamnida.
(Kahm-sah-hahm-nee-dah)
Also:
Komapsumnida.
(Koe-mop-sume-nee-dah)

Don't mention it./You're welcome.
Ch'on manui malssumimnida.
(Chan mah-nuu-e mahl-ssume-eem-nee-dah)
Also:
Chonmaneyo.
(Chahn-mahn-eh-yoe)

I'm sorry.
Mianhamnida.
(Mee-ahn-hahm-nee-dah)
Also:
Mianhaeyo.
(Mee-ahn-hay-yoe)

Excuse me.
Shillyehamnida.
(Sheel-yeh-hahm-nee-dah)

Pardon me.
Joesonghamnida.
(Joe-eh-song-hahm-nee-dah)

Just a moment, please.
Jamkkanman kidaryeo jushipshio.
(Jahm khan-mahn kee-dah-ryah juu-ship-she-oh)
Also:
Jamkkanmanyo.
(Jahm-kahn-mahn-yoe)

Do you like it?
Maum-e du seyo?
(Mah-uum-eh due say-yoe?)
Also:
Choahashimnikka?
(Choe-ah-hah-sheem nee-kkah?)

No, I don't like it.
Anio, choahaji an-ssumnida.
(Ah-nee-yoe, choe-ah-hah-jee ahn-ssume-nee-dah)

Do you want it?
Wonhashimnikka?
(Wahn-hah-sheem-nee-kkah?)

I don't want it.
Wonch'i anssumnida.
(Wone-chee ahn-ssume-nee-dah)

Never mind.
Yomnyo mashipshio.
(Yome-nyoe mah-ship-she-oh)

Are you ready?
Junbi toe ot ssumnikka?
(June-bee toe ah ssume-nee-kkah?)

Not yet.
Ajik.
(Ah-jeek)
Also:
Ajik an toe otssumnida.
(Ah-jeek ahn toe ah-ssume-nee-dah)

Let's go.
Kapshida (*polite*).
(Kahp-she-dah)
Also:
Kaja (*familiar*).
(Kah-jah)

Other Useful Phrases

May I introduce Mr. Ross?
Mr. Ross rul sogae hae turilkkayo?
(Mr. Ross ruul so-gay hay tuu-reel-kkah-yoe?)

I'm pleased to meet you.
Cho'um poepkessumnida.
(Choe-ume pep-kay-ssume-nee-dah)

21

It was nice meeting you.
Manna poeoso pangawo ssumnida.
(Mahn-nah pay-oh-so pahn-gah-woe
   ssume-nee-dah)

Please come again.
Tto oshipshiyo.
(Ttoe oh-ship-she-yoe)

I'm home! (announcing your return from work,
   shopping, etc.)
Tanyowassumnida!
(Tahn-yo-wah-ssume-nee-dah!)

Welcome home! (said to a returning family member)
Chigum toraoshimnikka!
(Chee-gume toe-rah-oh-sheem-nee-kkah!)

I'm going out now (formal expression used when
   leaving home for work, etc.).
Chigŭm naganun kilimnida.
(Chee-gume nah-gah-nuun keel-eem-nee-dah)

Sorry to disturb you (formal expression used
   when entering someone's home or office).
Sillyehamnida.
(Sheel-lay-hahm-nee-dah)

Thanks for your hospitality.
Yorokajiro kamsahamnida.
(Yoe-roe-kah-jee-roe kahm-sah-hahm-nee-dah)

When Using Taxis

Do you know this address?
I jusoka odinji aseyo?
(Ee juu-soe-kah ah-deen-jee ah-say-yoe?)

Wait here, please.
Chom kidaryo chuseyo.
(Chome kee-dah-rio chuu-say-yoe)

Please drive slower.
Soktorul chom nutchyo chuseyo.
(Soak-toe-ruul chome nute-choe chuu-say-yoe)

Stop here.
Yogiso torachushipshiyo.
(Yoe-ghee-so toe-rah-chuu-ship-she-yoe)

Go straight ahead.
Aphuro ttok paro kaseyo.
(Ahp-huu-roe ttoak pah-roe kah-say-yoe)

Please turn right.
Parun jjokuro tora chushipsiyo.
(Pah-ruun jjoe-kuu-roe toe-rah chuu-ship-she-yoe)

Please turn left.
Oen jjokuro tora chushipsiyo.
(Oh-ehnn jjoe-ku-roe toe-rah chuu-ship-she-yoe)

On the Telephone

Operator?
Kyohwansu imnikka?
(K'yoe-whan-sue eem-nee-kkah?)

Do you speak English?
Yong-o-rul haljul ashimnikka?
(Yong-oh-ruul hahl-juul ah-sheem-nee-kkah?)

May I speak to Mr. Ross?
Misuto Ross chom pakkwo chusipshiyo.
(Mees-tah Ross chome pahkk-woe chuu-ship-
    she-yoe.)

23

Who is calling, please?
Nugu simnikka?
(Nuu-guu sheem-nee-kkah?)

Just a moment, please.
Chamgan man kidari seyo.
(Cham-gahn mahn kee-dah-ree say-yoe)

He (she) is not here.
Yogi an kushimnida.
(Yoe-ghee ahn kuu-sheem-nee-dah)

You have the wrong number.
Chalmot kollyossumnida.
(Chahl-mot kole-yoe-ssume-nee-dah)

Please ask her (him) to call me.
Chonhwa hae tallago chon hae chuseyo.
(Choan-whah hay tahl-ah-go choan hay
    chuu-say-yoe)

Please.
Putakhamnida.
(Puu-tock-hahm-nee-dah)

Thank you very much.
Taedanhi kamsahamnida.
(Tay-dahn-hee kahm-sah-hahm-ne-dah)

You are welcome.
Chonmaneyo.
(Choan-mah-nay-yoe)

Excuse me
Mianhamnida
(Mee-ahn-hahm-nee-dah)

I want to reconfirm my reservation.
Yeyakul chaehwaginhago shipssumnida.
(Yay-yah-kull chay-whah-gheen-hah-go
  sheep-ssume-nee-dah)

Where can I change some money?
Odiso tonul pakkul suissumnikka?
(Ah-dee-so tone-null pahk-kuul sue-ee-sume-
  nee-kkah?)

Dining Vocabulary

  menu **menyu** (meh-nyuu)
  waiter **weita** (way-tah)
  waitress **weitress** (way-tress)
  Korean food **Hanguk yori** (Hahn-gook yoe-ree)
  Western food **Seoyang yori** (Sah-yahng yoe-ree)
  Chinese food **Jungguk yori** (Juung-gook-yoe-ree)
  Japanese food **Ilbon yori** (Eel-bone yoe-ree)
  meat **kogi** (koe-ghee)
  roast beef **pulgogi** (pule-goh-ghee)
  beef **soegogi** (soe-goh-ghee)
  pork **twaejigogi** (tway-jee-go-ghee)
  chicken **takkogi** (tock-koe-ghee)
  fish **saengseon** (sang-sahn)
  fish soup **saengseon guk** (sang-sahn gook)
  vegetables **yachae** (yah-chay)
  vegetable soup **yachae guk** (yay-chay gook)
  pickled cabbage **kimchi** (kim-chee)
  eggs **kyeran** (kay-rahn)
  bread **ppang** (pahng)
  milk **uyu** (uu-yuu)
  coffee **kopi** (koh-pee)
  black tea **hong cha** (hong-chah)
  ginseng tea **insam cha** (een-sahm chah)

beer **maekju** (make-juu)
wine **podoju** (poe-doe-juu)
fruit **kwail** (kwah-eel)
apples **sagwa** (sah-gwah)
peaches **poksunga** (poke-suung-ah)
pears **pae** (pay)
oranges **orenji/milgam** (oh-rane-jee/meel-gahm)
melon **chamoe** (cham-oh-eh)
watermelon **subak** (sue-bahk)
sugar **seoltang** (sahl-tang)
salt **sogum** (soe-gume)
pepper **huchu** (who-chuu)
red pepper **kochu** (koe-chu)
soy sauce **kanjang** (kahn-jahng)
mustard **kyeoja** (kyah-jah)
vinegar **cho/shikcho** (choe/sheek-choe)

Travel Vocabulary

passport **yokkwon** (yah-kwahn)
visa **pija** (pee-jaa)
reservations **yeyak** (yeh-yack)
tickets **pyo** (pyoe)
roundtrip tickets **wangbok pyo** (wang-bock pyoe)
first-class tickets **il-teung pyo** (eel-tung pyoe)
second-class tickets **i-teung pyo** (ee-tung pyoe)
sightseeing **kwangwang** (kwahn-kwang)
tour **yeohaeng** (yah-hang)
tour guide **yeohaeng annaeso** (yah-hang
   ahn-nay-soe)
sightseeing bus **kwangwang peosu**
   (kwahn-kwang pah-sue)

Hotel Vocabulary

hotel **hot'el** (hotel)
room **pang** (pahng)

room charge **pang kap** (pahng kahp)
hotel charge **sukbak ryo** (suke-bahk rio)
room number **pang pon ho** (pahng bahn hoe)
key **yolswoe** (yahl-soeh)
single bed **ilinyong chimdae** (eel-een-yong cheem-day)
double bed **iinyong chimdae** (e-een-yong cheem-day)
front desk **chop sugyee** (chop sue-gay-ey)
bellboy **poi** (boy)
maid **ajumma** (ah-jumme-mah)
bath **mogyoktang** (moeg'yoke-tahng)
shower **syawoe** (sha-wah)

Transportation Vocabulary

airplane **pihaenggi** (pee-hang-ghee)
airport **konghang** (kong-hahng)
taxi **taek-shi** (tack-she)
car **jadongcha** (jah-dong-chah)
driver **kisa (unjeonsu)** (kee-sah/uun-jahn-suc)
slow down **cheon-cheon-hi** (chone-chone-hee)
stop sign **jeong jishinho** (jong jee-sheen-hoe)
speed limit **sokto jehan** (soke-toe jay-hahn)
service station **jadongcha juyuso** (jah-dong-chah juu-yuu-soe)
parking lot **jucha jang** (juu-chah jahng)
no parking **jucha geumji** (juu-chah guum-jee)
bicycle **jajeongo** (jah-jong-gah)
bus **poesu** (pah-suc)
express bus **kosok peosu** (koe-soke pah-sue)
bus stop **poesu jeongryujang** (pah-sue jong-rue-jahng)
train **kicha** (kee-chah)
railroad **cheol-to** (chole-toe)
conductor **chajang** (chah-jahng)

subway **jihacheol** (jee-hah-chole)
ship **pae** (pay)
street **keori** (kah-ree)
corner **motungi** (moe-tung-ee)
sidewalk **indo** (een-doe)

Clothing Vocabulary

dress **uibok/duresu** (we-boak/duu-ray-sue)
dress suit **yang bok** (yahng boak)
trousers **paji** (pah-jee)
shirt **syassue** (sha-ssue)
white shirt **wai syassue** (wie sha-ssue)
skirt **sukotu** (sue-kah-tuu)
jumper **jamba** (jahm-bah)
blouse **pullausu** (puul-lah-uu-sue)
sweater **seta** (say-tah)
overcoat **oba kotu** (oh-bah koe-tu)
raincoat **reinkotu/piot** (rain-koe-tu/pee-oat)
gloves **jangap** (jahn-gahp)
socks **yangmal** (yahng-mahl)

Shopping Vocabulary

department store **paekhwajeom**
(pake-whah-jome)
market **sijang** (she-jhang)
gift shop **kinyeompum sang** (kee-
n'yome-pume-sahng)
jewelry store **kwikeumsok sang** (kwee-kume-
soak sahng)
Also: **posok sang** (poe-sock sahng)
drugstore **yak kuk** (yahk-kuke)
tax-free goods **myeon-se pum** (m'yone-say
pume)

price list **jeongga pyo** (jhong-gah pyoe)
  Also: **kakyok pyo** (kah-kyahk pyoe)
how much? **Olma imnika?** (ahl-mah
  eem-nee-kah?)
receipt **yeongsujeung** (yohng-sue-jung)
change (money) **koseureumdon** (koh-
  suu-rume-doan)
  Also: **jandon** (jahn-done)

Telephone Vocabulary

telephone **jeonhwa** (john-whah)
public telephone **kongjung jeonwha** (kong-jung
  john-whah)
telephone operator **jeonwha gyowhansu** (john-
  whah g'yoe-hwahn-sue)
phone directory **jeonwha beonhobu** (john-whah
  bahn-hoe-buu)
phone number **jeonwha beonho** (john-whah
  bahn-hoe)
dial **daieol** (dah-ee-ahl)
long distance call **sioe jeonwha** (she-o-eh
  john-whah)
overseas call **kukje jeon hwa** (kuke-jay
  john-whah)

Post Office Vocabulary

Post Office **Uche Guk** (Uu-chay Gook)
Central Post Office **Jungang Uche Guk**
  (Jung-ahng Uu-chay Gook)
International Parcel Post Office **Kukje
  Sopho Uche Guk** (Kuke-jay Soe-poe Uu-chay
Gook)
letter **pyeonji** (pyahn-jee)

post card **yeop seo** (yahp sah)

picture postcard **keurim yeopseo** (kuu-reem yahp-sah)

envelope **pongthu** (pong-thuu)

postage **uphyeon yogeum** (uu-pyahn yoe-guum)

stamps **uphyo** (uu-pyah)

revenue stamp **suip inji** (sue-eep een-jee)

air mail **hanggong upyeon** (hahng-gong uu-pyahn)

surface mail **seonbak uphyeon** (sahn-bahk uu-pyahn)

foreign mail **oegug uphyeon** (ohh-gook uu-pyahn)

domestic mail **kungnae uphyeon** (koong-nay uu-pyahn)

registered mail **teunggi uphyeon** (tuung-ghee uu-pyahn)

express mail **soktal** (soak-tahl)

parcel post **so po** (soe poe)

printed matter **inswae mul** (een-sway muul)

address **juso** (juu-soe)

return address **palshinin juso** (pahl-sheen-een juu-soe)

P.O. Box **Sa Seo Ham** (Sah Suh Hahm)

Part Two: Glossary of Useful Vocabulary

A

A (indefinite article)
[There is no equivalent of the "a" in Korean. It is "understood."]

Aboard *Tapsung* **(Tahp-soong)**
All aboard please. *Yorobun tapsuenghae chuship-shio.* (Yoe-roe-bune tah-soong-hay chuu-ship-she-oh.)

Abroad *Oegugeso* **(Oh-eh guu-gay-soe);** also *Hae oe* (Hay oh-eh)
I went abroad last year. *Chinanhae haeoe-e kot-ssah ssumnida.* (Cheen-nahn-hay hay-oh-eh-eh koh-ssah sume-nee-day.)   Do you like living abroad? *Oegugeso sanumkotsul choahashi imnikka?* (Ohh-guu-gay-soe sah-nume-kah-ssuel cho-ah-hah-she emm-nee-kkah?).

Accident *Sago* **(Saah-go)**
There has been an accident. *Sago-ga palssaenghae ssumnida.* (Sah-go-gah pahl-sang-hay sume-nee-dah.) Please call an ambulance. *Ueng kuep charul pulleo chuseyo* (Wang-koop cha-rule puul-lah chuu-say-yoe.)

Account *Yegumtongjang* **(Yeh-gume-tong-jang)**
Do you have an account with this bank? *I unhang yeguemtongjang-ul kajigo issum nikka?* (Ee wane-hang yeh-gume-tong-jahng-ule kah-jee-go ee-sume nee-kah?)

Accountant *Hoegyesa* **(Hoe-gay-sah)**
What is your accountant's name *Tangshin-ui hoe-gyesa-ue irum un muot imnikka?* (Tahng-sheen-we hoe-gay-sah-we ee-ruuem-une muu ah eem-nee-kkah?)

Ache *Apum* **(Ah-pume)**; Headache *Tutong* (Tute-tong); Stomachache *Poktong* (Poke-tong); Toothache *Chitong* (Chee-tong)
I have a bad headache. *Nanun moriga mopshi apumnida.* (Nah-noon mah-ree-gah mope-she ah pume-nee-dah.)

Acquaintance *Anun saram* **(Ah-noon sah-rahm)**;
Relative *Chinji* (Cheen-jee); An old acquaint-ance *Kumyon* (Kuu-myahn)
He is an old acquantance. *Kunun kumyon imnida. (Kuu-nuun kuu-myahn eem-nee-dah.)*

Address *Chuso* **(Chuu-soe); or** *Juso* (Juu-soe)
May I have your address, please. *Juso-rul karu-ch'yo chushipshio.* (Juu-soe-rule kah-rue-chah chuu-ship-she-oh.) Write your address here. *Yo-gie tanghsin-ui juso-rul ssuh chuseyo.* (Yoe-ghee-eh tahng-sheen-we juu-soe-ruul ssuh chu-say-yoe.)

Admission *Ipchang* **(Eep-chang)**; Admission fee *Ipchang nyo* (Eeep-chang nyo)
What is the admission fee? *Ipchang nyo ga olma imnikka?* (Eep-chang nyo gah ahl-mah eem-nee-kkah?) Admission is free. *Ipchang-un muryo im-nida.* (Eep-chang-uun muu-rio eem-nee-dah.)

Adult *Orun* **(Ah-rune);** also *Song-imn* (Sahng-een)
The admission fee for adults is one thousand won. *Orun-ui ipchang nyonun chon won imnida.* (Ah-rune-we eep-chang nyo-nune chan wahn eem-nee-dah.)

Advance payment *Sonbul* **(Sahn-bule);** Pay in advance *Sonbulhada* (Sahn-bule-hah-dah); also *Sonbul lo naeda* (Sahn-bule low nah-dah)
Please pay in advance. *Sonbul lo chuseyo.* (Sahn-bule low chuu-say-yoe.)

Advertise *Kwanggohada* **(Kwahng-go-hah-dah);** Advertisement *Kwanggo* (Kwahng-go); Help-wanted ad *Kuin kwanggo* (Kuu-een kwahng-go); Work-wanted ad *kujik kwanggo* (Kuu-jeek kwahng-go)
I want to place an ad in the newspaper. *Nanun shinmun-e kwanggo-rul naego shipssunnida.* (Nah-nune sheen-moon-eh kwang-goh-rule nay-go ship-ssume-nee-dah.) I saw your ad in the newspaper. *Nanun shinmun esuh tangshin-ui kwanggo rul boassumnida.* (Nah-nune sheen-muun eh-sah tahng-sheen-we kwang-goh rule boh-ah-ssume-nee-dah.)

Aerogram *Hanggong pongham yoppso* **(Hahng-gong pong-hahm yope-soe)**
May I have two aerograms, please. *Hanggong pongham yopso-rul tu chang chuseyo.* (Hahng-gong pong-hahm yahp-sah-rule tuu chahng chuu-say-yoe.)

Afford *Hal yoyuga itta* **(Hahl yoe-yuu-gah eet-tah)**
I cannot afford that. *Nanun kugossul hal yoyuga uhpssumnida.* (Nan-nune kuu-gah-ssule hahl yah-yuu-gah ahp-ssume-nee-dah.) I can't afford

to go. *Nanun kal yoyuga uhpssumnida.* (Nan-nune kahl yah-yuu-gah ahp-ssume-nee-dah.)

Afraid *Musoun* **(Muu-soe-uun);** *Turyoum* (Tuu-ryo-uum)
I am afraid to eat this. *Nanun igosul mong nun goshi musopssumnida.* (Nah-nune ee-go-sule mohng nune gah-she muu-sahp ssume-nee-dah.) Are you afraid to go? *Tangshin un kanun goshi musopssumnikka?* (Tahng-sheen-une kah-nune gah-she muu-sahp-ssume-nee-kka?)

Afternnoon *Ohu* **(Oh-huu);** This afternoon *Onul ohu* (Oh-nule oh-huu)
She will arrive this afternoon. *Kunyonun onul ohue tochak hal goshimnida.* (Kuu-nyo-nune oh-nule oh-huu toe-chak hahl guh-sheem-nee-dah.) It will be ready this afternoon. *Ku gossun onul ohu junbi doel goshimnida.* (Kuu gah-ssune oh-nule oh-huu june-bee doehl guh-sheem-nee-dah.) Let's go this afternoon. *Onul ohu-e kapshida.* (Oh-nule oh-huu eh kahp-she-dah.)

Again *Tashi* **(Tah-she)**
Please say it again. *Tashi malssum haechuseyo.* (Tah-she mahl-ssume hay-chuu-say-yoe.) Let's do this again sometime. *Onjenga tashi igossul hapshida.* (Ahn-jane-gah tah-she ee-guh-ssule hahp-she-dah.) Would you like to go again? *Tashi kashigetssoyo?* (Tah-she kah-she gay-ssah yoe?)

Age (polite) *Yonse* **(Yone-say);** (familiar) *Nai* (Nie)
What is your age, please? *Yonse-ga myoch'ishimnikka?* (Yone-say-gah myuh-chee sheem-nee-kkah?) also *Naiga olma imnikka?* (Nie-gah ahl-mah eem-nee-kkah?)

Agent *Taeriin* **(Tay-ree-een)**
Do you have an agent in Korea? *Hanguk-e taeriini issumnikka?* (Hahn-gook-eh tay-ree-een-ee ee-ssume nee-kkah?) Please check with a travel agent. *Yohangsae munihae chushipsio.* (Yoe-hang-sah-eh muu-nee-hay chuu-ship-she-oh.)

Agreement, contract *Kyeyak* **(Kay-yahck)**
We must have an agreement. *Urinun kyeyak haeyahapnida.* (Uu-ree-nune kay-yahck hay-yah-hahp-nee-day.) Please sign this agreement. *I kyeyak-e somyong hashipshio.* (Ee kay-yahck-eh sah-myang hah-sheep-she-oh.)

Air *Konggi* **(Kong-ghee);** Fresh air *shinsonhan konggi* (Sheen-sone-hahn kong-ghee)
Let's get some fresh air. *Shinsonhan konggirul kajipshida.* (Sheen-shan-hahn kong-ghee-rule kah-jeep-she-dah.) The air is fresh in the mountains. *Sansog-e shinsonhan konggiga issumnida.* (Sahn-sog-eh sheen-sahn-hahn kong-ghee-gah ee-ssume-nee-dah.)

Airline *Hanggong hoesa* **(Hahng-gong hoe-eh-sah)**
Which airline are you taking? *Tangshin un uhnue hanggong hoesa?* (Tahng-sheen uun uh-nuu hahng-gong hoe-eh-sah?)

Air conditioning *Nangbang changchi* **(Nang-bang chang-chee)**
We want a hotel with air conditioning. *Urinun nangbang changchiga innun hotel-ul wonhapnida.* (Uu-ree-nune nang-bang chahng-chee-gah een-nune hoe-tay-rule wahn-hahp-nee-dah.) Please turn the air conditioning on. *Nangbang changchi-rul kkyo chuseyo.* (Nang-bang chahng-chee-rule kkyah chuu-say-yoe.)

Airmail *Hanggong upyon* **(Hahng-gong uu-pyan)**
Please send this by airmail. *Igossul hanggong
upyon uro ponae chuseyo.* (Ee-gah-ssule hahng-
gohng uu-pyahn uu-roe poe-nay chuu-say-yoe.)
How much does airmail cost? *Hanggong yogumi
olma imnikka?* (Hahng-gohng yoe-gume-ee ahl-
mah eem-nee-kkah?)

Airsick *Pihaenggi molmiga nan* **(Pee-hayng-ghee
muhl-me-gah nahn)**
I am airsick. *Nanun pihanggi molmi-ga namnida.*
(Nah-nune pee-hayng-ghee mahl-mee-gah
nahm-nee-dah.)   Please bring me some medicine. *Naege yakjjom kattachuseyo.* (Nay-gay yahk-
jome kah-ttah-chuu-say-yoe.)

Alarm clock *Chamyongjong* **(Chahm-yang-jong)**
Do you have an alarm clock? *Tangshin un chamyongjong shigyerul kajigo issumnikka?* (Tahng-sheen
uun chahm-yong-jong she-gay-rule kah-jee-go
ee-ssume-nee-kkah?)   Please set the alarm clock
for 6 A.M. *Ojon yososshie chamyongjongul ma ch'o
chuseo.* (Oh-jahn yah-sah-she-eh chahm-yahng-
jong-ule mah-chuu-ah chuu-say-yoe.)

All *Modun* **(Moe-dune);** also *Modu* (Moe-due);
Chonbu (Chone-buu); *Chon* (Chone)
Is this all? *Igoshi chonbu imnikka?* (Ee-gah-sshe
chone-buu eem-nee-kkah?)   I'll take all of the
books. *Naega modun chaekul kajilgoshi-imnida.* (Nay-
gah moe-dune chake-ule kah-jeel-gah-sheem-
nee-dah.)

Almost *Koui* **(kah-we);** also *Taech'ero* (Tay-chay-
roe)
I'm almost ready. *Nanun junbi ga koui da doeossumnida.* (Nah-nune june-bee gah kah-we dah
doe-ah-ssume-nee-dah.)   Have you almost finished. *Tangshin-un koui da machossumnikka?*

(Tahng-sheen-uun kah-we dah mah-chuh ssume-
nee-kkah?)

Alone *Hollo* **(Hole-low);** also *Honjaso* (Hone-jah-
soe)
Are you alone? *Honja kyeshimnikka?* (Hone-jah
kay-sheem-nee-kkah?)   Are you going alone?
Tangshin honja gashimnikka? (Tahng-sheen hone-
jah gah-sheem-nee-kkah?)

Aloud *K'un soriro* **(Kune soe-ree-roe)**
Please read the book aloud. *Chak-eul k'un soriro
ilgo chusio.* (Chake-ule kune soe-ree-roe eel-gah
chuu-she-oh.)

Alphabet *Alp'abet* **(Al-pah-bet;** also *Chamo
munjja* (Chah-moe moon-jah)
The Korean alphabet is called hangul. *Hanguk
chamo munjja-nun hangul ira purunda.* (Hahn-gook
chah-moe moon-jah nuun hahn-guul ee-rah
puu-rune-dah.)

Already *Imi* **(E-me);** also *Polsso* (Pole-soe)
The train has already left. *Kicha-nun imi ttonago
opsossumnida.* (Kee-chah-nune e-me ttah-nah-
go up-suh-sume-nee-dah.)   Have you already
had lunch? *Polsso chomshimul mogossumnikka?*
(Pahl-ssah chahm-sheem-ule mah-gah-ssume-
nee-kkah?)

Also *Yokshi* **(yack-she);** also *Ttohan* (Toe-hahn)
Are you also going? *Tangshin ttohan kashimnikka?*
(Tahng-sheen ttoe-hahn kah-sheem-nee-kkah?)
Have you also been to Japan? *Tangshin ttohan Ilbon-e kabon jogi issum nikka?* (Tahng-sheen ttoe-
hahn Eel-bohn-eh kah-bohn jah-ghee ee-sume
nee-kkah?)

Altitude *Nop'i* **(Nope-ee);** also *Haebal* (Haybahl)
At what altitude are we flying? *Urinun olma-ui*

nopi-ro nargo issumnikka? (Uu-ree-nune ahl-mah-we nohp-ee-roe nahr-goh ee-sume-nee-kkah?) We are flying at 10,000 meters. *Urinun man mitero nargo issumnida.* (Uu-ree-nune mahn mee-tuh-roe nahr-go ee-sume-nee-dah.)

Ambassador   *Taesa* **(Tie-sah)**
Who is the American ambassador in Japan? *Ilbon chujae Miguk taesa nun nugu imnikka?* (Eel-bohn chuu-jay Mee-gook tie-sah nuu-en nuu-guu eem-nee-kkah?) I would like to meet the Korean ambassador to the U.S. *Nanun Miguk chujae Hanguk taesarul mannago shipssumnida.* (Nah-nune Mee-gook chuu-jay Hahn-gook tie-sah-rul mahn-nah-go sheep-ssume-nee-dah.)

Ambulance   *Aembyullonsu* **(Ahm-beu-lonse);**   also *Kugupch'a*   (Kuu-gupe-chah)
Please call an ambulance, quickly! *Ppalli kugupcharul pullo chuseyo!* (Ppahl-lee kuu-goop-chah-ruel pull-ah chuu-say-yoe!)

America   *Miguk* **(Me-gook);**   North America *Pungmi* (Puung-me);   South America *Nammi* (Nahm-me)
Mr. Lee has been to America many times. *Isshi nun Yoroban Miguk-e kabon jogi issumnida.* (Ee-she nune Yuh-ruh-bahn Me-gook-eh kah-bohn joe-ghee ee-sume-nee-dah.)

American   *Miguk-ui* **(Me-gook-we);**   also *Migukin* (Me-gook-een)
Are you an American? *Tangshin un Migukin imnikka?* (Tahn-sheen uun Me-gook-een eem-nee-kkah?) He is American. *Kunun Migukin imnida.* (Kuu-nune Mee-gook-een eem-nee-dah.) I am American. *Nanun Migukin imnida.* (Nah nune Mee-gook-een eem-nee-dah.)

American Embassy *Miguk Taesagwan* **(Me-gook Tay-sah-gwahn)**
I must go to the American Embassy. *Nanun Miguk Taesagwan-e kaya hamnida.* (Nah-nune Me-gook Tay-sah-gwahn-eh kah-yah hahm-nee-dah.)   Please take me to the American Embassy. *Narul Miguk Taesagwan-e teryoda chusio.* (Nah-rul Mee-gook Tay-sah-gwahn-eh tay-ryoh-dah chuu-she-oh.)

Amount (total) *Chonggye* **(Chong-gay)**
How much is the whole amount? *Chongae-ga olmana toemnikka?* (Chong-gay-gah uhl-mah-nah tome-nee-kkah?)

Animal *Tongmul* **(Tong-mule);**   Wild animals *Yasu* (Yah-sue); *Yasoeng tongmul* (Yah-song tong-mule)
Are there many wild animals in Korea? *Hanguk-e nun yasong tongmul i olmana manssumnikka?* (Hahn-gook-eh nuun yah-song tong-mule ee ahl-mah-nah mahn-ssume-nee-kkah?)

Anniversary *Kinyomil* **(Kee-nyuhm-eel);**   Wedding anniversary *Kyolhon Kinyomil* (Kyahll-hohn kee-nyuhm-eel)
Today is our anniversary. *Onurun chohidul-ui kinyomil imnida.* (Oh-nuu-rune choe-he-dul-we keen-yoe-meel eem-nee-dah.)

Announce *Palp'yohada* **(Pahl-pyoh-hah-dah);**   *allida* (Ahl-lee-dah)
Please announce our departure time. *Uriui chulbal shiganul allyo chuseyo.* (Uu-ree-we chuul-bahl shee-ghan-ule ahl-lyah chuu-say-yoe.)

Announcement *Kongp'yo* **(Kong-p'yoe);**   also *Songmyong* (Song-myong); *Kong go* (khong go)
Did you hear the announcement? *Tangshin un ku*

konggorul turossumnikka? (Tahng-sheen uun kuu khong-go-rul tur-ah-ssume nee-kkah?) What was that announcement? *Ku konggonun mwo-shimnikka?* (Kuu khong-go-nune mwah-sheem-nee-kkah?

Answer *Hoedap* (Hay-dahp); *Taedap hada* (Tay-dahp hah-dah)
I do not know the answer. *Nanun ku haedapul morupnida.* (Nah-nune kuu hay-dahp-ule moh-rupe-nee-dah.) What is your answer? *Tangshin-ui taedapun mwossimnikka?* (Tahng-sheen-we tay-dahp-ueun mwah-sheem-nee-kkah?)

Antique *Kolttongp'um* (Kole-tong-pume); Antique dealer *Kolttongp'um sang* (Kole-tong-pume sahng)
I would like to buy some antiques. *Nanun kol-tongpumul sagoshipssumnida.* (Nah-nune kohl-tohng puum-ule sah-go-sheep-ssume-nee-dah.)

Apartment *Apatu* (Ah-pah-tuu)
I live in an apartment. *Nanun apatu eso salgois-sumnida.* (Nah-nune ah-pah-tu eh-sah sahl-go-ee-ssume-nee-dah.) I have a two-bedroom apartment. *Nanun I-inyong chimshili itnun apatu-ga issumnida.* (Nah-nune ee-een-yohng cheem-sheel-ee eet-nune ah-pah-tu-gah ee-ssume-nee-dah.)

Appendicitis *Maengjangyom* (Mang-jang-yahm)
I think I have appendicitis. *Nanun maengjangyom-i ittago soenggakhamnida.* (Nah-nune mang-jang-yahm-ee ee-ttah-gah sang-gah-hahm-nee-dah.)
I think you have appendicitis. *Nanun tangshin-i maengjangyom-ul kajigo ittago saenggakhamnida.* (Nah-nune tahng-sheen-ee mang-jang-yahm-ul kah-jee-go ee-ttah-go sang-gack-hahm-nee-dah.)

Appetite *Shigyok* **(Sheeg-yoke)**
How is your appetite? *Shigyogun ottossumnikka?*
(Sheeg-yoe-goon aht-tah-ssume-nee-kkah?)

Applaud *Paksu kalch'aehada* **(Pahk-sue kahl-chay-hah-dah);** *Paksu chida* (Pahk-suu chee-dah)
Is it all right to applaud? *Paksu chyodo doemnikka?*
(Pahk-suu chyah-doe dome-nee-kkah?)

Apple *Sagwa* **(Sah-gwah)**
Are many apples eaten in Korea? *Hanguk-e sonun sagwa-rul mani mogssumnikka?* (Hahn-gook-eh sah-nune sah-gwah-rul mah-nee mohg-sume-nee-kkah?) Do you have any apples? *Tangshin un sagwa-rul jome kajigo issumnikka?* (Tahng-sheen uun sah-gwah-rul johm kah-jee-go ee-sume nee-kkah?) We have apple pie. *Urinum sagwa pai-rul kajigo issumnida.* (Uu-ree-nume sah-gwah pah-ee-rul kah-jee-go ee-ssume-nee-dah.)

Application *Shinchong* **(Sheen-chong);** Request *Shinch'ong* (Sheen-chong); Application form *Shinch'ong so* (Sheen-chong soe); Written application *Wonso* (Wone-soe)
You must fill out an application. *Tangshin un shinchong-so-rul sso yahamnida.* (Tahng-sheen uun sheen-chung-sah-rul ssah yah-ham-nee-dah.) Where are the application forms? *Shinchong so nun odie issum nikka?* (Sheen-chong sah nuun ah-dee-eh ee-ssume-nee-kkah?)

Appointment *Yaksok* **(Yahk-soke)**
I have an appointment at one o'clock. *Nanun hanshi-e yakssok-i issumnida.* (Nah-nune hahn-she-eh yahk-soak-ee ee-ssume-nee-dah). What time is your appointment? *Tangshin-ui yakssok un myossi-e issumnikka?* (Tahng-sheen-we yahk-soak-uun myah-she-eh ee-ssume-nee-kkah?)

Architecture *Konchuk* **(Kahn-chuke);** also *Konchukgga* (Kahn-chuke-gah)
I am interested in the architecture of Korean temples. *Nanun Hanguk sawondul-e konchuk-e kwanshimi issumnida.* (Nah-nune Hahn-gook sah-wuhn-duel-eh kahn-chuke-eh kwan-sheem-ee ee-ssume-nee-dah.)

Area *Chiyok* **(Chee-yoke);** also *Chigu* (Chee-guu); *Chidae* (Chee-day)
I want to see an industrial area. *Kongop chidaerul pogo shipssumnida.* (Kohng-up chee-day-rul poe-go sheep-ssume-nee-dah.) Where are the residential areas? *Chutaek chigu nun odi imnika?* (Chuu-take chee-guu nune ah-dee eem-nee-kkah?)

Arrangements *Chongdon* **(Chong-doan);** *Junbi* (June-bee)
Have you made arrangements for your trip? *Yohang junbi-nun toeossumnikka?* (Yuh-hang june-bee-nuu-en doe-ah-ssume-nee-kkah?)

Arrival *Tochak* (Toe-chock)
I will let you know my arrival time. *Na-ui tochak shiganul allyo turigessumnida.* (Nah-we toe-chock she-gah-nule ahl-yoe tuu-ree-gay-sume-nee-dah.) What time are you arriving? *Onje tochak hashimnikka?* (Ahn-jay toe-chock hah-sheem-nee-kkah?) I just arrived. *Banggum tochak hassumnida.* (Bahng-gume toe-chock hah-ssume-nee-dah.)

Asia *Asia;* Continent of Asia *Asia taeryuk* (Tay-ruke)
This is my first time in Asia. *Asia nun Iboni chouemimnida.* (Ah-shee-ah nune ee-bohn-ee chah-uum-eem-nee-dah.)

Aspirin *Asupirin* **(Ahsu-pee-reen)**
Do you have any aspirin? *(Asupirin-ul kajigo is-sumnikka?* (Ahsu-pee-reen-ule kah-jee-go ee-ssume-nee-kkah?) I need an aspirin. *Asupirin-ul chuseyo.* (Ahsu-pee-reen-ule chuu-say-yoe.)

Atlantic Ocean *Taesoyang* **(Tay-soe-yang)**

Attention *Chuui* **(Chuu-ee);** *Choshim* (Choe-sheem)
Look out! *Chuui haseyo!* (Chuu-we hah-sey-yoe!); *Choshim haseyo!* (Choe-sheem hah-sey-yoe!) May I have your attention please! *(Chamkkan shillye hamnida!* (Chahm-kahn sheel-yay hahm-nee-dah!)

Attorney *Pyonhosa* **(Pyahn-hoe-sah)**
Are there many attorneys in Korea? *Hanguk-e nun pyonhosa duli manssumnikka?* (Hahn-gook-eh nune pyahn-hoe-sah duel-ee mahn-ssume-nee-kkah?)

Aunt *Ajumoni* **(Ah-juu-moe-nee)**
This is my aunt [maternal]. *Imo imnida.* (Ee-moe eem-nee-dah.) also *Ibun un naui komo* [paternal] *imnida.* (Ee-buun un nah-we koh-moe eem-nee-dah.) I am going to visit my aunt. *Nanun naui komo-rul pangmun hal yejong imnida.* (Nah-nune nah-we koe-moe-rul pahng-muun hahl yeh-juhng eem-nee-dah.)

Australia *Osutureillia* **(Oss-trail-yah);** also *Hoju* (Hoe-juu)
Korean products are popular in Australia. *Hanguk jepum duli hoju eso inkki imnida.* (Hahn-gook jeh-pume duel-ee hon-juu eh-sah een-kee eem-nee-dah).

Author *Choja* **(Choe-jah);** also *Chakka* (Chackkah)
I would like to meet some authors. *Myot-myot*

chakkahdurul mannago shipssumnida. (Myaht-myaht
chahk-kah-due-rul mahn-nah-go sheep-ssume-
nee-dah.)   Mr. Lee is a famous author. *I Son-
saeng-nim un yumyonghan chakka imnida.* (Ee Sahn-
sang-neem uun yuu-myahng-hahn chahk-kah
eem-nee-dah.)

Automobile   *Chadongcha* (Chah-dong-chah)
Is this your automobile? *Igossun tangshin-ui chadongcha imnikka?* (Ee-gah-ssu-en tahng-sheen-we
chah-dohng-chah eem-nee-kkah?)   Was this
automobile made in Korea? *I chadongcha num
Hanguk-san imnikka?* (Ee chah-dong-chah nume
Hahn-gook-sahn eem-nee-kkah?)

Avenue   *Karosukil* (Kah-roe-sue-keel);   also *Taero*
(Tay-roe)
What is the name of this avenue? *(I taero-e irumi
mwoshimnikka?* (Ee-tay-roe-eh ee-rume-ee
mwah-sheem-nee-kkah?)

Average   *Pyonggyun* (P'yong-gyune);   also *Potong*
(Poe-tong)
What is the average rainfall in Seoul? *Seoul-e
pyonggyun kanguryang un olma imnikka?* (Sah-uul-
eh pyuhng-pyuun kohng-uu-ryang uun ahl-mah
eem-nee-kkah?)   The average summer temperature is thirty degrees centigrade *Pyonggyum
yorun ondo-nun shopssi shamshipdo imnida.*
(Pyahng-gyuum yah-rune own-doe-nune shuhp-
sshe shahm-sheep-doe eem-nee-dah.)

Awake   *Kkaeda* (Kkay-dah):   also *Kkaonada* (Kkay-
ah-nay-dah)
What time do you usually wake up? *Tangshin un
myossie kkaeonamnikka?* (Tahng-sheen uun myah-
sshe-eh kkay-ah-nahm-nee-kkah?)   I usually
wake up at six. *Nanun yosossie kkaeonamninda.*

(Nah-nune Yah-sah-shee-eh kkay-ah-nahm-nee-dah.)   Get up! *Ironaseyo!* (Ee-rah-nah-say-yoe!)

B

Baby   *Agi* **(Ah-ghee);**   also *Kannanagi* (Kahn-nahn-ah-ghee);   Baby carriage *Yumocha* (Yuu-moe-chah)
How old is your baby? *Tangshin-ui aginun myot sal imnikka?* (Tang-sheen-we ah-ghee-nune myaht sahl eem-nee-kkah?)   What is your baby's name? *Agi-ui irumi mwossimnikka?* (Ah-ghee-we ee-rume-ee mwah-sheem-nee-kkah?)

Bachelor   *Tokshin namja* **(Toke-sheen nahm-jah);**   also *Chonggak* (Chong-gahck)
Are you still a bachelor? *Tangshin-un ajik chonggak imnikka?* (Tahng-sheen-uun ah-jeek chong-gahck eem-nee-kkah?)

Bad   *Nappun* **(Nahp-poon)**
Drinking is a bad habit. *Umjunun nappun poru-shimnida.* (Umm-juu-nuun nahp-poon puh-rue-sheem-nee-dah.)   That's too bad. *Kugot cham andwaetkkunyo.* (Kuu-gaht chahm ahn-dwate-kune-yoe.)   The weather is bad today. *Onul-un nalssiga nappumnida.* (Oh-nule-uun nahl-sshe-gah nah-ppume-nee-dah.)

Bag, briefcase   *Kabang* **(Kah-bahng);**   also *Paek* (Pake)
Please open your briefcase. *Kabang-ul yoro chu-shilkkayo.* (Kah-bahng-ule yoe-roe chuu-sheel-kah-yoe.)   I left my briefcase in the restaurant. *Kabang-ul umshikchom-e tugo watssumnida.* (Kah-bahng-ule umm-sheek-chome-eh tuu-go waht-ssume-nee-dah.)

Baggage *Suhamul* **(Sue-hah-mul);** Baggage car
Suhamul cha (Sue-hah-mul chah); Baggage
room *Suhamul pogwanso* (Sue-hah-mul poe-
gwahn-soe); Baggage claim *Suhamul yoguem*
(Sue-hah-muul yoh-gume)
Is this your baggage? *Igossun tangshin-e kabang
imnikka?* (Ee-go-ssune tahng-sheen-eh kah-
bahng eem-nee-kkah.) I cannot find my baggage.
Nae kabang-ul chatjji mottaessumnida. (Nay kah-
bahng-ule chaht-jee moh-ttay-ssume-nee-dah.)
Please take my baggage to the hotel. *Nae kabang-
ul hotele katta chuseyo.* (Nay kah-bahng-ule hoh-
tehl-eh kah-ttah chuu-say-yoe.)

Bakery *Ppangchip* **(Pahng-cheep)**
Is there a bakery nearby? *Kuencho-e ppangchip-i issumnikka?* (Kuu-en-choe-eh ppahng-cheep-ee
ee-ssume-nee-kkah?)

Bandage *Pungdae* **(Poong-day);** also *Baend* (Band)
Do you have a bandage? *Pungdae-rul kajigo issumnikka?* (Poong-day-rule kah-jee-go ee-ssume-
nee-kkah?) I need a bandage. *Pungdae-rul
chuseyo.* (Poong-day-rule chuu-say-yoe.)

Bank *Unhaeng* **(Uun-hang);** Commercial bank
Sangop unhaeng (Sahng-up unn-hang)
I must go to the bank. *Nanun unhaeng-e kaya
hamnida.* (Nah-nune uun-hang-eh-kah-yah
hahm-nee-dah.) What time do the banks open?
Unhangun myossie yamnikka? (Uun-hang-uun
myah-sshe-eh yahm-nee-kkah?)

Banquet *Yonhoe* **(Yone-hoe);** Banquet room *Yonhoe jang* (Yone-hoe jahng)
I went to a banquet last night. *Nanun jinanbam
yanhoae-e kassossumnida.* (Nah-nune jee-nahn
bahm yahn hoe-eh kah-ssah-ssume-nee-dah.)
Banquets are popular in Korea. *Yanhoega Hanguk-*

eso inggi imnida. (Yahn-hoe-gah Hahn-gook-eh-soe een-ghee eem-nee-dah.)

Bar (drinking) *Ppa* **(Ppah)**
I'll meet you in the bar. *Nanun tangshin-ul ppa-eso mannal gosshimnida.* (Nah-nuun tahng-sheen-ule ppah-eh-soe mahn-nahl gah-sheem-nee-dah.)
Let's stop by the bar for a drink. *Hanjan hagiwihae ppae yope mamchupshida.* (Hahn-jahn hah-ghee-wee-hay ppay yahp-eh mahm-chuup-shee-dah.)

Barber *Ibalssa* **(E-bahl-sah)**
She is a good barber. *Kunyo-nun hullyunghan ibalssa imnida.* (Kune-yoe-nuun huul-lyuung-hahn ee-bahl-sah eem-nee-dah.)

Barbershop *Ibalsso* **(E-bahl-soe)**
Is there a barbershop in the hotel? *Hotele ibalsso-ga issumnikka?* (Hoh-tehl-eh ee-bahl-soh-gah ee-ssume-nee-kkah?) What time does it open? *Myossie munul yomnikka?* (Myah-sshe-eh muun-ule yahm-nee-kkah?) How much for a haircut? *Iballyoga olma imnikka?* (Ee-bahl-lyoh-gah ahl-mah eem-nee-kkah?)

Bargain *Hungjong* **(Hung-jong);** also *Ssaguryo mulgon* (Sah-guu-rio mul-goan); To bargain *Enurihada* (E-nuu-ree-hah-dah); Bargain sale *pagen seil* (pah-gain-sale)
Are you having a bargain sale? *Chigum pagen seil hanun chung imnika?* (Chee-gume pah-gain-sale hah-noon chuung eem-nee-kkah?) This is really a bargain. *Igosun chongmal chal sashinun koshimnida.* (Ee-go-soon chong-mahl chahl sah-she-nune koe-sheem-nee-dah.)

Baseball *Yagu* **(Yah-guu);** To play baseball *Yagu-rul hada* (Yah-guu-rule hah-dah)
Would you like to go to a baseball game? *Yagu*

game-e kashigessoyo? (Yah-guu game-eh kah-shee-gay-ssah-yoe?)

Basketball *Nonggu* **(Nohng-guu)**
Basketball is popular in Korea. Let's go see a game. *Nonggu-nun Hanguk-eso inkki imnida. Kkaeim poro kapshida.* (Nohng-guu-nuun Hahn-gook-eh-soe een-kee eem-nee-dah. Game poe-rah kahp-shee-dah.)

Bath *Mogyok* **(Moag-yoke);** Sunbath *Ilgwangyok* (Eel-gwhang-yoke)
I'm going to take a bath. *Nanun mogyok hal yejong imnida.* (Nah-nuun moag-yoke hahl yeh-juhng eem-nee-dah.) I'd like a single room with bath, please. *Mogyok tang-i innun tokbbang-ul chuseyo.* (Moag-yoke tahng-ee een-nuun tohk-bahng-ule chuu-say-yoe.)

Bathroom *Mogyoktang* **(Moag-yoke-tahng);** also *Yokshil* (Yoke-sheel); *Hwajangshil* (Hwah- jahng-sheel)
I need to go to the bathroom. *Hwajangshil-e kago shipssumnida.* (Hwah-jahng-sheel-eh kah-go sheep-ssume-nee-dah.) Where is the bathroom? *Hwajangshil-i odi imnikka?* (Hwah-jahng-sheel-ee ah-dee eem-nee-kkah?)

Bay *Man* **(Mahn);** also *Hanggu* (Hahn-guu)
What is the name of this bay? *I hanggu-e irumi mwoshimnikka?* (Ee hahng-guu-eh ee-rume-ee mwah-ssheem nee-kkah?)

Be (present tense) *Imnida* **(Eem-nee-dah);** Past tense *Ossumnida* (Uh-sume-nee-dah); also *Is-sumnida* (Ee-sume-nee-dah); Negative tense *Opssumnida* (Up-ssume-nee-hah); Polite present tense *Kyeshimnida* (Kay-sheem-nee-dah); Polite past tense *Kyesyossumnida* (Kay-shah-ssume-nee-dah); Negative past tense *An-kye syo ssum-nida* (Ahn-kay-shah-ssume-nee-dah); In a question *Imnikka?* (Eem-nee-kkah?)

Beach *Haebyon* **(Hay-b'yahn)**
I would like to go to the beach. *Haebyon-e kago shipssumnida.* (Hay-b'yahn-eh kah-go sheep-ssume-nee-dah.) Is there a beach near Seoul? *Seoul kuncho-e haebyon-i issumnikka?* (Sah-uul kune-chah-eh hay-b'yahn-ee ee-ssume-nee-kkah?) There are several good beaches around Pusan. *Pusan kuncho-e joun haebyon-duli issumnida.* (Puu-sahn kune-chah-eh joe-uun hay-b'yahn duel-ee ee-ssume-nee-dah.)

Bean *Kong* **(Kong);** Soy bean *Taedu* (Tay-duu); Red beans *Pat* (Paht)
Do you like beans? *Kong-ul joa haseyo?* (Kohng-ule joe-ah hah-say-yoe?)

Beard *Suyom* **(Sue-yome)**
I am growing a beard. *Nanun suyom-ul kirugo is-sumnida.* (Nah-noon sue-yome-uul kee-rue-goh ee-ssume-nee-dah.) He has a beard. *Kunun suyom-i itta.* (Kuu-nune sue-yome-ee ee-ttah.)

Beautiful *Arumdaun* **(Ah-rume-dah-uun)**
You are beautiful. *Tangshin-un arumdapgunyo.* (Tahn-sheen-uun ah-rume-dahp-guun-yoe.) The weather is beautiful today. *Onul-un nalssiga arumdapssumnida.* (Oh-nule uun nahl-sshee-gah ah-rume-dahp-ssume nee-dah.)

Beauty contest *Miin taehoe* **(Me-een tay-hoe-eh)**
There will be a beauty contest tonight. *Onul bam-e miin taehoega issul goshimnida.* (Oh-nule bahm-eh mee-een tay-hoe-gah ees-suul gah-sheem-nee-dah.)

Beauty parlor/shop *Mi jangwon* **(Me jahng-won)**
The beauty shop is in the arcade *Mi jangwon-i kue arcade-e issumnida.* (Mee-jahng-wahn-eh kue ah-kaid-eh ees-sume-nee-dah.) I want to go to the beauty shop this afternoon. *Onul ohu-e migang-won-e kagoja hamnida.* (Oh-nule oh-huu-eh mee-jahng-wahn-eh kah-joe-gah hahm-nee-dah.)

Bed *Chimdae* **(Cheem-day);** To go to bed *Cham-charie tulda* **(Chahm-cha-ree-eh tule-dah)**
What time do you go to bed? *Tangshin-un myossie cham charie tumnikka?* (Tahng-sheen-uun myah-sshee-eh chahm-cha-ree-eh tume-nee-kkah?) I'm still in bed. *Nanun ajik chimdae-e issumnida.* (Nan-nune ah-jeek cheem-day-eh ee-ssume-nee-day.)

Beef *Soegogi* **(Soeh-go-ghee)**
How about a beef dish? *Soegogi han jopshi tue-shigessoyo?* (Soeh-go-ghee hahn johp-shee tue-shee-gay-ssah-yoe?)

Beer *Maekchu* **(Make-chuu)**
May I have a beer, please. *Maekchu-rul han chan chuseyo.* (Make-chuu-rule hahn chahn chuu-say-yoe.) Two beers, please. *Maekchu-rul tu jan chuseyo.* (Make-chuu-rule too jahn chuu-say-yoe.)

Before (time) *Chone* **(Choe-nay)**
We will arrive before noon. *Urinun chongo chone tochak halgoshimnida.* (Uu-ree-nune chohng-oh chohn-eh toe-chak hahl-gah-sheem-nee-dah.) I want to go before lunch. *Nanun jomshim chon-e kago shipssumnida.* (Nah-nune jahm-sheem chahn-eh kah-go sheep-ssume-nee-dah.)

Bellboy (at a hotel) *Poi* **(Poy);** also *Sahwan* **(Sah-whaan)**
Please send a bellboy for my bags. *Nae kabang-ul*

wihae poi-rul ponae chuseyo. (Nay kah-bahng-ule wee-hay poy rule poe-nay chuu-say-yoe.) The bellboy will show you to your room. *Poi-ga pangkkaji annaehae turil kkomnida.* (Poy-gah pahng-kah-jee ahn-nay-hay tuu-reel kkome-nee-dah.)

Best *Kajang choun* **(Kah-jahng choe-uun)**
Is this the best one? *Igoshi kajang choun goshimnikka?* (Ee-go-shee kah-jahng choh-uun gah-sheem-nee-kkah?) Let me see the best one you have. *Kajang choun kosul poyo chushipshio.* (Kah-jahng choe-uun kah-sul poe-yoe chuu-sheep-she-oh.)

Better *To choun* **(Tah choe-uun);** also *Poda naun* (Poe-dah nah-uun)
Which one is better? *Onu koshi to chossumnikka?* (Ah-nuu kah-she tah choe-ssume-nee-kkah?)

Between *Sai* **(Sah-ee);** also *Chunggan* (Chung-ghan)
Is Taegu between Seoul and Pusan? *Taegu-nun Seoul kwa Pusan sai-e issumnikka?* (Tay-guu-nune Sah-uul kwah Puu-sahn sie-eh ees-sume-nee-kkah?) Let's meet between six and six-thirty. *Yoshoshi eso yoshoshi ban-saie mannapshida.* (Yuh-shah-shee eh-soe yah-shah-shee bahn-sah-ee-eh mahn-nap-shee-dah.)

Bicycle *Chajonga* **(Chah-jahn-gah)**
Can we rent bicycles here? *Yogiso chajongo-rul pillilssu issumnikka?* (Yoe-ghee-sah chah-jahn-gah-rule peel-leel-suu ees-sume-nee-kkah?) Let's go by bicycle. *Chajongo-ro kapshida.* (Chah-jahn-gah-roe kahp-shee-dah.)

Big *Kun* **(Kune)**
That is too big. *Kugosun nomu kumnida.* (Kuu-go-sune nah-muu kume-nee-dah.) Do you have a

bigger one? *To kungosul kajigo issumnikka?* (Tah kung-go-suul kah-jee-go ees-sume nee-kkah?) How big is it? *Olmana kumnikka?* (Ahl-mah-nah kume-nee-kkah?)

Bill (for payment) Kyesanso (Kay-sahn-sah)
Please bring the bill. *Kyesanso-rul kajyo shipshio.* (Kay-sahn-sah-rule kah-joe sheep-she-oh.)   How much is the bill? *Keysanso-ga olma jio?* (Kay-sahn-sah-gah ahl-mah jee-oh?)

Birthday Saengil (Sang-eel);   Birthday present *Saengil sonmul* (Sang-eel soan-muul)
My birthday is next week. *Nae saengili taum chue issumnida.* (Nay sang-eel-ee tah-uum chuu-eh ees-sume-nee-dah.)   When is your birthday? *Saengirun onjeimnikka?* (Sang-ee-rune own-jay-eem-nee-kkah?)   Happy birthday! *Saengirul chukkahamnida!* (Sang-ee-rule chuke-kah-hahm-nee-dah!)

Birthplace Chulssaengji (Chule-sang-jee)
Where is your birthplace? *Chulssaengji-ga odi imnikka?* (Chule-sang-jee-gah ah-dee eem-nee-kkah?)

Black Komun (Kohm-uun);   also *Oduun* (Oh-duu-uun)
Do you have black shoes in this style? *I noyange komun kudurul kajigo issumnikka? (Ee no yahng-eh koh-muun kuu-duu-rule kah-jee-go ees-sume-nee-kkah?)*

Blanket Tamnyo (Tom-nyoh)
Please bring another blanket. *Tarun tamnyo-rul katta chuseyo.* (Tah-rune tom-nyoh-rule kah-ttah chuu-say-yoe.)

Blue Purun (Puu-rune)
Do you have a blue one? *Purun gosul kajigo issum-*

nikka? (Puu-rune go-suul kah-jee-go ees-sume-nee-kkah?)   The sky is blue today. *Onul-un hanuli purumnidu.* (Oh-nuul-uun hah-nuul-ee puu-rume-nee-dah.)

Boat *Pae* **(Pay);**   also *Potu* (Poe-tuu);   Boat race *Potu kyoju* (Poe-tuu k'yoe-juu)
I want to go to Cheju Island by boat. *Nanun Chejudo-e pae-ro kago shipssumnida.* (Nan-nune Cheh-juu-doe-eh pay-roe kah-go sheep-ssume-nee-dah.)

Book *Chaek* **(Chake);**   also *Sojok* (Sah-jahk);   Bookstore *Sojom* (Soe-jome);   Bookstand *Soga* (Soe-gah)
Where is the closest bookstore? *Kajang kakkaun sojom-i odi imnikka?* (Kah-jahng kahk-ka-uun soe-jahm-ee ah-dee eem-nee-kkah?)

Boots *Changhwa* **(Chahng-whah);**   also *Kudu* (Kuu-duu);   Leather boots *Kajuk kudu* (Kah-juke kuu-duu)
I want to buy a pair of leather boots. *Nanun kajuk kudu han kyulye-rul sago shipssumnida.* (Nah-nune kah-juke kuu-duu hahn kyuhl-lyeh-rule sah-go sheep-ssume-nee-dah.)

Border (country) *Kukggyong* **(Kuke-kyahng)**
How far is the border from here? *Yogiso kukggyong kkaji olmana momnikka?* (Yah-ghee-sah kuke-kyahng kkah-jee ahl-mah-nah mahm-nee-kkah?)

Born *Taeonan* **(Tay-uh-nahn)**
Where were you born? *Odiso taeona ssumnikka?* (Ah-dee-soe tay-ah-nah ssume-nee-kkah?)   What year were you born? *Tangshin-un myonnyon-e taeona ssumnikka?* (Tahng-sheen-uun myahn-nyahn-eh tay-ah-nah ssume-nee-kkah?)

Bottle *Pyong* **(P'yong);** Bottle opener *Pyongdda-gae* (P'yong-dah-gay)
I need a bottle opener. *Pyongddagae chuseyo.*
(P'yong-dah-gay chuu-say-yoe.)

Bow (greeting) *Morirul sugida* **(Moe-ree-rule sue-ghee-dah);** also *Insahada* (Een-sah-had-dah)
I am learning how to bow Korean style. *Nanun Hanguk shik insa pangbop-ul paeugo issumnida.*
(Nah-nune Hahn-gook sheek een-sah pahng-bahp-ule pay-uu-go ees-sume-nee-dah.)

Bowl *Konggi* **(Kong-ghee);** Rice bowl *Pap konggi* (Pahp kong-ghee)
Please bring two more bowls. *Tu Konggi to kajyo oseyo.* (Tuu kohng-ghee tah kah-jyah oh-say-yoe.) Would you like a bowl of rice? *Pab han konggi dushigetssoyo?* (Pahb hahn kohng-ghee due-shee-gay-ssah-yoe?)

Box *Sangja* **(Sahng-jah)**
I need a box to mail these books. *I chaek durul pu-chil sangja-ga pilyohamnida.* (Ee chake duu-rule puu-cheel sahng-jah-gah peel-yoe-hahm-nee-dah.)

Boy *Sonyon* **(Soh-nyuhn);** Son *Adul* (Ah-dule); Teenage boy *Shiptae sonyon* (Sheep-tay soh-nyuhn)
Ask the boy to go with us. *Ku sonyonege uriwa ka-chi kaljji-rul mulo poseyo.* (Kuu sah-nyahn-eh-geh uu-ree-wah kah-chee kahl-jee-rule muul-ah poe-say-yoe.)

Brand *Sangpyo* **(Sahng-p'yoe)**
Several Korean brands are now well-known in the U.S. *Yoro Hanguk sangpyoduri Miguk-eso jigum jal alyojyo itta.* (Yuh-rah Hahn-gook sahng-pyoh-due-ree Mee-gook-eh-so jee-gume jahl ahl-yah-jyah ee-ttah.)

Brass *Notssoe* **(not-soeh)**
Is there a brassware shop in this area? *I kuncho-e notssoe kurut sangjom-i issumnikka?* (Ee kune-choe-eh not-so-eh kuu-rute sahng-jahm-ee ees-sume-nee-kkah?)

Bread *Ppang* **(Ppahng)**
Would you like bread or rice? *Ppang dushigetssoyo, pab dushigetssoyo?* (Pphang due-shee-geh-ssuh-yoe, pahb due-shee-geh-ssuh-yoe?) Bread, please. *Ppang chuseyo.* (Pphang chuu-say-yoe.)

Break *Kkaetturida* **(Kkay-tuu-ree-dah)**
Is there anything breakable in your luggage? *Tangshin ui suhwamulssoke kkaejinun got issunikka?* (Tahng-sheen-we soh-hwa-muul-so-kay kkay-jee-nune got ee-ssume-nee-kkah?)

Breakfast *Choban* **(Choe-bahn)**
What time is breakfast? *Choban-un myossie issumnikka?* (Choe-bahn-uun myah-she-eh ee-ssume-nee-kkah?) I'll meet you after breakfast. *Choban hue tangshin-ul mannal goshimnida.* (Choe-bahn huu-eh tahng-sheen-ule mahn-nahl go-sheem-nee-dah.)

Bride *Shinbu* **(Sheen-buu);** Bridegroom Shilrang (Sheel-rahng)
Many brides and bridegrooms go to Cheju Island for their honeymoon. *Manun shinbuwa shilrangduri shinhon yohangul Chejudo-ro ganda.* (Mahn-une sheen-buu-wah sheel-rahng due-ree sheen-hohn yah-hang-uel Cheh-juu-doe-roe gahn-dah.)

Bridge *Tari* **(Tah-ree)**
There are many bridges across the Han River in Seoul. *Seoul-ui Han Kang-ul karojirunun manun tari-duri itta.* (Suh-uul-we Hahn Kahng-ule kah-roh-jee-ruh-nuun mah-nuun tah-ree-duu-ree ee-

ttah.)   It's just beyond the bridge. *Kagosun paro ku tari nomoe itta.* (Kah-gah-suun pah-roe kue tah-ree nah-mah-eh ee-ttah.)

Britain   *Yongguk* **(Yong-gook);**   British   *Yongguk-ui* (Yong-gook-we)   British Embassy *Yongguk Tae-sagwan* (Yong-gook Tays-ah-g'wahn)
Please take me to the British Embassy. *Narul Yongguk Taesagwanuro teryoda chusey.* (Nah-rule Yahng-gook Tay-sah-gwahn-uu-roe teh-ryah-dah chuu-say-yoe.)

Brochure   *Pampulret* **(Pahm-puu-ret)**
Do you have any travel brochures on Kyongju? *Kyongju-e gwanhan yohang pampulret issumnikka?* (Kyahng-juu-eh gwahn-hahn yah-hahng pahm-puu-ret ee-ssume-nee-kkah?)

Brother   *Hyongje* **(H'yong-jay);**   Elder brother *Hyong* (H'yong);   Younger brother   *Au* (Ah-uu); Brothers and sisters   *Hyongje chamae* (H'yong-jay chah-may)

Brown   *Kalssaega* **(Kahl-say-gay)**
Let me see a brown jacket, please. *Kalsaege jaket-ul poyo chuseyo.* (Kahl-say-gay jah-ket-ule poe-yah chuu-say-yoe.)

Buddha   *Pucho* **(Puu-choe);**   also *Pulta* (Pul-tah)

Buddhism   *Pulgyo* **(Pul-g'yoe);**   Buddhist   *Pulgyo-shinja* (Pul-g'yoe-sheen-jah)
Is Buddhism the most popular religion in Korea? *Pulgyoga Hanguk-eso kajang taejungjogin chonggyo imnikka?* (Puul-gyoh-gah Hahn-gook-eh-sah kah-jahng tay-juung-jah-geen chohng-gyoh eem-nee-kkah?)   Some Americans also follow the Buddhist religion. *Yakkan-ui Miguk induldo Pulgyorul missumnida.* (Yah-kkahn-we Mee-gook een-duel-doe Puul-gyoh-rule mee-ssume-nee-dah.)

Budget   *Yesan* **(Yay-sahn)**
What is your budget for this evening? *Onul jon-yok yesanun olma imnikka?* (Oh-nulc jah-nyoke yeh-sah-nuun ahl-mah eem-nee-kkah?)   I do not have a budget for shopping. *Shijang gal yesani opssumnida.* (Shee-jahng gahl yeh-sahn-ee ahp-ssume-nee-dah.)

Building   *Konmul* **(Kone-mule);**   also *Pilding* (Bill-deeng)
What is the name of the building? *Ku konmul-ui irumi mwosshimnikka?* (Kuu kahn-muul we ee-rue-mee mwah-sheem-nee-kkah?)   Where is the building located? *Ku konmul-un odie wichi hago is-sumnikka?* (Kuu kahn-muul-uun ah-dee-eh wee-chee hah-go ee-sume-nee-kkah?)   The office is on the second floor of the Chosun Hotel build-ing. *Ku samushil-un Chosun Hotel Pilding i-chung-e issumnida.* (Kuu sah-muu-sheel-uun Choe-sahn hohtehl peel-deeng eechung-eh ee-sume-nee-dah.)

Burglar   *Toduk* **(Toe-duke)**
It is best to be careful of burglars. *(Toduk-ul cho-shim hanun goshi choesun imnida.* (Toe-duke-ule choe-sheem hah-nune go-she choe-sahn eem-nee-dah.)

Bus   *Posu* **(Bah-sue)**
What is the bus fare? *Posu yogumi olma imnikka?* (Bah-sue yoe-guu-mee ahl-ma eem-nee-kkah?)   Does this bus go to Seoul Station? *I posu-ga Seoul yoge kamnikka?* (Ee bah-sue gah Sah-uul yah-gay kahm-nee-kkah?)   Where do I catch a bus to go to Olympic Village: *Olympic Chon-uro ganun posu-rul odiso tamnikaa?* (Ohl-leem-peck Chohn-uu-roe gah-nuun pah-sue-rule ah-dee-suh tahm-nee-kkah?)

Business *Yongop* **(Yong-ope);** Buiness hours
Yongop shigan (Yong-ope she-gahn); Occupation *Chigop* (Chee-gop)
What business are you in? *Chigopi mwoshimnikka?*
(Chee-guh-pee mwah-sheem-nee-kkah?) I
would like to do business with you. *Tangshin-gwa*
tongop hago shipssumnida. (Tahng-sheen-gwah
tohng-ahp hah-go sheep-ssume-nee-dah.)

Business drink *Kyojesul* **(Kyoh-jeh-suul)**
Let's have a business drink this evening. *Onul*
pame kyojesul hanjan hapshida. (Oh-nule pahm-eh
kyoh-jeh-suul hahn-jahn hahp-shee-da.)

Businessman *Shiropgga* **(She-rahp-gah):** also
Sangin (Sahng-een)
The Chosun Hotel is very popular with businessmen. *Chosun Hotel-un shiropgga-dulege taedanhi*
inkki imnida. (Choe-sahn Hoh-tehl-uun shee-
rahp-gah-dul-eh-geh tay-dahn-hee een-kkee
eem-nee-dah.)

Busy *Pabbun* **(Pah-boon)**
Are you busy now? *Chigum pabbu shimnikka?*
(Chee-gume pah-bbuu sheem-nee-kkah?) No,
I'm not busy. *Anio, nanun pabbu-ji anssumnida.*
(Ah-nee-oh, nah-nune pah-bbuu-jee ahn-ssume-
nee-dah.) Yes, I'm very busy right now. *Yeh,*
nanun jigum maeu pabbumnida. (Yeh, nah-nune
may-uu pah-bboom nee-dah.)

Butter *Poto* **(Pah-tah)**
May we have some butter, please? *Poto jom chu-*
seyo. (Pah-tah johm chuu-say-yoe.)

Buy *Sada* **(Sah-dah)**
I want to buy a fur coat. *Nanun mopi coat-rul sago*
shipssumnida. (Nah-nune moe-pee koh-tue-rule
sah-go sheep-ssume-nee-dah.) Where did you

buy this? *Tangshin-un igossul odiso sassumnikka?*
(Tahng-sheen-uun ee-gah-sule ah-dee-suh sah-
ssume-nee-kkah?) I have bought too much.
Nanun nomu mani satta. (Nah-nune nah-muu
mahn-ee sah-ttah.)

C

Cabbage *Yangbaechu* **(yahng-bay-chuu)** also
K'aebiji (Kae-bee-jii)
Cabbage is the main ingredient in kimchi. *(Yang-
baechuga kimchi-e chusongbun imnida.* (Yahng-bay-
chuu-gah kimchi-eh chuu-suhng-buun eem-nee-
dah.)

Cablecar *Keibulka* **(Kay-bul-kah);**   Cablegram
Haeoe chonbo (Hay-oh chuhn-boh)
Let's take the cablecar. *Keibulka-rul tapshida.* (Kay-
buul-kah-rule tahp-shee-dah.) I'd like to send a
cablegram to the U.S. *Miguk-e haeoe chonbo-rul
ponaego shipssumnida.* (Mee-gook-eh hay-oh
chuhn-boh-rule poh-nay-goh sheep-ssume-nee-
dah.)

Cake *Keiku* **(Kay-kuu)**
Would you like a piece of cake? *Keiku hanjogak
dushigessoyo?* (Kay-kuu hahn-joh-gak due-shee-
gay-ssah-yoh?) What kind of cake do you have?
Otton keiku-rul dushigessumnikka? (Ah-ttahn kay-
kuu-rule duu-she-gay-ssume-nee-kkah?) We
have chocolate cake and coconut cake. *Chocolate
keiku wa coconut keiku-ga issumnida.* (Choh-kohl-
leit kay-kuu wah koh-koh-nuht kay-kuu-gah ees-
sume-nee-dah.)

Calendar *Tallyok* **(Tall-yoke);** Lunar calendar
Umnyok (Umm-n'yoke)
Let me check the calendar. *Tallyok-ul poaya ges-
sumnida.* (Tahl-lyuhk-ule poh-ah-yah geh-
ssume-nee-dah.)

Call *Puruda* **(Pue-rue-dah)**
Please call a taxi. *Taxi-rul pulo chuseyo.* (Tack-
shee-rule puul-ah chuu-say-yoe.) What do you
call this in Korean? *Igosul Hangung mallo muorage
hamnikka?* (Ee-go-sule Hahn-gung mahl-loh mu-
uh-rah-go hahm-nee-kkah?) Who is calling,
please? *Chonhwa koshinun punun nugu-shimnikka?*
(Chahn-whah kah-she-noon puu-noon nuu-guu
sheem-nee-kkah?)

Camera *Kamera* **(Kah-meh-rah)**
Don't forget your camera. *Kamera-rul ijji mashipshio* [or] *maseyo.* (Kah-meh-rah-rule ee-jjee mah-
sheep-shee-oh [or] mah-say-yoe.) Shall I take a
camera? *Noega kamera-rul kajyodo doemnikka?*
(Naeh-gah kah-meh-rah-rule kah-jyo-doh dome-
nee-kkah?) Whose camera is this? *Igossun nugu-e
kamera imnikka?* (Ee-goh-sune nuu-guu-eh kah-
meh-rah eem-nee-kkah?)

Can *Hal ssu itta* **(Hahl suu ee-tah)**
Can you do it? *Kugossul halsu issumnikka?* (Kuu-
goh-sule hahl-suu-ee-ssume-nee-kkah?) What
can I do for you? *Mwosul towa turilkkayo?* (Mwah-
sule toh-wah tuu-reel-kkah-yoh?) Can you
speak English? *Yongo-rul mal halsu issumnikka?*
(Yohng-ah-rule mahl hahl-suu ee-ssume-nee-
kkah?) Can you help me? *Narul towa julsu issumnikka?* (Nah-rule tah-wah juul-suu ee-
ssume-nee-kkah?) Can you take me to the
Chosen Hotel? *Narul Chosun Hotelo teryoda julsu
issumnikka?* (Nah-rule Choh-sahn Hoh-tehl-oh
tay-ryah-dah juul-suu ee-ssume-nee-kkah?)

Cancel *Ch'wisohada* **(Chwee-soh-ha-dah)**
Please cancel my reservation. *Yeyak-ul chwiso hae chuseyo.* (Yeh-yahk-ulc chwee-soh hay-chuu-say-yoe.) Shall I cancel tomorrow's reservation? *Naeil-e yeyak-ul chwiso haedo doemnikka?* (Nay-eel-eh yeh-yahk-ule chwee-soh hay-doh dome-nee-kkah?) It's raining, so let's cancel the tour. *Piga oni, kwangwang-ul chwiso hapshida.* (Pee-gah oh-nee, kwahng-wahng-ule chwee-soh hahp-shee-dah.)

Candy *K'aendi* **(Kahn-dee);** also *Kwaja* (Kwah-jah)
Would you like some chocolate candy? *Chocolate kaendi dushigessoyo?* (Choh-kohl-leit kahn-dee due-shee-geh-ssuh-yoh?

Capital (city) *Sudo* **(Sue-doe);** Money *Chabon* (Chah-bone)
Seoul is the capital of Korea. *Seoul-un Taehanmin-guk-e sudoimnida.* (Suh-uu-rune Tay-hahn-meen-gook-eh suh-doh-eem-nee-dah.)

Car *Cha* **(Chah);** Motorcar *Chadongcha* (Chah-dong-chah); Sleeping car *Chimdae cha* (Cheem-day chah)
I would like to rent a car. *Charul piligo shipssumnida.* (Chah-rule peel-ee-goh sheep-ssume-nee-dah.) What number is the sleeping car? *Chimdae chanun myoppon imnikka?* (Cheem-day-chah-nune myuh-ppahn eem-nee-kkah?)

Careful *Choshimsong innun* **(Choe-sheem-song een-noon)**
Careful it isn't broken! *Kkaeji antorok choshimhashio!* (Kay-jee ahn-toe-roke choe-sheem-hah-she-oh!)

Carrot *Tanggun* **(Tahng-goon)**
Do you have fresh carrots? *Shinsonhan tanggun is-*

sumnikka? (Sheen-suhn-hahn tahng-gune ee-ssume-nee-kkah?)   May I have some carrots, please? *Tanggun jom chuseyo.* (Tahng-gune johm chuu-say-yoe.)

Carry   *Unbanhada* **(Uun-bahn-hah-dah);**   also *Naruda* (Nah-rue-dah)
Please carry this for me. *Nae taeshin igosul unban hae chuseyo.* (Nay tay-sheen ee-go-suul uun-bahn hay chuu-say-yoe.)   Can you carry that by yourself? *Tangshin susuro kugosul unban halssu issumnikka?* (Tahn-sheen sue-sue-roh kuu-go-suul uun-bahn hahl-suu ee-ssume-nee-kkah?)   I'll carry it. *Kugosul unban halssu issumnida.* (Kuu-go-suul uuhn-bahn hahl-suu ee-ssume-nee-dah.)

Cash   *Hyongum* **(H'yone-gume)**
I'll pay cash. *Hyongum-uro chibul hal goshimnida.* (Hyahn-gume-uu-roh chee-buul hahl go-sheem-nee-dah.)   We accept only cash. *Hyongum man passumnida.* (Hyahn-gume-mahn pah-ssume-nee-dah.)   Can you cash this check, please? *(I supyo-rul hyongu-muro paqwo chulssu issumnikka?* (Ee suu-pyah-rule hyon-guu-muu-roe pah-qwo chuul-suu ee-ssume-nee-kkah?)

Cashier   *Chullapkye* **(Chull-ahp-kay);**   also *Hoegyegye* (Hoh-gay-gay)
Please pay the cashier. *Hoegyegye-e chibul-hahshipshio.* (Hoh-gay-gay-eh chee-bull-hah-ship-she-oh.)   Please leave it at the cashier's desk. *Kugosul hoegye-ui chaekssange noachuseyo.* (Kuu-go-suul hoh-gay-we chaek-sahng-eh noh-ah-chuu-say-yoe.)

Castle   *Song* **(Song)**
Are there many castles in Korea? *Hanguk-enun manun songdueri issumnikka?* (Hahn-gook-eh-nune mah-nuun song-duu-eh-ree ee-ssume-nee-kkah?)

Catholic Church *Chonju kyohoe* **(Chone-juu Kyoh-huh)**; Catholicism *Chonjugyo* (Chone-juu-g'yoe)
Are there many Catholic churches in Korea? *Hanguk-enun manun chonju kyohoeduri issumnikka?* (Hahn-gook-eh-nune mah-nune chone-juu kyoh-hoh-duu-ree ee-ssume-nee-kkah?)

Celadon *Chongja* **(Chonge-jah)**
I would like to see some of Korea's famous celadon pottery. *Hanguk-e yumyonghan chongja tojagiruel pogo shipssumnida.* (Hahn-gook-eh yuu-myuhng-hahn chonge-jah-toh-jah-ghee-rule poh-goh sheep-ssume-nee-dah.)

Change *Pakkuda* **(Pah-kkuu-dah)**; Small coins *Chandon* (Chahn-doan); Money returned as balance *Kosurumton* (Koe-sue-rume-tone)
Where do I change buses? *Odiso posu-rul pakkwo tam nikka?* (Ah-dee-suh poe-sue-rule pah-kkwoh tahm nee-kkah?) Here is your change. *Chandon yogi issumnida.* (Chahn-dohn yah-ghee ee-ssume-nee-dah.) Do you have change for this? *Igo pakkulgot issumnikka?* (Ee-guh pah-kuul-guht ee-ssume-nee-kkah?) Keep the change. *Kosurumtonon-un kajishio.* (Koe-sue-rume-tone-uun kah-jee-she-oh.)

Charge (expenses) *Piyong* **(Pee-yong)**; also *Yogum* (Yoh-gume)
What are the charges? *Piyong-i olma imnikka?* (Pee-yong-ee ahl-mah eem-nee-kkah?) There is a delivery charge. *Paedal yogumi issumnida.* (Pay-dahl yoh-gume-ee ee-ssume-nee-dah.)

Charming *Maeryokchogin* **(May-ryuk-chah-geen)**
The children are charming. *Ku yoja nun maeryokchogimnida.* (Kuu yoe-jah nuun may-ryuk-chuh-gheem-nee-dah.)

Chauffeur *Koyong unjonsa* **(Koh-yohng uun-juhn-sah)**
I would like to hire a chauffeur. *Unjonsa-rul koyong hago shipssumnida.* (Uun-jahn-sah-rule koh-yohng hah-goh sheep-ssume nee-dah.)
Please tell the chauffeur to wait for me. *Na rul kidarirago unjonsaege malhaseyo.* (Nah-rule kee-dah-ree-rah-goh uun-juhn-sah-eh-geh mahl-hah-say-yoh.)

Cheap *Ssan* **(Sahn);** also *Kapssan* (Kahp-sahn)
Do you have anything cheaper than this? *Igot-poda to ssan kosun opsumnikka?* (Ee-gote-poe-dah toe sahn koe-soon ope-sume-nee-kkah?) That is too cheap. *Kugosun nomu ssamnida.* (Kuu-gah-sune nah-muu ssahm-nee-dah.)

Check (personal/bank) *Sup'yo* **(Supe-yoe);** Bill at restaurant *Kyesan* **(Kay-sahn)**
Do you accept checks? *Supyo-rul passumnikka?* (Suu-pyoh-rule pah-ssume-nee-kkah?) I'd like to cash this check. *Isupyo-rul hyon gumuro pakkuo chushige-ssumnikka?* (Ee supe-yoe-rule h'yone gume-uu-roe pahk-uu-oh chuu-she-gay-sume-nee-kkah?) Check, please. *Kyesanhae chushipshio.* (Kay-sahn-hay chuu-sheep-she-oh.)

Checkbook *Supyochang* **(Suu-pyoh-chang);** also *Supyochake* (Suu-pyoh-chake)
I forgot my checkbook. *Supyochaekul punshil haessumnida.* (Suu-pyoh-chake-ule puun-sheel hay-ssume-nee-dah.) Don't forget your checkbook. *Supyochaek-ul punshil haji mashipshio.* (Suu-pyoh-chake-ule puun-sheel hah-jee mah-sheep-shee-oh.)

Cheese *Chiju* **(Chee-jue)**
What kind of cheese do you have? *Otton chijuga*

issumnikka? (Ah-ttahn chee-juu-gah ee-ssume-nee-kkah?)

Chestnut *Pam* (Pahm)

Would you like some roasted chestnuts? *Kun pam-ul dushigessoyo?* (Kuun pahm-ule due-shee-geh-ssuh-yoe?) Chestnuts are used in some Korean dishes. *Pami Hanguk umshike mani ssuimnida.* (Pahm-ee Hahn-gook umm-shee-keh mahn-ee ssue-eem-nee-dah.)

Chewing gum *Kkom* (Kome)

Do you have any gum? *Kkom-ul kajigo issumnikka?* (Kome-ule kah-jee-goh ee-ssume-nee-kkah?)

Chicken *Tak* (Tahk)

Let's have a chicken dish. *Takyori-rul mogupshida.* (Tahk-yoh-ree-rule muh-gupe-shee-dah.) Do you have barbecued chicken? *Barbecue tak issumnikka?* (Bah-bee-kyu tahk ee-ssume-nee-kkah?)

Chilly *Sonsonhan* (Suhn-sahn-hahn); also *Ususuhan* (Ue-sue-sue-hahn)

It is chilly today. *Onul-un sonsonhamnida.* (Oh-nule uun suhn-suhn-hahm-nee-dah.)

China *Chungguk* (Chung-gook); Chinese *Chunggugin* (Chung-goog-een)

Have you been to China? *Tangshin-un Chunguk-e kabonjogi issumnikka?* (Tahng-sheen-uun Chung-gook-eh kah-bohn-jah-ghee ees-sume-nee-kkah?) I'm going to China from here. *Nanun yogiso Chungguk-uro kamnida.* (Nah-nune yah-ghee-suh Chuung-gook-uu-roh kahm-nee-dah.)

Chopsticks *Chotkarak* (Chuht-kah-rahk)

May we have chopsticks, please. *Chotkarak-ul chushipshio* [or] *chuseyo.* (chuht-kah-rahk-ule chuu-sheep-shee-oh [or] chuu-say-yoe.)

Christmas *Songtanjol* **(Song-tahn-jole);** also
Kurisumasu (Kue-ree-sue-mah-sue)
Is Christmas celebrated in Korea? *Hanguk-eso
songtanjol-ul chukha hamnikka?* (Hahn-gook-eh-suh
song-tahn-jole-ule chuuk-hah hahm-nee-kkah?)

Church *Kyohoe* **(Kyoh-hoh-eh);** Church service
Yebae (Yay-bay)
What time do church services start? *Yebae-nun
myot sshi-e shijaktoemnikka?* (Yeh-beh-nune myuht
she-eh she-jahk-tome-nee-kkah?)

Circus *Kongmadan* **(Kong-mah-dahn);** also *So-
kosu* (Suh-kuh-sue)
There is a circus today. *Onul sokosuga issumnida.*
(Oh-nule suh-kah-sue-gah ee-ssume-nee-dah.)
Let's go to the circus. *Kongmadan kugyong kapshida.* (Kong-mah-dahn kuu-gyohng kahp-shee-
dah.)

Citizen *Shimin* **(She-meen);** Citizenship *Shimin
kwon* (She-meen k'won)
Are you a citizen of Korea? *Tangshin-un Hanguk
shimin imnikka?* (Tahng-sheen-uun Hahn-gook
shee-meen eem-nee-kkah?) What is your citizenship? *Tangshin-un onu nara shimin imnikka?* (Tahng-
sheen-uun uh-nue nah-rah shee-meen eem-nee-
kkah?)

Clam *Taehapchogae* **(Tay-hop-choe-gay)**
Would you like some raw clams? *Saeng taehapcho-
gae-rul tushigessoyo?* (Sang tay-hop-choh-gay-rule
tuu-shee-geh-ssuh-yoe?)

Class (kind) *Chongnyu* **(Chong-nyuu);** Rank
Tunggup (Tung-gupe); Social status *Kyegup*
(Kay-gupe); Lesson *Hakkup* (Hahk-up)
How much is first class? *Iltunggup-un olma im-
nikka?* (Eel-tung-gupe-uum ahl-mah eem-nee-

kkah?) Two first-class tickets to Seoul, please. *Seoul-hang il tunggup pyo-rul tujang chuseyo.* (Sah-uul-hang eel-tung-gupe pyoh-rule tuu-jahng chuu-say-yoe.)

Clean *Kkaekkutan* **(Kake-kuu-tahn);** To clean *Chongsohada* (Chong-soe-hah-dah)
Please clean my room. *Naebang-ul chongsohaseyo.* (Nay-bahng-ule chahng-soh-hah-say-yoe.)
Please give me a clean fork. *Kkaekkutan fork-rul chuseyo.* (Kkay-kuu-tahn poh-kue-rule chuu-seh-yoh.) Please have this suit cleaned. *I yangbo-gul setakhae chushipshio.* (Ee yang-boe-gule say-tahk-hay chuu-sheep-she-oh.)

Clerk *Samuwon* **(Sah-muu-won);** also *Sogi* (Soe-ghee)
Please ask the clerk at the front desk. *Annaegye-e samuwonge mulo poseyo.* (Ahn-nae-gay-eh sah-muu-won-geh muul-ah poh-say-yoe.)

Climate *Kihu* **(Kee-hun)**
What kind of climate does Korea have? *Hanguk-e kihunun ottossumnikka?* (Hahn-gook-eh kee-huu-nune ah-ttah-ssume-nee-kkah?) The climate is mild in Pusan. *Pusan-e kihunun onhwa hamnida.* (Puu-sahn-eh kee-huu-nune own-hwa hahm-nee-dah.)

Clinic (medical office) *Chiryoso* **(Chee-ryo-sho);** also *Ui-won* (We-wahn)
Is there a clinic nearby? *Kuncho-e uiwon-i issumnikka?* (Kune-chan-eh we-wahn-ee ee-sume-nee-kkah?)

Clock *Shigye* **(She-gay)**
Is there a clock in the room? *Ku bange shigyega issumnikka?* (Kuu bahng-eh shee-gay-gah ee-ssume-nee-kkah?) This clock is slow. *I shigye-*

nun nurimnida. (Ee shee-gay-nune nuu-reem-nee-dah.)

Clogs (wooden shoes) *Namakshin* **(Nah-mahk-sheen)**
I'd like to buy some clogs as souvenirs. *Kinyom-pum-uro namakshin-ul shago shipssumnida.* (Kee-nyahm-puum-uu-roh nahmahk-sheen-ule shah-goh sheep-ssume-nee-dah.)

Close (near) *Kakkai* **(Kah-kkai);** also *Kunchoe* (Kune-choe); Shut *Tatchido* (Taht-chee-dah)
Is it close to here? *Yogiso kakkapssumnikka?* (Yah-ghee-suh kah-kkahp-ssume-nee-kkah?) The shopping center is close to your hotel. *Shopping center-nun hotel kuncho imnida.* (Shoh-pping shen-tah-nune hoh-tehl kune-cha eem-nee-dah.) Please close the window. *Changmun-ul tada chuseyo.* (Chahng-muun-ule tah-dah chuu-say-yoe.)

Cloth *Chon* **(Chone);** Woven fabric *Otkam* (Oat-kham)
I'd like to buy some cloth for a suit. *Yangbok chon-ul shago shipssumnida.* (Yahng-bohk-chahn-ule shah-goh sheep-ssume-nee-dah.) May I see some cloth samples? *Otkam kyonbon chom poyo chushipshio.* (Oat-kham k'yone-bone chohm poh-yuh chuu-sheep-she-oh.)

Cloudy *Hurin* **(Hue-reen)**
Unfortunately, it is cloudy today. *Pulhanghi, onul-un hurimnida.* (Puul-hahng-hee, oh-nule-uun hue-reem-nee-dah.) Is it going to be cloudy to-morrow? *Naeil-un hurimnikka?* (Nay-eel-uun hue-reem-nee-kkah?)

Coat *Kotu* **(Koh-tue)**
Don't forget your coat. *Kotu-rul ijji maseyo.* (Koh-tuu-rule ee-jjee mah-say-yoe.) It's going to be

cold, so take a coat. *Chuulgoshini, kotu-rul kajoga-shipshio.* (Chuu-uul-gah-shee-nee, koh-tuu-rule kah-jyah-gah-sheep-shee-oh.)

Cocktail   *Kakteil* **(Kahk-teil)**
Let's have a cocktail before dinner. *Shiksha chone kakteil-ul tupshida.* (Sheek-shah chahn-eh kahk-teh-eel-ule tupe-shee-dah.)   Would you like a cocktail? *Kakteil tushigessumnikka?* (Kahk-teh-eel tuu-shee-geh-ssume-nee-kkah?)

Coffee   *Kopi* **(Koe-pee)**
Coffee, please. *Kopi-rul chuseyo* [or] *chushipshio.* (Koh-pee-rule chuu-say-yoe [or] chuu-sheep-shee-oh.)   How do you like your coffee? *Kopi mashi maume tumnikka?* (Koh-pee mah-shee mah-ume tume-nee-kkah?)

Coke (Coca-Cola)   *Koka kolla* **(Koe-kah koe-la)**
Two cokes, please. *Koka kolla tujan chuseyo.* (Koh-kah kohll-ah tuu-jahn chuu-say-yoe.)

Cold   *Chuun* **(Chuu-uun);**   also *Ssanulhan* **(Ssah-nuel-hahn);**   *Kamgi* **(kahm-ghee)**
It's really cold today! *Onul-un cham chupssumnida!* (Ohn-nule-uun chahm chuup-ssume-nee-dah!)   I caught a cold. *Kamgi kolyossum nida.* (Kahm-ghee kuhl-lyah-ssume nee-dah.)   It will get much colder tonight. *Onul pam-enun jomdu chuwojil ko-simnida.* (Oh-nule pahm-eh-nuun johm-duh chuu-wuh-jeel kuh-sheem-nee-dah.)

Color   *Saek* **(Sake)**
What colors do you have? *Otton saek-ul kajigo is-sumnikka?* (Ah-ttahn sake-ule kah-jee-goh ee-ssume-nee-kkah?)   This color looks good on you. *I saegi tangshin-ege oulrimnida.* (Ee say-ghee tahng-sheen eh-gay ah-uul-reem-nee-dah.)

Comb *Pit* **(Peet)**
I'm looking for a comb. *Pit-ul chatgo issumnida.*
(Peet-ule chaht-goh ee-ssume-nee-dah.)

Come *Oda* **(Oh-dah)**
What time are they coming? *Kudul-un myossie omnikka?* (Kuu-duel-uun myuh-she-eh ohm-nee-kkah?) What time shall I come? *Myot shie kalkkayo?* (M'yote she-eh kahl-kah-yoe?) Come in! *Duro oseyo!* (Du-roe oh-seh-yoh!) Are you coming? *Oshigessum nikka?* (Oh-shee-gay-ssume nee-kkah?) Where do you come from? *Kohyang-un odishimnikka?* (Koe-yahng-uun oh-dee-sheem-nee-kkah?) also *Chulshin-un odishimnikka?* (Chuul-sheen-uun oh-dee-sheem-nee-kkah?)

Comfortable *Kibun choun* **(Kee-boon choe-uun);** also *Anukan* (Ah-nue-kahn); *Pyonhan* (Pyohn-hahn)
Is it comfortable? *Pyonhan nikka?* (Pyohn-hahn nee-kkah?) Please make yourself comfortable. *Pudi maum puk noushipshio.* (Puu-dee mah-uum pook no-uu-sheep-she-oh.) also *Pyonani swiseyo.* (Pyo-nah-nee swee-say-yoe.)

Common *Potonge* **(Poh-tohng-eh)**
That is a common sight in Korea. *Kugosun Hanguk-esonun potonge punggyong imnida.* (Kuu-gah-sune Hahn-gook-eh-sah-nuun poh-tohng-eh puung-yong eem-nee-dah.)

Communication *Chondal* **(Chone-dahl)**
Communication is very good between Korea and the rest of the world. *Chondal-un Hanguk gwa segye saie maeu chungyohan goshimnida.* (Chahn-dahl-uun Hahn-gook gwah say-gay sah-ee-eh may-uu chuung-yoh-hahn gah-sheem-nee-dah.)

Communist *Kongsanjuuija* **(Kong-sahn-juu-we-jah)**

Are those people Communists? *Cho saram dulun kongsanjuuijadul imnikka?* (Chah sah-rahm duel-une kohng-sahn-juu-we-jah-duel eem-nee-kkah?)

Companion *Chingu* **(Cheen-guu);** also *Tongbanja* (Tong-bahn-jah)

These are my companions. *I saram dulun nae chingudul imnida.* (Ee-sah-rahm-duel-uun nay cheen-guu-duel eem-nee-dah.)

Company (firm) *Hoesa* **(Ho-eh-sah);** Guests *Sonnim* (Sone-neem)

What is the name of your company? *Tangshin-e hoesa irum-un mwoshimnikka?* (Tahng-sheen-eh hoe-eh-sah ee-rume-uun mwah-sheem-nee-kkah?) Do you have company now? *Tangshim-un jigum sonnim-gwa issumnikka?* (Tahng-sheen-unn jee-gume soan-neem-gwah es-sume-nee-kkah?)

Concert *Yonjuhoe* **(Yahn-juu-hoeh)**

There is a concert tonight. *Onul pam yonjuhoega issumnida.* (Oh-nule pahm yahn-juu-hoeh-gah ee-ssume-nee dah.) Where is the concert going to be? *Yonjuhoega odi-eso yolimnikka?* (Yahn-juu-hoeh-gah ah-dee-eh-suh yahl-eem-nee-kkah?)

Conductor (of a train) *Chajang* **(Chah-jahng)**

Excuse me, are you the conductor? *Shillye hamnidama, tangshimi chajang imnikka?* (Sheel-yeh hahm-nee-dah-mah, tahng-sheem-ee chah-jahng eem-nee-kkah?)

Confirm *Hwaginhada* **(Hwah-gheen-hah-dah)**

I would like to confirm my plane reservations. *Nae pihaenggi yeyak-ul hwaginhago shipssumnida.* (Nay pee-hang-ghee yeh-yahk-ule hwah-geen-hah-go sheep-ssume-nee-dah.)

Confucious *Kongja* **(Kohng-jah)**
Does this temple have some connection with
Confucius? *I sawan-un kongjawa kwallyon issum
nikka?* (Ee sah-wahn-uun Kohng-jah-wah kwal-
lyuhn ee-ssume-nee-kkah?)

Congratulate *Chukahada* **(Chuke-ah-hah-dah)**
Congratulations! *Chukahamnida!* (Chuke-ah-
hahm-nee-dah!)

Consulate *Yongsagwan* **(Yahng-sagh-wahn)**
Is there a Korean Consulate here? *Yogie Hanguk
Yongsagwani issumnikka?* (Yah-ghee-eh Hahn-gook
Yahng-sah-gwahn-ee ee-ssume-nee-kkah?)
Where is the consulate? *Yongsagwani odie issum-
nikka?* (Yahng-sah-gwahn-ee ah-dee-eh ee-
ssume-nee-kkah?)

Contract *Kyeyak* **(Kay-yahk)**
It is better to have a contract. *Kyeyak hanungoshi
chokessumnida.* (Kay-yahk hah-nune-guh-shee
choh-keh-ssume-nee-dah.)   Please sign the contract here. *Yogi kyeyake somyong hashipshio.* (Yah-
ghee kay-yahk-eh sah-myahng hah-sheep-shee-
oh.)

Conversation *Hoehwa* **(Hoe-whah);** also *Taehwa*
(Tay-whah)
I want to study Korean conversation. *Hanguk
hoehwa-rul kongbu hago shipssumnida.* (Hahn-gook
hoe-whah-rule kohng-buu hah-goh sheep-
ssume-nee-dah.)   Did you study English conversation at school? *Tangshin-un hakgyoeso yongo
hoehwa-rul kongbu haessumnikka?* (Tahng-sheen-
uun hahk-gyo-eh-sah yahng-ah hoe-whah-rule
kohng-buu hay-ssume-nee-kkah?)

Cook *Yorisa* **(Yoh-ree-sah)**
The cook here is very good. *Yogi yorisa-nun tae-*

danni hullyung hamnida. (Yah-ghee yoh-ree-sah-
nune tay-dahn-nee huul-yung hahm-nee-dah.)
Do you know how to cook? *Yorihaljul ashimnikka?*
(Yoh-ree-hahl-juul ah-sheem-nee-kkah?)

Cool *Sonulhan* **(Sah-nuel-hahn);** also *Shiwonhan*
(Shee-won-hahn)
It is nice and cool today. *Onul-un sangknaehago
shiwonhamnida.* (Oh-nule-uun sahng-knay-hah-
goh shee-wahn-hahm-nee-dah.) It will get cool
this evening. *Onul bam-un sonul halgoshimnida.*
(Oh-nule bahm-uun sah-nule hahl-gah-sheem-
nee-dah.)

Copyright *Pankwon* **(pahn-kwahn)**
Is this book copyrighted in Korea? *I chaekun Hanguk-eso pankwon-i issumnikka?* (Ee chack-uun
Hahn-gook-eh-sah pahn-kwahn-ee ee-ssume-
nee-kkah?)

Cost (price) *Kap* **(Kahp);** also *Kagyok* (Kah-
gyuhk); *Piyong* (Pee-yong)
How much does this cost? *Igosun kagyoki olma imnikka?* (Ee-gah-sune kah-gyuhk-ee ahl-mah eem-
nee-kkah?)

Country *Shigol* **(She-gole);** also *Nara* (Nah-rah)
What country are you from? *Onu nara chulshin
imnikka?* (Uh-nuu nah-rah chuul-sheen eem-
nee-kkah?) Is Korea your native country? *Hanguk-un tangshin-e kohyang imnikka?* (Hahn-gook-
uun tahng-sheen-eh koh-yahng eem-nee-kkah?)

Couple (husband and wife) *Pubu* **(Puu-buu)**
They are husband and wife. *Kudulun pubu imnida.* (Kue-duel-uun puu-buu eem-nee-dah.)

Cow *Amso* **(Ahm-soe);** Milk cow *Chosso* (Choe-
soe)
Do many farm families in Korea have milk cows?

Hanguk-e nongganun chosso-rul kajigo issumnikka?
(Hahn-gook-eh nohng-gah-nuun chah-ssoe-rule
kah-jee-goh ee-sume-nee-kkah?)

Cream *Kurim* **(Kue-reem)**
May I have some cream, please? *Kurim jom chu-seyo.* (Kue-reem johm chuu-say-yoe.) Would
you like cream? *Kurim dushigessoyo?* (Kuu-reem
due-shee-gay-ssah-yoh?)

Credit card *Krejit kadu* **(kray-jeet kah-duh);** also
Shinyong kadu (Sheen-yong kah-due)

Cross (the street) *Karojilrogada* **(Kah-roh-jeel-roe-gah-dah)**
Walk straight until you cross three streets. *Ne-gori-rul set chinal ttaekkaji kotchang korogashio.*
(Nay-go-ree-rule sate che-nal take-kah-jee kote-chahng koe-roe-gah-she-oh.)

Crossroad *Negori* **(Nay-go-ree);** also *Kyocharo*
(Kyoh-chah-roh)
Make a left turn at the crossroad. *Kyocharo-eso
jwahoejon hashipshio.* (Kyoh-chah-roh-eh-sah
jwah-hoh-jahn hah-sheep-shee-oh.)

Culture (civilization) *Munhwa* **(Moon-whah)**
I want to learn something about Korea's culture.
Hanguk-e munhwa-rul paeugo shipssumnida. (Hahn-gook-eh moon-whah-rule paeh-uu-goh sheep-ssume-nee-dah.)

Curtain *Koten* **(Kah-tehn)**
Please leave the curtains open. *Koten-ul yoryo
nouseyo.* (Kah-tehn-ule yah-rio noh-uu-say-yoe.)

Cushion *Pangsok* **(Pahng-suhk);** also *K'ushyon*
(Kuu-shone)
Please bring another cushion. *Tarun pangsok-ul*

kajyo oseyo. (Tah-ruun pahng-sahk-ule kah-joe oh-seh-yah.)

Custom *Pungsup* **(Puung-supe);** also *Kwansup* (Kwahn-supe)
Traditional customs are still common in Korea. *Chontongjok pungsupi ajik Hanguk-e nama issumnida.* (Chahn-tohng-jahk puung-supe-ee ah-jeek Hahn-gook-eh nahm-ah ee-ssume-nee-dah.) Is this a Korean custom? *Igosun Hanguk pungsup imnikka?* (Ee-go-suun Hahn-gook puung-supe eem-nee-kkah?)

Customer *Sonnim* **(Sone-neem);** also *Kogaek* (Koe-gake)
Do you have many customers in summer? *Yorume manun kogaeki issumnikka?* (Yah-rum-eh mah-nuun koh-gay-kee ee-ssume-nee-kkah?)

Cuttlefish *Ojingo* **(Oh-jeeng-ah)**
Would you like to try some cuttlefish? *Ojingo-rul hanbon tushoboshiget ssumnikka?* Oh-jccng-ah-rule hahn-bone tuu-sho-bow-she-gate ssume-nee-kkah?)

D

Dad, daddy *Appa* **(Ahp-pah);** also *Aboji* (Ah-bah-jee); Polite form *Abonim* (Ah-bah-neem)
Is your dad still alive and well? *Tangshin-e abonim-un saragyeshimyo kongang hashimnikka?* (Tahng-sheen-eh ah-bah-neem-uun sah-rah-gay-shee-myah kahn-gahng hah-sheem-nee-kkah?)

Daily *Maeil-e* **(May-eel-eh);** also *Ilssang-e* (Eel-sahng-eh)
The train leaves daily at 8 A.M. *Kicha-nun maeil*

yodolshie tonamnida. (Kee-chah-nune may-eel yah-dal-shee-eh tah-nahm-nee-dah.) Is this a daily newspaper? *Igosun ilgan shimmun imnikka?* (Ee-go-sune eel-gahn sheem-muun eem-nee-kkah?)

Dance *Ch'um* **(Chuum);** also *Taenssu* (Daen-sue)
Do you dance? *Chum chuseyo?* (Chuum chuu-say-yoe? Would you like to dance? *Chum chushiges-sumnikka?* (Chuum chuu-shee-geh-ssume-nee-kkah?)

Date (appointment) *Teit'u* **(Day-tuu);** also *Yaksok* (Yhak-soke)
We have a date tomorrow. *Naeil mannal yakssogi issumnida.* (Nay-eel kuu-wah mahn-nahl yahk-soe-ghee ees-sume-nee-dah.)

Daughter *Ttal* **(Tahl);** also *Yoshik* (Yoe-sheek)
This is my daughter. *Nae ttal imnida.* (Nay ttahl eem-nee-dah.) Do you have any daughters? *Ttalduri issumnikka?* (Ttahl-due-ree ee-ssume-nee-kkah?)

Dawn *Saebyok* **(Say-b'yoke)**
Let's leave at dawn. *Saebyoke ttonapshida.* (Say-byah-kay ttah-nahp-she-dah.)

Day (day time) *Nat* **(Naht);** also *Chugan* (Chuu-ghan); One day (24 hours) *Haru* (hah-rue); also *Nal* (Nahl)
Today is the 10th of June. *Onul-un Yuwol shibil imnida.* (Oh-nule-uun yuu-wahl shee-beel eem-nee-dah.) What day is today? *Onul-un musun nal imnikka?* (Oh-nule-uun muu-sune nahl eem-nee-kah?)

Decision *Kyolchong* **(Kyahl-chahng)**
I cannot make a decision now. *Chigum kyolchong halssu opssumnida.* (Chee-gume kyahl-chahng hahl-suu ahp-ssume-nee-dah.) The decision has

already been made. *Imi kyolchong nassumnida.*
(Ee-mee kyahl-chahng nah-ssume-nee-dah.)

Declare (report) *Shingohada* **(Sheen-go-hah-dah);** also *Pogohada* (Poh-goh-hah-dah)
Do you have anything to declare? *Shingohal koshi issumnikka?* (Sheen-go-hahl kah-she ees-sume-nee-kkah?)

Deep *Kipun* **(Kee-pune)**
Is the water deep here? *Yogi imul-un kipssumnikka?* (Yah-ghee ee-muul-uun keep-ssume-nee-kkah?) Is the river deep? *I kang-un olmana kipsumnikka?* (Ee-kahng-uun ahl-mah-nah keep-sume-nee-kkah?)

Deer *Sasum* **(Sah-sume)**
Are there any deer in Korea? *Hanguk-enun-sasumi issumnikka?* (Hahn-gook-eh-nune sah-sue-mee ee-ssume-nee-kkah?)

Degrees (temperature) *Ondo* **(Ohn-doh)**
It is now twenty-eight degrees Centigrade. *Chigum shopssi ishippal do imnida.* (Chee-gume shahp-ssee-ee-sheep-pahl doh eem-nee-dah.)

Delicious *Madinnun* **(Mah-deen-noon);** also *Chinmiui* (Cheen-me-we)
It is delicious. *Madinneyo.* (Mah-deen-nay-yoe.) [or] *Madissumnida.* (Mah-dee-ssume-nee-dah.)

Delightful *Kippun* **(Keep-poon);** also *Chulgoun* (Chuul-gah-uun)
I had a delightful time. *Chulgoun shiganul ponaessumnida.* (Chuul-gah-uun shee-gah-nule poh-nay-ssume-nee-dah.)

Deliver *Chonhada* **(Chone-hah-dah);** also *Paedalhada* (Pay-dahl-hah-dah)
Can you deliver it? *Kugosul chonhalsu issumnikka?*

(Kuu-go-sule chahn-hahl-ssu ee-ssume-nee-
kkah?) Please deliver this. *Igosul chonhaechuseyo.*
(Ee-go-sule chahn-hay-chuu-seh-yoh.)

Dentist   *Chikwaui* (Chee-kwah-we)
I need to go to a dentist. *Chikwae kago chipssum-
nida.* (Chee-kwah-eh kah-goh sheep-ssume nee-
dah.) Do you know a dentist who speaks
English? *Yongo-rul malhanum chikwauisarul ashimnikka?* (Yahng-ah-ruel mahl-hah-nune chee-kwa-
we-sah-rule ah-sheem nee-kkah?)

Depart (leave)   *Chubalhada* (Chuul-bahl-hah-dah)
What time does the train depart? *Kicha-nun myossie ttonamnikka?* (Kee-chah-nune myah-ssee-eh
ttah-nahm-nee-kkah?)

Department store   *Paekhwajom* (Pake-wha-jahm)
What time do the department stores open?
Paekhwajomun myossie yomnikka? (Pake-wha-jahm-
uun myah-sshe-eh yahm-nee-kkah?) Which department store do you recommend? *Onu
paekhwajomul sogae hashi gessumnikka?* (Ah-nuu
pake-wha-jahm-ule soh-gay hah-shee geh-
ssume-nee-kkah?) Can you direct me to the Midopa Department Store? *Midopa paekhwajomul
karuchyo chushigessumnikka?* (Mee-doh-pah pake-
wha-jahm-ule kah-rue-chyah chuu-shee-geh-
ssume nee-kkah?)

Departure   *Chulbal* (Chuul-bahl)
Is this the departure platform for Pusan? *Igoshi
Pusanhaeng chulbal platform imnikka?* (Ee-go-shee
puu-sahn-hang chuul-bahl plaet-form eem-nee-
kkah?) What time is your departure? *Myossie
chulbal hamnikka?* (Myah-shee-eh chuul-bahl
hahm-nee-kkah?)

Dessert *Tijotu* **(Dee-jah-tue);** also *Hushik* (Huu-sheek)
What kind of dessert do you have? *Tijotu nun otton koshi issumnikka?* (Dee-jah-tue-nune aht-toan koe-she ees-sume-nee-kkah?) What would you like for dessert? *Tijoturo mwosul tushigessumnikka?* (Dee-jah-tuu-roh mwah-sule tuu-she-geh-sume-nee-kkah?)

Destination *Haengsonji* **(Hang-soan-jee)**
What is your destination? *Haengsonjiga odi imnikka?* (Hang-sahn-jee-gah ah-dee eem-nee-kkah?)

Devilfish *Ojingo* **(Oh-jeeng-ah)**
Have you ever eaten devilfish? *Ojingorul mogo poassumnikka?* (Oh-jeeng-ah-rule mah-gah poh-ah-ssume-nee-kkah?)

Dial *Taiol* **(Tah-ee-ahl)**
What number did you dial? *Myot pone kosyossumnikka?* (Myaht-pahn-eh kah-shyah sume-nee-kkah?)

Diarrhea *Solssa* **(Sahl-sah)**
I have diarrhea. *Solssa-rul hamnida.* (Sahl-sah-rule hahm-nee-dah.)

Dictionary *Sajon* **(Sah-joan);** English-Korean dictionary *Yong-han sajon* (Yong-hahn-sah-joan); Korean-English dictionary *Han-yong sajon* (Hahn-yong sah-joan)
May I borrow your dictionary for a moment? *Jamkkan sajanul pilnyodo doegessum nikka?* (Jahm-kkahn sah-jah-nule peel-nyah-doh doh-geh-ssume nee-kkah?) Which language dictionary do you recommend? *Onu ohwi sajo-nul sogae hashigessumnikka?* (Ah-nuu ah-hwee sah-jah-nule soh-gay hah-shee-geh-ssume-nee-kkah?)

Dining car *Shiktang cha* **(Sheek-tahng chah);**
Dining room *Shiktang* (Sheek-tahng)
What number is the dining car? *Shiktang cha-nun myopon imnikka?* (Sheek- tahng-chah-nune myah-pahn eem-nee-kkah?) I'll meet you in the dining room. *Shiktang-eso mana poepgessumnida.* (Sheek-tahng-eh-sah mahn-nah pep-geh-ssume-nee-dah.)

Dinner (evening meal) *Chonyok shikssa* **(Chah-nyahk sheek-sah)**
What are the dinner hours? *Chonyok shikssa-nun myossie issumnikka?* (Chah-nyahk sheek-sah-nune myah-shee-eh ee-ssume-nee-kkah?) What time would you like to have dinner? *Chonyok shiksanun myossie tushigessumnikka?* (Chah-nyahk sheek-sah-nune myah-shee-eh tuu-shee-geh-ssume-nee-kkah?) Please join me for dinner tonight. *Onul ppame chonyok shikssa-rul kachi hapshida.* (Oh-nule pahm-eh chah-nyahk sheek-sah-rule kah-chee hahp-shee-dah.)

Direction *Panghyang* **(Pahng-hyang);** also *Chok* (Chohk)
Which direction is the Chosun Hotel? *Chosun Hotel-un onu panghyang imnikka?* (Choh-sahn Hoh-tehl-uun ah-nue pahng-hyahng eem-nee-kkah?) What direction are we going in now? *Uri-nun jigum onu panghyange issumnikka?* (Uu-ree-nune jee-gume ah-nue pahng-hyang-eh es-sume-nee-kkah?)

Dirty *Toroun* **(Tah-rah-uun)**
My shoes are dirty. *Nae kudu nun toropssumnida.* (Nay kuu-duu-nune tah-rahp-ssume-nee-dah.) This plate is dirty. *I panun toropssumnida.* (Ee pah-nune tah-rahp-ssume-nee-dah.)

Discount *Hwarin* **(Hwah-reen)**
Can you give me a discount? *Hwarin-hae chu-shigessumnikka?* (Hwah-reen-hay chu-she-geh-sume-nee-kkah?) A ten percent discount is not enough. *Ship percent hwarinun chungbunchi an-summnida.* (Sheep pah-shent hwah-ree-nune chuung-buun-chee ahn-ssume-nee-dah.)

Dish *Chopshi* **(Chop-she);** Food *Yori* (Yoe-ree); Dishcloth *Hangju* (Hang-juu); Vegetable dish *Yachae yori* (Yah-chie yoe-ree)
Please bring another dish. *Tarun yori-rul katta chuseyo.* (Tah-rune yoh-ree-rule kah-ttah chuu-say-yoe.) Let's have a meat dish, a vegetable dish and a noodle dish. *Kogi yori, yachae yori, myon-rul mogupshida.* (Koe-ghee yoe-ree yah-chay yoe-ree, me-yone-rule moe-gupe-she-dah.)

Do (act) *Hada* **(hah-dah);** Deal with *Chori hada* (Chah-ree hah-dah)
What are you going to do? *Mwosul hal yejong im-nikka?* (Mwah-sule hahl yeh-jahng eem-nee-kkah?) What are you doing now? *Chigum mwosul hago kyeshimnikka?* (Chee-gume mwah-sule hah-go kay-sheem-nee-kkah?)

Doctor *Uisa* **(We-sah);** Title of doctor *Pakssa* (Pahk-sah); Female doctor *Youisa* (Yoh-we-sah)
Please send for a doctor. *Uisa-rul pulro chuseyo.* (We-sah-rule puul-roe chuu-say-yoe.)

Dog *Kae* **(Kay);** Mad dog *Michin kae* (Me-cheen-kay)
I couldn't sleep last night because of a noisy dog. *Shikkuroun gae ttaemune chinan pam jam-ul mochassumnida.* (Shee-kkue-rah-uun gay ttay-muun-eh chee-nahn-pahm jahm-ule moh-chah-ssume-nee-dah.)

Doll *Inhyong* **(Een-hyong)**
I would like to buy a Korean doll as a souvenir.
Kinyompum-uro Hanguk inhyongul sago shipssum-nida. (Kee-nyahm-puum-uh-roe Hahn-gook een-hyong-ule sah-goh sheep-ssume-nee-dah.)

Dollar *Dalla* **(Dahl-lah)**
How much is that in dollars? *Kugosun dollaro olma imnikka?* (Kuu-go-sune dahl-lah-roh ahl-mah eem-nee-kkah?) I have only twenty dollars. *Tanji iship dalla issumnida.* (Tahn-jee ee-sheep dahl-lah ee-ssume-nee-dah.)

Door *Mun* **(moon);** Entrance *Churipku* (Chuu-reep-kuu); Front door *Ammun* (Ahm-moon); Back door *Twin-mun* (Tween-moon)
Please open the door. *Munul yoro chuseyo.* (Muun-ule yah-rah chuu-say-yoe.) Is the door locked? *Muni chamgyossumnikka?* (Muun-ee chahm-gyah-ssume-nee-kkah?) Lock the door. *Munul chamguseyo.* (Muun-ule chahmguu-say-yoe.)

Doorbell *Hyongwanpel* **(Hyahn-gwahn-pehll)**
When you arrive, ring the doorbell. *Tochak ha-myon, hyongwan perul nuruseyo.* (Toh-chahk hah-myahn hyahn-gwahn peh-rule nuu-ruu-say-yoe.)

Doorman (or bellboy) *Munjigi* **(Moon-jee-ghee)**
The doorman will get you a taxi. *Munjigiga tang-shin-ege taxi-rul taewojul goshimnida.* (Muun-jee-ghee-gah tahng-sheen-eh-gay taxi-rule tay-woe-juul go-sheem-nee-dah.)

Doorway *Churipku* **(Chuu-reep-kuu)**
Please don't block the doorway. *Churipku-rul makji mashipshio.* (Chuu-reep-kuu-rule mahk-jee mah-sheep-shee-oh.)

Downtown *Toshimji* **(Toe-sheem-jee);** also
Sangga chidae (Sahng-gah chee-die)
I'd like to see the downtown area. *Toshimji-rul
pogo shipssumnida.* (Toh-sheem-jee-rule poh-goh
sheep-ssume-nee-dah.)   Are there any restaurants downtown? *Toshimji-e shiktangi issumnikka?*
(Toh-sheem-jee-eh sheek-tahng-ee ee-ssume-nee-
kkah?)

Dozen *Tasu* **(Tah-sue)**
Two dozen, please. *Tu tasu chushipshio.* (Tuu tah-
sue chuu-sheep-shee-oh.)   What is the price of
one dozen? *Han tasu-ui kagyogi olma imnikka?*
(Hahn tah-sue-we kah-gyo-ghee ahl-mah eem-
nee-kkah?)

Dress *Uibok* **(We-boke);** also *Duressu* (Duu-ray-
sue);   Get dressed *Osul ip'ida* (Oh-sule eep-dah)
Your dress is beautiful. *Oshi arumdapssumnida.*
(Oh-shee ah-rume-dahp-ssume-nee-dah.)   Do
you like this dress? *I oshi maume tumnikka?* (Ee
oh-shee mah-uum-eh tume-nee-kkah?)

Drink *Umnyo* **(Uum-n'yoe);** To drink *Mushida*
(Mah-she-dah);   Soft drink *Chongnyang umnyo*
(Chong-nyang uum-n'yoe)
Would you like something to drink? *Muot jom
mashigessumnikka?* (Muu-aht johm mah-shee-
geh-ssume-nee-kkah?)   Let's get something to
drink. *Muot jom mashipshida.* (Muu-aht johm mah-
sheep-shee-dah.)

Drive *Unjon* **(Uun-jahn);** also *Turaibu* (Tue-rie-
buu);   Driver *Unjonsa* (Uun-jahn-sah)
Let's drive out into the countryside. *Shigol-ro turaibu hapshida.* (Shee-gohl-roh tue-rie-buu hahp-
shee-dah.)   Can you drive? *Unjon haljul
ashimnikka?* (Uun-jahn hahl-juul ah-sheem-nee-
kkah?)

85

Drugstore *Yakpang* **(Yahk-pahng);** also *Yakkuk* (Yahk-kuuk)
Where is the nearest drustore? *Kajang kakkaun yakkuki odie issumnikka?* (Kah-jahng kah-kkah-uun yahk-kuu-kee ah-dee-eh ee-ssume-nee-kkah?)

Dry-clean *Turai kurininghada* **(Tu-rie kuu-ree-neeng-hah-dah)**
Please have these dry-cleaned. *Igosul turai kurininghae chuseyo.* (Ee-go-sule tuu-rie kuu-ree-ning-hay chuu-say-yoe.)

Dust *Monji* **(Mahn-jee);** To dust *Chongsohada* (Chahng-soh-hah-dah)
There is a lot of dust in the air. *Kongkichunge monjiga mani itta.* (Kohng-kee-chuung-eh mahn-jee-gah mah-nee ee-tah.)

Duty (tax) *Chose* **(Choe-say);** also *Shegum* (Sheh-gume)
You must pay duty on those items. *I mulgone taehan shegum-ul naeyahamnida.* (Ee muul-gahn-eh tay-hahn sheh-gume-ule nay-yah-hahm-nee-dah.) These things are duty-free. *Imulgon durun myonse imnida.* (Ee-muul-gahn due-rune myahn-seh eem-nee-dah.)

Dysentery *Ijil* **(Ee-jeel);** also *Solsapyong* (Sahl-sah-pyahng)
There is no danger from dysentery in Korea. *Hanguk-enun ijil-e wihom-un opssumnida.* (Hahn-gook-eh-nune ee-jeel-eh wee-hahm-uun ahp-ssume-nee-dah.)

E

Ear *Kwi* **(Kwe);** Earring *Kwigori* (kwe-gah-ree)
May I see those earrings, please? *Jo Kwigori-rul*

poyo chuseyo. (Juh kwee-gah-ree-rule poh-yah chuu-say-yoe.)

Early *Irun* **(E-roon);** also *Iltchigi* (Eel-chee-ghee)
I get up early every morning. *Maeil achim iljjik ironamnida.* (May-eel ah-cheem eel-jeek ee-rah-nahm-nee-dah.) Let's start early. *Iljjik chulbal hapshida.* (Eel-jeek chuul-bahl hahp-shee-dah.) It is still early. *Ajik irumnida.* (Ah-jeek ee-rume-nee-dah.)

Earthenware *T'ogi* **(Toe-ghee);** also *Chilgurut* (Cheel-gue-ruet)
I would like to visit an earthenware factory. *Togi konjang-ul pangmun hagoshipssumnida.* (Toe-ghee kohng-jahng-ule pahng-muun hah-goh-sheep-ssume-nee-dah.) Is this earthenware very old? *I togi-nun oraedoeossumnikka?* (Ee toe-ghee-nune oh-rae-doe-ah-ssume-nee-kkah?)

Earthquake *Chijin* **(Chee-jeen)**
There was a small earthquake last night. *Jinan bam-e yakan chijin-i issossumnida.* (Jee-nahn bahm-eh yah-kahn chee-jeen-ee ee-ssuh-ssume-nee-dah.) Korea has very few earthquakes. *Hanguk-enun chijin-i koui opssumnida.* (Hahn-gook-eh-nune chee-jeen-ee kah-we ahp-ssume-nee-dah.)

East *Tongtchok* **(Tong-tchok);** East coast *Tong haean* (Tong hay-ahn); Far East *Kuk tong* (Kuek tohng)
Which way is east? *Onu kiri tongtchok imnikka?* (Ah-nuu kee-ree tong-tchok eem-nee-kkah?) Go east on this street for two blocks. *I kori-eso tu blok tongtcho-kuro kashipshio.* (Ee kah-ree-eh-sah tuu blohk tohng-tchok-kuu-roh kah-sheep-shee-oh.)

Eat *Mokta* **(Moke-tah);** also *Chapsushida* (Chop-sue-she-dah)
Are you ready to eat? *Mokul junbi doeossumnikka?*

(Mah-kule june-bee doeh-ah-ssume-nee-kkah?)
What would you like to eat? *Mwosul chapsu-shigessumnikka?* (Mwah-sule chahp-suu-shee-gay-ssume-nee-kkah?) Is there anything you can't eat? *Mongmog-nun goshi issumnikka?* (Mohn-mong-nune gah-shee ee-ssume-nee-kkah?)

Economy *Kyongje* **(Kyahng-jeh);** Economic
Kyongjesang-e (Kyahng-jeh-sahng-eh)
Korea's economy depends on foreign trade. *Han-guk kyongi-nun oeguk muyoke uichon hago issum-nida.* (Hahn-gook kyahng-ee-nune oh-gook muu-yahk-eh we-chohn-hah-goh ee-ssume-nee-dah.)

Eel *Paemjango* **(Pame-jahng-ah)**
Baked eel is one of my favorite dishes. *Kun pame-jango-nun naega cheil choa hanun yori chunge hana imnida.* (Kune pame-jahng-ah-nune nay-gah cheh-eel choh-ah-hah-nune yoh-ree chuung-eh hah-nah eem-nee-dah.)

Egg *Talgyal* **(Tahl-gyal);** Raw egg *Nal dalgyal* (Nahl dahl-gyal)
How do you like your eggs? *Kyeranul ottoke hae-durilkkayo?* (Kay-rahn-ule ah-ttah-kay hay-due-reel kkah-yoh?)

Electric *Chongi-e* **(Chahn-ghee-eh);** Electric car *Choncha* (Chahn-chah); Electric fan *Sonpunggi* (Sohn-pung-ghee); Electric heater *Chonyolgi* (Chahn-yahl-ghee)
Do you have an electric fan? *Songpunggi-ga is-sumnikka?* (Sohn-pung-gee-gah ee-ssume-nee-kkah?)

Electricity *Chongi* **(Chahn-ghee)**
Is the electricity 110 watts? *Chongi-nun paekship watchu imnikka?* (Chahn-ghee-nune pake-sheep wah-chuu eem-nee-kkah?)

Electronic *Chonja-e* **(Chone-jah-eh);** Electronic
calculator *Chonja kyesangi* (Chone-jah kay-sahn-
ghee)
May I use your electronic calculator? *Chonja kye-
sangi-rul sayong haedo doemnikka?* (Chone-jah kay-
sahn-ghee-rule sah-yohng hay-do dome-nee-
kkah?)

Elementary school *Kungmin hakkyo* **(Kuung-
meen hahk-k'yoe)**
Is that an elementary school? *Jogosun Kungmin
hakkyo imnikka?* (Jah-gah-sune kuung-meen hahk-
kyo eem-nee-kkah?)

Elephant *Kokkiri* **(Koh-kkee-ree)**

Elevator *Elribeito* **(Ehl-ree-bei-tah)**
Where are the elevators? *Elribeito-nun odie issumnikka?* (Ehl-ree-bei-tah-nune ah-dee-eh ee-
ssume-nee-kkah?) Take the elevator to the
twelfth floor and turn right. *Shipichung kkaji elri-
beito-rul tashigo orunchoguro tora kaseyo.* (Sheep-ee-
chuung kkah-jee ehl-ree-bei-tah-rul tashee-goh
oh-rune-choh-gue-roh toh-rah kah-say-yoe.)

Embassy *Taesagwan* **(Tie-sah-gwahn)**
Where is the American Embassy? *Miguk Taesag-
wan-un odie issumnikka?* (Mee-gook Tie-sah-
gwahn-uun ah-dee-eh ee-ssume-nee-kkah?)
Please take me to the American Embassy. *Narul
Miguk Taesagwan-uro teryoda chuseyo.* (Nah-rule
Mee-gook Tie-sah-gwahn-uu-roh teh-ryah-dah
chuu-say-yoe.)

Emergency *Pisang satae* **(Pee-sahng sah-tay);**
also *Kingup satae* (Keen-gupe sah-tay); Emergency call *Pisang sojip* (Pee-sahng soe-jeep); Emergency exit *Pisanggu* (Pee-sahng-guu)
This is an emergency. *Jigum pisang satae imnida.*
(Jee-gume pee-sahng sah-tay eem-nee-dah.)

Where is the emergency exit? *Pisanggu-nun odie issumnikka?* (Pee-sahng-guu-nune ah-dee-eh ee-ssume-nee-kkah?)

Empty *Pin* **(Peen);** Vacant *Konghohan* (Kong-hah-hahn); Empty box *Pin sangja* (Peen sahng-jah)
Do you have any vacant rooms? *Pin pangi issum-nikka?* (Peen pahng-ee ee-ssume-nee-kkah?) Do you have an empty box? *Pin sangja issumnikka?* (Peen sahng-jah ee-ssume-nee-kkah?)

Endorse *Isohada* **(Ee-sah-hah-dah)**
Will you please endorse the check? *Supyoe isohae chushigessumnikka?* (Suu-pyoh ee-sah-hay chuu-she-gay-sume-nee-kkah?) I have already endorsed it. *Imi kugosul isonhaessumnida.* (Ee-mee kuu-gah-sule ee-soan-hay-ssume-nee-dah.)

England *Yongguk* **(Yong-gook);** English language *Yongu-ko* (Yon-guu-koe); Englishman *Yongguk saram* (Yong-gook sah-rahm); English dictionary *Yongo sajon* (Yon-go sah-joan)
Do you speak English? *Yongo-rul haljul ashim-nikka?* (Yahng-ah-rule hahl-juul ah-sheem-nee-kkah?) Your English is very good. *Tangshin-e Yongo-num maeu hullyung hamnida.* (Tahng-sheen-eh Yong-oh-nune may-uu huul-lyung hahm-nee-dah.) Are you English? *Tangshin-un Yongguk saram imnikka?* (Tahng-sheen-uun Yong-gook sah-rahm eem-nee-kkah?)

Enjoy *Chulgida* **(Chule-ghee-dah)**
Did you enjoy the meal? *Shiksha-rul chulgisos-sumnikka?* (Sheek-shah-rule chuul-ghee-soh-ssume-nee-kkah?) Did you enjoy the trip? *Yohang-un chulgo-wotssumnikka?* (Yah-hang-uun chuul-gah-waht-sume-nee-kkah?)

Enough *Chungbunhan* **(Chung-boon-hahn);** also
Chungbunhi (Chung-boon-hee)
That is enough. *Kugosun chungbunhamnida.* (Kuu-
go-sune chung-buun-hahm-nee-dah.) Is that
enough? *Kugosun chungbun hamnikka?* (Kuu-go-
sune chung-buun hahm-nee-kkah?) I've had
enough, thank you. *Komapsumnida, shilkot mo-
gossumnida.* (Koh-mahp-sume-nee-dah, sheel-
kote mah-gah-sume-nee-dah.)

Entertainment (hospitality) *Taejop* **(Tay-jope);**
Reception *Yonhoe* (Yone-hoe-eh); Public entertainment *Yohung* (Yoe-hung)
Thank you for the entertainment. *Taejophae chu-
shyoso kamsahamnida.* (Tay-jope-hay chuu-shyah-
sah kahm-sah-hahm-nee-dah.) What time is the
reception going to be? *Yonhoe-nun myossie issul yejong imnikka?* (Yahn-hoe-nune myah-shee-eh ee-
ssule yeh-jahng eem-nee-kkah?)

Entrance *Ipku* **(Eep-kuu);** Admission *Ipchangk-
won* (Eep-chahng-kwon)
Is this the entrance? *Igoshi ipku imnikka?* (Ee-gah-
shee eep-kuu eem-nee-kkah?) Is there an admission fee? *Ipchangryo-ga issumnikka?* (Eep-
chahng-rio-gah ee-sume-nee-kkah?)

Envelope *Pongtu* **(Pong-tuu)**
Do you have any envelopes? *Pongtu issumnikka?*
(Pohng-tuu ee-ssume-nee-kkah?) I need an airmail envelope. *Hangkong pongtu chuseyo.* (Hahng-
kahng pohng-tuu chuu-say-yoe.)

Equator *Chokto* **(Choke-toe)**

Equinox (spring) *Chunbun* **(Chune-boon);** Fall
equinox *Chubun* (Chuu-boon)
Do you have any festivals connected with the
spring equinox? *Chunhun-e kwangye doen chukje-ga*

issumnikka? (Chuun-buun-eh kwahn-gay-doan chuuk-jeh-gah ee-ssume-nee-kkah?)

Error *Chalmot* **(Chahl-mot);** also *Oryu* (Oh-ryuu)
I think there is an error in this bill. *I soryu-enun chalmoshi ittago nanun saenggak hamnida.* (Ee sah-ryuu-eh-nune chahl-moh-shee it-tah-goh nah-nune sang-gahk hahm-nee-dah.)

Escalator *Esukalreito* **(Es-kahl-rei-tah)**
Take the escalator to the third floor. *Sam chung kkaji esukalreito-rul tashipshio.* (Sahm-chung kkah-jee es-kahl-rei-tah-rule tah-sheep-shee-oh.)

Etiquette *Yeui pomjol* **(Yay-we pom-jole);** also *Yepop* (Yay-pope); *Etiket* (E-tee-ket)
Korean etiquette is very formal. *Hanguk-e yepopun maeu hyongshik jogida.* (Hahn-gook-eh yeh-poh-pune may-uu hyahng-sheek jah-ghee-dah.)
I want to learn something about Korean etiquette. *Hanguk yepopul paeugo shipssumnida.* (Hahn-guuk yeh-poh-puul pay-uu-goh sheep-ssume-nee-dah.)

Europe *Yurop* **(Yuu-rope);** European *Yurop saram* (Yuu-rope sah-rahm); European (thing) *Yurop-e* (Yuu-rope-eh)
Have you been to Europe? *Yurop-e kabonjogi issumnikka?* (Yuu-rope-eh kah-bohm-jah-ghee ee-ssume-nee-kkah?) Is this made in Europe? *Igosun Yuropssan imnikka?* (Ee-go-sune Yuu-rope-sahn eem-nee-kkah?)

Evening *Chonyok* **(Chone-yoke);** also *Pam* (Pahm); This evening *Onul chonyok* (Oh-nule chone-yoke); Tomorrow evening *Naeil chonyok* (Nay-eel chone-yoke)
Are you free this evening? *Onul chonyoke shigani issumnikka?* (Oh-nule chone-yoke-eh shee-gah-

nee ee-ssume-nee-kkah?) How about tomorrow evening? *Naeil chonyok-un ottossumnikka?* (Nay-eel chone-yoke-uun ah-ttah-ssume-nee-kkah?) Let's go out this evening. *Onul pame nagapshida.* (Oh-nule pahm-eh nah-gahp-shee-dah.)

Everybody *Nugudunji* **(Nuu-guu-dune-jee);** also *Nuguna* (Nuu-guu-nah); *Modunsaram* (Moh-dune-sah-rahm); *Chonbu* (Chahn-buu) Where is everybody? *Modu* [or] *chonbu odie issumnikka?* (Moh-duu [or] chahn-buu ah-dee-eh ee-ssume-nee-kkah?) Is everybody ready? *Modu junbi doeossumnikka?* (Moh-duu june-bee doeh-ah-ssume-nee-kkah?)

Everyday (daily) *Nalmada-e* **(Nal-mah-dah-eh);** also *Maeil-e* (May-eel-eh) The bus leaves at 8:00 A.M. every day. *I posu-nun maeil ojon yodolshie chulbal hamnida.* (Ee pah-sue-nune may-eel oh-jahn yah-dahl-shee-eh chuul-bahl hahm-nee-dah.)

Exchange rate *Hwanyul* **(Hwahn-yuul)**

Exempt *Myonjehada* **(M'yone-jay-hah-dah)** Are these items exempt from customs duties? *I mulgondurun kwanssega myonje doemnikka?* (Ee muul-gahn-due-rune kwahn-say-gah myahn-jeh dome-nee-kkah?) This is not exempt from customs duties. *Igosun myonse doeji anssumnida.* (Ee-go-sune myahn-say doe-jee ahn-ssume-nee-dah.)

Exhibition *Pangnamhoe* **(Pahng-nahm-hoe);** also *Chonshihoe* (Chone-she-hoe); Art exhibition *Misul chonshihoe* (Me-sule chone-she-hoe); Industrial exhibition *Sanop pangnamhoe* (Sah-nope pahng-nahm-hoe) Would you like to see an art exhibit? *Misul chonshihoe-rul poshigessumnikka?* (Mee-suul chone-

shee-hoe-rule poh-shee-gay-ssume-nee-kkah?)
What time does the exhibition open? *Chonshihoe-nun myoshie yomnikka?* (Chone-she-hoe-nune myah-shee-eh yahm-nee-kkah?)

Exit *Chulgu* **(Chule-guu);** Emergency exit
Pisang-gu (Pee-sahng-guu)
Where is the station exit? *Chonggojang chulgu-nun odimnikka?* (Chahng-go-jahng chuul-guu-nune ah-dee-eem-nee-kkah?) Make sure you know where the emergency exit is located. *Pisanggu-ui wichi-rul pandushi ara nouseyo.* (Pee-sahng-guu-we wee-chee-rule pahn-due-shee ah-rah noh-u-say-yoe.)

Expense (cost) *Piyong* **(Pee-yong);** Traveling expenses *Yobi* (Yoe-bee)
How much should I allow for food expenses? *Umshikpiyong-un olmana turoya hamnikka?* (Uum-sheek-pee-yohng-uun ahl-mah-nah tuu-rah-yah hahm-nee-kkah?)

Expensive *Pissan* **(Pee-sahn)** also *Kappisan* (Kahp-pee-sahn)
That is too expensive. *Kugosun nomu pissamnida.* (Kuu-go-sune nah-muu pee-ssahm-nee-dah.)
Do you have a less expensive room? *Chom tol pissan pang-un opsumnikka?* (Chome tahl pee-sahn pahng-uun ope-sume-nee-kkah?)

Explain *Solmyong-hada* **(Sole-myahng-hah-dah)**
I cannot explain in Korean. *Hanguk-oro solmyong halsu opssumnida.* (Hahn-gook-oh-roh sole-myahng hahl-suu ahp-ssume-nee-dah.) Please explain in English. *Yongo-ro solmyonghae chushio.* (Yong-ah-roh sole-myahng-hay chuu-she-oh.)

Export (item) *Suchul* **(Sue-chule);** To export
Suchulhada (Suu-chuul-hah-dah); Export duty

Suchul sse (Sue-chule say)
Is this exported? *Igosun suchulpum imnikka?* (Ee-go-sune suu-chuul-puum eem-nee-kkah?)

Exporter *Suchurop-cha* (**Sue-chu-rahp-chah**)
Are you also an exporter? *Tangshin-do suchuropcha imnikka?* (Tahng-sheen-doh suu-chuu-rahp-chah eem-nee-kkah?)

Express train *Tukkup yolcha* (**Tuke-kupe yahl-chah**)
Is this the express train for Pusan? *Igoshi Pusan-haeng tukkup yolcha imnikka?* (Ee-go-shee Puu-sahn-hang tuke-kupe-yahl-chah eem-nee-kkah?)
What is the track number of the express train? *Tukkup yolcha-nun myopon son imnikka?* (Tuke-kupe-yahl-chah-nune myah-pahn-sahn eem-nee-kkah?)

Extension number (phone) *Ponhonun* (**Pone-hoe-noon**)
What is your extension number? *Tangshin-e yongyol chonwha ponho-nun muoshimnikka?* (Tahng-sheen-eh yahn-gyahl chahn-whah-pahn-hyoh-nune muu-ah-sheem-nee-kkah?)   Call extension number 213. *Yongyol chonwha ibaek shipsam-uro chonwha haseyo.* (Yahn-gyahl chahn-whah ee-bake sheep-sahm-uu-roh chahn-whah hah-say-yoe.)

Eye *Nun* (**Noon**)
I have something in my eye. *Nanun ane mwoshi issumnida.* (Nah-nune ah-nay mwah-shee ee-ssume-nce-dah.)   Your eyes are very pretty. *Tangshin-e nu-nun maeu kwiyopssumnida.* (Tahng-sheen-eh nuu-nune may-uu kwee-yaph-ssume-nee-dah.)

F

Fabric *Chingmul* **(Cheeng-mule);** also *Piryuk* (Peer-yuke)
Is this silk fabric? *Igosun myongju chingmul imnikka?* (Ee-go-sune myahng-juu cheeng-muul eem-nee-kkah?) What kind of fabric is this? *Igosun otton chongyu-e chingmul imnikka?* (Ee-go-sune ah-ttahn chohng-yuu-eh cheeng-muul eem-nee-kkah?)

Face *Olgul* **(Ole-guul);** Face massage *Olgul massaji* (Ole-guul mah-sah-jee)
I'd like to wash my face. *Sean hago shipssumnida.* (Say-ahn hah-goh sheep-ssume-nee-dah.) Would you like a face massage? *Olgul massaji hashigessumnikka?* (Ole-guul mah-sah-jee hah-shee-geh-ssume-nee-kkah?)

Factory *Kongjang* **(Kong-jahng)**
Where is your factory? *Tangshin-e kongjang-un odie issumnikka?* (Tahng-sheen-eh kong-jahng-uun ah-dee-eh ee-ssume-nee-kkah?) I'd like to visit your factory. *Tangshin-e kongjang-ul pangmun hago shipssumnida.* (Tahng-sheen-eh kong-jahng-ule pahng-muun hah-goh sheep-ssume-nee-dah.)

Family *Kajong* **(Kah-jong);** also *Kajok* (Kah-joke)
Is this your family? *Ibunduri tangshin-e kajok imnikka?* (Ee-buun-duu-ree tahng-sheen-eh kah-johk eem-nee-kkah?) Do you have a large family? *Tangshin kajok-un taekajok imnikka?* (Tahng-sheen kah-johk-uun tay-kah-johk eem-nee-kkah?) How many in your family? *Tangshin-e kajokun olmana doemnikka?* (Tahng-sheen-eh kah-joe-kuun ahl-mah-nah dome-nee-kkah?) What is your family name? *Tangshin-e song-un mwoshim-*

nikka? (Tahng-sheen-eh sahng-uun mwah-sheem-nee-kkah?)

Famous *Yumyonghan* **(Yume-yong-hahn)**
Which is the most famous temple in Korea? *Hangkuk-eso kajang yumyonghan sawonun onu koshimnikka?* (Hahn-gook-eh-sah kah-jahng yuu-myong-hahn sah-wohn-un oh-nuu kah-sheem-nee-kkah?) There are hundreds of famous landmarks in Korea. *Hanguk-enun subaekgac-e yumyonghan punggyongduri issumnida.* (Hahn-gook-eh-nune suu-bake-gay-eh yuu-myohng-hahn puung-gyahng-duc-ree ee-ssume-nee-dah.)

Far *Mon* **(Mahn);** also *Monamon (Mah-nah-man)*
How far is it from here? *Yogiso olmana momnikka?* (Yah-ghee-sah ahl-mah-nah mahm-nee-kah?) That's too far to go in one day. *Haruane kagi-enun nomu momnida.* Hah-ruu-ahn-eh kah-ghee-eh-nune nah-muu mahm-nee-dah.)

Fare (charge) *Yogum* **(Yoh-gume);** Taxi fare *Taekshi yogum* (Tack-she yoe-gume); Food *Umshingmul* (Uem-sheeng-muul)
How much is the fare? *Yogum-un olmaimnikka?* (Yoh-gume-uun ahl-mah-eem-nee-kkah?) Do I pay the fare in advance? *Yogum-un sonburimnikkah?* (Yoh-gume-uun sahn-buu-reem-nee-kkah?)

Farewell *Chakpyol* **(Chock-p'yole);** also *Songbyol* (Sohng-byahl)
I'm going to a farewell party this evening. *Onulbbam songbyol patie kamnida.* (Oh-nule-bahm sohng-byahl pah-tee-eh kahm-nee-dah.)

Farm *Nongjang* **(Nong-jhang);** also *Nongji* (Nong-jee); Farm house *Nong ga* (Nong gah); Farmer *Nongbu* (Nong-buu)

I would like to visit a farm before leaving Korea. *Hanguk-ul ttonagichone nongjang-ul pangmun hago shipssuminda.* (Hahn-gook-ule ttah-nah-ghee-chahn-eh nohng-jahng-ule pahng-muun hah-goh sheep-ssume-nee-dah.)

Fashion (vogue) *Yuhaeng* **(Yuu-hang);** Style *Hyong* (h'yong)
This dress is the latest fashion. *I dress-nun choe-gun yuhaengimnida.* (Ee-dress-nune choe-guun yuu-hang-eem-nee-dah.)

Fast (quick) *Chaepparun* **(Chape-pah-rune)**
Is the train very fast? *I kicha-nun maeu pparum-nikka?* (Ee kee-chah-nune may-uu ppah-rume-nee-kkah?) Don't drive so fast! *Kuroke ppali unjonhaji mashipshio!* (Kuu-rah-keh ppahl-ee uun-jahn-hah-jee mah-sheep-she-oh!)

Fat (person) *Saltchin* **(Salt-cheen);** Fat lady *Ttungttunghan yoin* (Ttung-ttung-hahn yoe-een); Animal fat *Pigye* (Pee-gay)
It is unusual to see fat people in Korea. *Hanguk-eso ttungttunghan saram-ul ponun kosun tuemulda.* (Hahn-gook-eh-sah ttuung-ttuung-hahn sah-rahm-ule poh-nune kah-sune tue-muul-dah.) I don't want to get fat. *Saltchinungoshi shilssum-nida.* (Sahl-cchee-nune-gah-shee sheel-ssume-nee-dah.)

Father (familiar usage) *Aboji* **(Ah-bah-jee);** also *Abonim* (Ah-bah-neem); Father-in-law *Changgin* (Chahng-geen); also *Shiaboji* (She-ah-bah-jee)
My father was in Korea many years ago. *Nae abonim-un myotaejone Hanguk-e kyeshyossumnida.* (Nay ah-bah-neem-uun myah-tay-jahn-eh Hahn-gook-eh kay-shyah-ssume-nee-dah.) I would like to accompany my father to Korea. *Abonim-ul ttara Hanguk-e kagoshipssumnida.* (Ah-bah-neem-

ule ttah-rah Hahn-gook-eh kah-goh-sheep-
ssume-nee-dah.)

Favor *Putak* **(Puu-tahk)**
Will you do me a favor? *Putak hana turo chushigessumnikka?* (Puu-tahk hah-nah tuu-rah chuu-she-
gah-sume-nee-kkah?)

Favorite *Aju choahanun* **(Ah-juu choe-ah-hah-
noon)**; also *Cheil choahanun* (Cheh-eel choh-ah-
hah-noon)
This is my favorite food. *I gosun naega cheilchoa-
hanun umshikimnida.* (Ee-go-sune nay-gah cheh-
eel-choh-ah-hah-noon uum-sheek-eem-nee-
dah.) What is your favorite food? *Otton umshikul
choahashimnikka?* (Ah-ttahn uum-sheek-ul choe-
ah-hah-sheem-nee-kkah?)

Feast (banquet) *Chanchi* **(Chahn-chee)**; also *Yonhoe* (Yahn-hoe)
This was really a feast! *Igosun chintcha chanchi imnida!* (Ee-go-sune cheen-tchah chahn-chee eem-
nee-dah!)

Fee (charge) *Yogum (Yoe-gume)*; also *Susuryo*
(Sue-sue-rio); Admission fee *Ipchangnyo* (Eep-
chahng-n'yoe)
Do we have to pay an admission fee? *Ipchangnyo-
rul naeya hamnikka?* (Eep-chahng-nyoh-rule nay-
yah hahm-nee-kkah?) I have already paid the
admission fee. *Imi ipchangnyo-rul chibul haessumnida.* (Ee-mee eep-chahng-nyoh-rule chee-buul
hay-ssume-nee-dah.)

Female (woman) *Yoja* **(Yoe-jah)**; Animal *Amkot*
(Ahm-kot); also *Yosong* (Yoe-sahng)
The female population of Cheju Island far out-
numbers the male population. *Cheju do-e yoja
ingu-nun namja ingu poda manssumnida.* (Cheh-

juu-doh-eh yoe-jah een-guu-nune nahm-jah een-
guu poh-dah mahn-ssume-nee-dah.)

Ferry *Narutpae* **(Nah-root-pay);** also *Pae* (Pay);
Ferry boat *Yolrakson* (Yoe-rock-soan)
Let's go by ferry. *Pae-ro kapshida.* (Pay-roh kahp-
shee-dah.) How much does the ferry cost? *Pae
yogumi olma imnikka?* (Pay-yoh-gume-ee ahl-mah
eem-nee-kkah?)

Festival *Chukche* **(Chuuk-cheh)**
Are there going to be any festivals this week?
Ibon chuile otton chukche-ga yolrimnikka? (Ee-bahn
chuu-eel-eh ah-ttahn chuuk-cheh-gah yahl-reem-
nee-kkah?) The festival starts at 10 A.M.
Chukche-nun ojon yolshie shijak hamnida. (Chuuk-
cheh-nune oh-jahn yahl-shee-eh shee-jahk-
hahm-nee-dah.)

Fever *Yol* **(Yole);** High fever *Koyol* (Koh-yole)
Do you have a fever? *Shinyori issumnikka?*
(Sheen-yoh-ree ees-sume-nee-kkah?) I have a
little fever. *Yakkan issumnida.* (Yahk-kahn ee-
sume-nee-dah.)

Fiance (male) *Yakonja* **(Yah-kone-jah);** Female
Yakonnyo (Yahk-own-'n-yoe)
This is my fiancee. *I saram-un na-ui yakonja* [or]
yakonyo imnida. (Ee sah-rahm-uun nah-we yahk-
own-jah [or] yahk-own-nyo eem-nee dah.)

Filling (gas) station *Chuyuso* **(Chu-yuu-soe)**
Is there a gas station nearby? *Kuncho-e chuyuso-ga
issumnikka?* (Kuun-chah-eh chuu-yuu-soh-gah ee-
ssume-nee-kkah?)

Film (for camera) *Pilrum* **(Peel-rume)**
Do you have color film for this camera? *I kamera-
e matnun chonyonsaek pilrum-i issumnikka?* (Ee kah-

meh-rah-eh mahn-nuhn chahn-yahn-sake peel-rume-ee ee-ssume-nee-kkah?)

Finger *Sonkarak* **(Soan-kah-rahk);** Fingernail *Sont'op* (Sohn-tohp); Fingerprint *Chimun* (Chee-moon)
You must have your fingerprints taken. *Chimun-ul jjigoya hamnida.* (Chee-muun-ule jjee-gah-yah hahm-nee-dah.)

Finish (complete) *Walryohada* **(Wall-rio-hah-dah);** also *Machida* (Mah-chee-dah); Stop *Kkunnaeda* (Kune-nay-dah)
When will you finish my suit? *Onje nae yangpok-i tadoemnikka?* (Ahn-jeh nay yahng-pohk-ee tah-dome-nee-kkah?) Is my room finished? *Nae pangi tadoeossumnikka?* (Nay-pahng-ee tah-doeh-ah-ssume-nee-kkah?)

Fire (conflagration) *Hwajae* (Hwah-jay); Fire alarm *Hwajae Kyongbogi* (Hwah-jay k'yong-boe-ghee); Fireman *Sobangsu* (Soh-bahng-suu); Fire insurance *Hwajae pohom* (Hwah-jay poh-hahm)
Beware of fires. *Pulchoshim hashipshio.* (Puul-choh-sheem hah-sheep-shee-oh.) Sound the fire alarm. *Hwajae kyongbogi-rul ulrishipshio.* (Hwah-jay kyahng-boh-ghee-rule uul-ree-sheep-she-oh.)

Firm (company) *Sanghoe* **(Sahng-hoe);** also *Hoesa* (Hoe-eh-sah)
What kind of firm do you work for? *Otton hoesa-eso ilhamnikka?* (Ah-ttahn hoeh-sah-eh-sah eel-hahm-nee-kkah?)

First class *Iltung* **(Eel-tung);** First time *Iboni choumimnida* (Ee-bone-nee chah-uum-eem-nee-dah)
This is my first time in Korea. *Hanguk-un iboni*

choumimnida. (Hahn-gook-uun ee-bahn-ee chah-uum-eem-nee-dah.) Shall we go first class? *Il-tung-uro kalkkayo?* (Eel-tung-uu-roh kahl-kkah-yoh?)

Fish *Mulkogi* **(Mul-koe-ghee);** also *Saengson* (Sang-sahn); Fish market *Saengson shijang* (Sang-soan she-jahng)
Do you like raw fish? *Saengsonhoe-rul choahashim-nikka?* (Sang-sahn-ho-eh-rule choh-ah-hah-sheem-nee-kkah?) How do you like your fish cooked? *Saengsom yori-rul tushigessumnikka?* (Sang-sahn yoh-ree-rule tuu-shee-geh-ssume-nee-kkah?)

Fishing *Nakshijil* **(Nahk-she-jeel);** Fishing boat *Oson* (Oh-soan); Fishing rod *Nakshi-ttae* (Nahk-she-tay)
Would you like to go fishing? *Nakshiharo kashiges-sumnikka?* (Nahk-shee-hah-rah kah-shee-geh-ssume-nee-kkah?) Fishing is a popular sport here. *Nakshijil-un jogieso imggiin-nun spochu im-nida.* (Nahk-shee-jeel-uun jah-ghee-eh-sah eem-ghee-een-nune spoh-chuu eem-nee-kah.)

Flag *Kipal* **(Kee-pahl);** National flag *Kukggi* (Kuke-ghee)
Koreans are very respectful of their national flag. *Hanguk-indurun kukggi-rul maeu chonjunghamnida.* (Hahn-gook-een-due-rune kuuk-ghee-rule may-uu chohn-juung hahm-nee-dah.)

Flavor (taste) *Mat* **(Maht);** also *Pungmi* (Poong-me)
Do you like the flavor? *Kumasul choahashimnikka?* (Kuu-mah-sule choh-ah-hah-sheem-nee-kkah? What kind of flavor is it? *Kugosun otton chongnyu-e mat imnikka?* (Kuu-go-sune ah-ttahn chohng-yuu-eh maht-eem-nee-kkah?)

Flight (airline) *Pihaeng* **(Pee-hang)**; Morning flight *Achim pihaenggi* (Ah-cheem pee-hang-ghee); Night flight *Yagan pihaeng* (Yah-gahn pee-hang)
Would you prefer a morning flight? *Achim pihaenggi-rul tashigessumnikka?* (Ah-cheem pee-hang-ghee-rule tah-shee-geh-ssume-nee-kkah?)
What flight number is that? *Kugosun myopom pihaenggi imnikka?* (Kuu go-sune myah-pahn pee-hang-ghee eem-nee-kkah?)

Floor (of a building) *Chung* **(Chuung)**; also *Maru* (Mah-rue)
The gift department is on the fourth floor. *Kinyompumjomun sachunge issumnida.* (Kee-nyahm-puum-jahm-uun sah-chuung-eh ee-ssume-nee-dah.) What floor, please? *Myochung imnikka?* (Myah-chuung eem-nee-kkah?)

Flower *Kkot* **(Kote)**; Flower arrangement *Kkot kkoji* (Kote koe-jee); Artificial flowers *Chowha* (Choe-whah)

Fluent *Yuchanghage* **(Yuu-chahng-hah-gay)**
Your English is very fluent. *Yongo-rul yuchanghage chalhashimnida.* (Yahng-ah-rule yuu-chahng-hah-gay chahl-hah-sheem-nee-dah.) I wish I spoke Korean fluently. *Hanguk-malul yuchanghage hago shipssumnida.* (Hahn-gook-mahl-ule yuu-chahng-hah-geh hah-goh sheep-ssume-nee-dah.)

Fog *Angae* **(Ahn-gay)**; Dense fog *Chitun angae* (Chee-tune ahn-gay)
It is often foggy here. *Yoginun kakkum angaega kkimnida.* (Yah-ghee-nuun kah-kkume ahn-gay-gah kkeem-nee-dah.) Fog is common in Seoul. *Seoul-enun angaega nul kkimnida.* (Sah-uul-eh-nune ahn-gay-gah nule kkeem-nee-dah.)

Food *Umshik* **(Uum-sheek);** also *Shingnyang* (Sheeng-nyang); Korean food *Hanguk umshik* (Hahn-gook uum-sheek)

Do you like Korean food? *Hanguk umshigul choahashimnikka?* (Hahn-gook uum-shee-guul choh-ah-hah-sheem-nee-kkah?) Would you like to eat Korean food tonight? *Onulbbame Hanguk umshigul tushigessumnikka?* (Oh-nule-bahm-eh Hahn-gook uum-sheek-ule tuu-shee-geh-ssume-nee-kkah?)

Foot *Pal* **(Pahl);** Measure of length *Pitu* (Pee-tuu)

Is it near enough to go on foot? *Koroso kagie chungbunhi kakkap ssumnikka?* (Kah-rah-sah kah-ghee-eh chuung-buun-he kah-kkahp ssume-nee-kkah?)

Forecast *Yebo* **(Yay-boe);** Weather forecast *Ilgi yebo* (Eel-ghee yay-boe)

Did you hear the weather forecast? *Ilgi yebo-rul turossumnikka?* (Eel-ghee yay-boh-rule tuu-rah-ssume-nee-kkah?) What is the weather forecast for tomorrow? *Naeil ilgi yebo-nun ottossumnikka?* (Nay-eel eel-ghee-yeh-boh-nune ah-ttah-ssume-nee-kkah?)

Foreign *Oegugui* **(Oeh-goog-we);** also *Oerae-e* (Oeh-ray-eh); Foreign language *Oegu go* (Oeh-guu-go); Foreign country *Oe guk* (Oeh-gook); Ministry of Foreign Affairs *Oe mu bu* (Oeh-muu-buu)

Do many Koreans study foreign languages? *Manun Hanguk-induri oeguko-rul kongbuhamnikka?* (Mah-nune Hahn-gook-een-due-ree oeh-guu-kah-rule kohng-buu hahm-nee-kkah?)

Foreigner *Oegukin* **(Oeh-gook-een);** also *Oeguk saram* (Oeh-gook sah-rahm)

Many foreigners live in Seoul. *Manun oegukin-*

duri Seoul-e salgo issumnida. (Mah-nune oeh-guu-keen-due-ree Sah-uul-eh sahl-goh ee-ssume-nee-dah.)

Forget *Itta* **(Eet-tah);** Leave behind *Noko oda* (Noke-koe oh-dah)
I forgot it in the taxi! *Kugosul taxi-e nokowatta* [or] *nokowassumnida* (polite)! (Kuu-go-sule taek-shee-eh noh-koh-wah-ttah [or] noke-koe-wah assume-nee-dah!) Don't forget our appointment! *Yakssogul ijji mashipshio!* (Yahk-soh-guul ee-jjee mah-sheep shee-oh!)

Forgive *Yongsohada* **(Yong-sah-hah-dah)**
Please forgive me for being so late. *Nomu nujungot yongsohashipshio.* (Nah-muu nuu-june-gaht yohng-sah-hah-sheep-shee-oh.)

Fork (for food) *Poku* **(Poe-kuu)**
Please bring us another fork. *Tarun poku-rul kajyo oshipshio.* (Tah-rune poke-kuu-rule kah-jyah oh-sheep-shee-oh.)

Fragile *Pusojigi shwiun* **(Puu-soe-jee-ghee schwe-uun);** also *Kkaejinun got* (Kkay-jee-nune gaht)
Do you have anything fragile in your suitcase? *Kabang-e kkaejinun got issumnikka?* (Kah-bahng-eh kkay-jee-nune gaht ee-ssume-nee-kkah?)

France *Purangsu* **(Pue-rahng-sue);** Frenchman *Purangsu-in* (Puu-rahng-sue-een)
Are you from France? *Purangsu chulshin imnikka?* (Pue-rahng-sue chuul-sheen eem-nee-kah?) [or] *Puransueso wassumnikka?* (Pue-rahng-sue-eh-sah wah-ssume-nee-kkah?)

Free (of charge) *Muryo-ui* **(Muu-rio-we);** At leisure *Hangahan* (Hahn-gah-hahn); Tax-free *Myon sero* (M'yone say-roe)
Are you free tonight? *Onul bbame shigan issum-*

nikka [or] *hangahamnikka?* (Oh-nule bahm-eh
shee-gahn ee-ssume-nee-kkah [or] hahn-gah-
hahm-nee-kkah?)   Is this tax-free? *Igosun myon-
sega doemnikka?* (Ee-go-sune myone-say-gah
dome-nee-kkah?)

Frequent *Pinbonhan* **(Peen-bone-hahn);**   Frequently *Pinbonhi* (Peen-bone-hee);   also *Chaju*
(Chah-juu)
Do you come here frequently? *Yogie chaju
ominkka?* (Yah-ghee-eh chah-juu ohm-nee-kkah?
Yes, I'm a frequent visitor. *Ye, chaju ominda.* (Yeh,
chah-juu ohm-nee-dah.)

Fresh (new) *Saeroun* **(Say-roe-uun);**   also *Shimson-
han* (Sheen-sahn-hahn)
Do you have any fresh fruit? *Shinsonhan gwaili issumnikka?* (Sheen-sahn-hahn gwah-eel-ee ee-
ssume-nee-kkah?)   Is this bread fresh? *I ppang-
un saegoshimnikka?* (Ee ppahng-uun say-gah-
sheem-nee-kkah?)

Friend *Chingu* **(Cheen-guu);**   also *Tongmu* (Tong-
muu)
This is my very good friend. *I saram-un na-ui cheil
choun chingu imnida.* (Ee sah-rahm-uun nah-we
cheh-eel choh-uun cheen-guu eem-nee-dah.)
Bring a girl friend along. *Yoja chingu-rul hamgge
teryo oseyo.* (Yah-jah cheen-guu-rule hahm-kkeh
teh-ryah oh-say-yoe.)

Frost *Sori* **(soe-ree)**
When do you generally have the first frost? *Chot
soriga potong onje omnikka?* (Chaht soe-ree-gah
poh-tohng ahn-jay ohm-nee-kkah?)

Fruit *Kwail* **(Kwah-eel);**   also *Kwashil* (Kwah-
sheel);   Fruit store *Kwail jjom* (Kwail jome)
Let's have some fresh fruit. *Shinsonhan gwail-ul*

kajiseyo. (Sheen-sahn-hahn gwah-eel-ule kah-jee-seh-yoh.) Would you like fruit for dessert? *Dessert-ro kwail-ul tushigessumnikku?* (Dee-jah-tuu-roh kwah-eel-ule tuu-shee-geh-ssume-nee-kkah?)

Fry *Kirume twigida* (Kee-rue-may twi-ghee-dah)
Please fry my fish. *Saengson-ul kirume twigyo chuseyo.* (Sang-sahn-ule kee-rume-eh twee-gyah chuu-say-yoe.)

Full (of food) *Kadukchahn* (Kah-duke-chahn);
also *Paega purun* (Paeh-gah puu-rune)
I'm full! *Paega purunnida.* (Paeh-gah puu-rune-nee-dah.) Is the box full? *I bax-nun kaduk chassumnikka?* (Ee bahx-nune kah-duke chah-ssume-nee-kkah?)

Funny (laughable) *Usuun* (Uu-soon)
That was really a funny movie. *Chongmallo usuun yonghwa imnida.* (Chahng-mahl-loh uu-sue-uun yahng-hwah eem-nee-dah.)

Fur coat *Mopi kotu* (Moh-pee koh-tue)
Korea is famous for its fur coats. *Hanguk-un mopi kotu-ro yumyong hamnida.* (Hahn-gook-uun moh-pee koh-tu-roh yume-yahng hahm-nee-dah.)

Furniture *Kagu* (Kah-guu)
I really like Korean-style furniture. *Hanguk-shik kago-rul chomgmallo choa hamnida.* (Hahn-gook-sheek kah-guu-rule chahng-mahl-loh choh-ah-hahm-nee-dah.) Please take me to a furniture store. *Kagujome teryoda chuseyo.* (Kah-guu-jahm-eh teh-ryah-dah chuu-say-yoe.)

Future *Mirae* (Me-rie); also *Changnae* (chahng-nie); Near future *Kakkaun changnaee* (Kah-kkah-uun chahng-nie-eh)
I will go back to Korea in the near future. *Kakkaun changnae-e Hanguk-uro tora kalgoshimnida.*

(Kah-kkah-uun chahng-nay-eh Hahn-gook-uu-roh toh-rah kahl-gah-sheem-nee-dah.)

G

Gallery (fine arts) *Hwarang* **(Hwah-rang);** National Gallery *Kungnip misulgwan* (Kuung-neep mee-sul-gwahn)
I would like to go to the National Gallery tomorrow. *Naeil kungnip misulgwane kago shipssumnida.* (Nay-eel kuung-neep mee-suul-gwahn-eh kah-goh sheep-ssume-nee-dah.)

Game (play) *Nori* **(No-ree);** Sporting contest *Shihap* (She-hahp)
Korean children love to play games. *Hanguk orin-idurun nori-rul choahanda.* (Hahn-gook ah-reen-ee-due-rune noh-ree-rule choh-ah-hahn-dah.)
What is the most popular game in Korea? *Hanguk-eso cheil inkki itnun nori-nun mwoshimnikka?* (Hahn-gook-eh-sah cheh-eel een-kee eet-nune noh-ree-nune mwah-sheem-nee-kkah?)

Garage (for parking) *Chago* **(Chah-go);** Repair garage *Chadongcha* (Chah-dong-chah)
Where is the nearest repair garage? *Kajang kak-kaun chadongcha suriso-nun odi issuminkka?* (Kah-jahng kah-kkah-uun chah-dong-chah sue-ree-soe-nune ah-dee es-sume-nee-kkah?) My car is still in the garage. *Nae chanun ajik chadongcha surisoe issumnida.* (Nay-chah-nune ah-jeek chah-dong-cha sue-ree-soe-eh es-sume-nee-dah.)

Garden *Chongwon* **(Chong-won);** Flower garden *Hwawon* (Hwah-won)
Do you have a garden at your home? *Chipe chongwoni issumnikka? (Cheep-eh chahng-wahn-ee ee-*

ssume-nee-kkah?) Landscaped gardens are famous in Korea. *Hanguk-enun yumyonghan chongwonduri mansumnida.* (Hahn-gook-eh-nune yume-yong-hahn choeng-wahn-duu-ree mahn-sume-nee-dah.)

Garlic *Manul* (Mah-nuel)

Garlic is good for you. *Manuli tangshin-ege cho-ssumnida.* (Mah-nuu-lee tahng-sheen-eh-geh choe-ssume-nee-dah.) Yes, but I don't like the taste or the smell. *Ne, kulona nanun ku naemsawa mashi shilssumnida.* (Neh, kuu-lah-nah nah-nuun kuu naehm-say-wah mah-she sheel-ssume-nee-dah.)

Gasoline *Kilum* (Kee-luum); also *Kasollin* (Kah-soe-leen); Gas station *Chuyuso* (chuu-yuu-soe)

Where is the nearest gas station? *Kajang kakkaun chuyusoga odie issumnikka?* (Kah-jahng kah-kkah-uun chuu-yuu-soh-gah ah-dee-eh ee-ssume-nee-kkah?) How much is one liter of gas? *Kilum illitul-nun olma imnikka?* (Kee-luum eel-lee-tuhl-nune ahl-mah eem-nee-kkah?)

Gate *Mun* (Munn); also *Ipku* (Eep-kuu); Front gate *Am mun* (Ahm-munn); Back gate *Twit mun* (Tweet-munn)

I will meet you at the temple gate. *Nanun tang-shin-ul chol muneso mannal koshimnida.* (Nah-nune tahng-sheen-ule chole muun-eh-sah mahn-nahl kah-sheem-nee-dah.)

Gentleman *Shinsa* (Sheen-sah)

Elderly Korean gentlemen often wear traditional clothing. *Naidun Hanguk shinsadurum kakkum chont'ong uibokul ipssumnida.* (Nay-dune Hahn-gook sheen-sah-due-rume kock-kume chahn-tong we-boh-kuul eep-ssume-nee-dah.)

Genuine *Chintchaui* **(Cheen-chah-we)**
Are these pearls genuine? *I chinjudurun chinchcha imnikka?* (Ee cheen-juu-due-rune cheen-chah eem-nee-kkah?) Is this genuine leather? *Igosun chinchcha kajuk imnikka?* (Ee-go-sune cheen-chah kah-juuk eem-nee-kkah?)

German (person) *Togil saram* **(Toe-gheel sah-rahm);** Germany *Togil* (Toe-gheel); West Germany *So dok* (Soe doke); Made-in-Germany *Togil-che* (Toe-gheel-cheh)
Many German businessmen visit Korea. *Manun Togil saopgaduri Hanguk-ul pangmun hamnida.* (Mah-nune Toh-gheel sah-ahp-gah-due-ree Hahn-gook-ule pahng-muun hahm-nee-dah.)

Gift *Sonmul* **(Soan-mule);** New Year's gift *Saehae sonmul* (Saeh-haeh sahn-muul)
I want to buy a gift for my wife. *Anaeegejul sonmurul sago shipssumnida.* (Ah-nay-eh-geh-juul sahn-muu-ruul sah-goh-sheep-ssume-nee-dah.)

Ginger *Saenggang* **(Sang-gahng)**
Would you like some fresh ginger? *Singsinghar saenggangul chushigessumnikka?* (Sheng-sheng-harh sang-gahng-ule chu-shee-geh-ssume-nee-kkah?)

Girl *Sonyo* **(Soh-nyah);** Girl friend *Yoja chingu* (Yah-jah cheen-guu)
Do most young Korean girls go to work after finishing school? *Taebubun-e Hanguk sonyodurun chorophue ilharo kamnikka?* (Tay-buu-buun-eh Hahn-gook soh-nyah-due-rune choe-rohp-huu-eh eel-hah-rah kahm-nee-kkah?)

Glass (for drinking) *Chan* **(Chahn)**
May I have a glass of water, please. *Mul hanchan chushipshio.* (Muul-hahn-chann chuu-sheep-shee-oh.) Is this your glass? *Igosun sonsaenge chan im-*

nikka? (Ee-go-sune song-sang-eh chahn eem-nee-kkah?)

Gloves *Changgap* (**Chahng-gahp**); also *Kullobu* (Kuu-loe-buu)
Don't forget your gloves. *Changgap-ul ijji maship-shio.* (Chahng-gahp-ule ee-jjee mah-sheep-shee-oh.)

Go *Kada* (**Kah-dah**)
Shall we go? *Kal kkayo?* (Kahl kkah-yoh?) Where do you want to go? *Odiro kagoshippssumnikka?* (Ah-dee-roh kah-goh-sheep-ssume-nee-kkah?) Let's go back to the hotel. *Hotelo tora kapshida.* (Hoh-tehl-oh toh-rah kahp-shee-dah.) Are you ready to go? *Kal jumbi-ga doetssumnikka?* (Kahl june-bee-gah dote-ssume-nee-kkah?)

Gold *Kum* (**Kume**); Gold coins *Kum hwa* (Kume hwah)
I would like to buy a gold ring. *Kumbanji-rul sa-goshippssumnida.* (Kume-bahn-jee-rule sah-goh-sheep-ssume-nee-dah.)

Goldfish *Kumbungo* (**Kume-buung-ah**)

Golf *Kolpu* (**Kole-puu**); Golf club *Kolpu chae* (Kole-puu chay); Golf course *Kolpu jang* (Kole-puu jahng)
Are there many golf courses in Korea? *Hanguk-e kolpu jangi manun issumnikka?* (Hahn-gook-eh kole-puu-jahng-ee mah-nune ee-ssume-nee-kkah?) Would you like to play golf tomorrow? *Neil kolpu chiro kashigessumnikka?* (Nay-eel kole-puu chee-rah kah-shee-geh-ssume-nee-kkah?)

Good *Choun* (**Choe-uun**)
This is very good. *Igosun maeu chossumnida.* (Ee-go-sune may-uu choh-ssume-nee-dah.)

Government *Chongbu* **(Chong-buu);** Government office *Kwan chong* (Kwahn chong); Government of Korea *Hanguk chongbu* (Hahn-gook chong-buu)

Governor (of a province) *Chisa* **(Chee-sah);** also *Dochisa* (Doh-chee-sah)
The governor is here to make a speech. *Dochisa-ga yonsol hagiwihaeso yogie issumnida.* (Doh-chee-sah-gah yahn-sahl hah-ghee-wee-hae-sah yah-ghee-eh ee-ssume-nee-dah.)

Graduate (from a university) *Choropsaeng* **(Choe-rope-sang)**
He is a graduate of Seoul National University. *Kunun Seoul taehakkyo choropsaeng imnida.* (Kuu-nune soul Tay-hahk-kyoh choe-rope-sang eem-nee-dah.)

Grandchild (male) *Sonja* **(Soan-jah);** Female *Sonnyo* (soan-yoe); Grandfather *Haraboji* (Hah-rah-boe-jee); Grandmother *Halmoni* (Hahl-moe-nee); Grandparent *Chobumo* (Choe-buu-moe)
Are your grandparents still alive? *Chobumonun ajik sara gyeshimnikka?* (Choh-buu-moh-nuen ah-jeek sah-rah gay-sheem-nee-kkah?)

Grapes *Podo* **(Poe-doe)**
Do you have any grapes? *Podo-ga issumnikka?* (Poh-doh-gah ee-ssume-nee-kkah?)

Greece *Kurisu* **(Kuu-ree-sue)**

Green *Noksaegui* **(Noke-say-gwee);** Greenhouse *Onshil* (Own-sheel)
Korea becomes very green in the spring. *Hanguk-un pome noksaeguro pyunhamnida.* (Hahn-gook-uun pohm-eh nohk-say-guu-roh pyahn-hahm-nee-dah.)

Ground (land) *Toji* **(Toe-jee)**

Group *Chiptan* **(Cheep-tahn);** also *Muri* **(Muu-ree);** *Group* **(Guu-ruup)**
Are you traveling with a group? *Tangshin-un group-uro yohaenghamnikka?* (Tahng-sheen-uun guu-rupe-uu-roh yah-hang-hahm-nee-kkah?) Which group are you with? *Onu group-e issumnikka?* (Ah-nuu guu-rupe-eh ee-ssume-nee-kkah?)

Guarantee *Pojung* **(Poe-jung)**
Is this guaranteed? *Igosun pojungi doemnikka?* (Ee-go-sune poh-jung-ee dome-nee-kkah?) How long does the guarantee last? *Pojungun olmagan imnikka?* (Poh-jung-uun ahl-mah-gahn eem-nee-kkah?)

Guest *Sonnim* **(Soan-neem);** Guest room *Kaek shil* (Kake-sheel)
You are my guest. *Tangshin-un nawi sonnim imnida.* (Tahng-sheen-uun nah-wee soan-neem eem-nee-dah.)

Guide *Annaeja* **(Ahn-nay-jah);** Guide book *Annae so* (Ahn-nay soe)
Do you have any guide books on Korea? *Hanguk-e gwanhan annaesoga issumnikka?* (Hahn-gook-eh gwahn-hahn ahn-nay-soe-gah es-sume-nee-kkah?) I need a guide who speaks English. *Yongo-rul hal su itnun annaeja-ga piryohamnida.* (Yong-go-rule hahl sue eet-nuun ahn-nay-jah-gah pee-rio-hahm-nee-dah.)

Gum (chewing) *Chuing gum* **(Chuu-eeng gome);** also *Kkum* **(Kkahm)**
Would you like some chewing gum? *Kkum-ui dushigessumnikka?* (Kkahm-we due-shee-gay-ssume-nee-kkah?) Do you have chewing gum? *Kkumi issumnikka?* (Kkahm-ee ee-ssume-nee-kkah?)

Gymnasium *Cheyukkwan* **(Chay-yuke-kwan)**
Are there many gyms in Seoul? *Seoul-e cheyukk-wani manun issumnikka?* (Seoul-eh cheh-yuuk-kwan-ee mah-nune ee-ssume-nee-kkah?)

Gynecologist *Puinkkwa uisa* **(Puu-een-kwah we-sah)**
Could you recommend a gynecologist? *Puinkkwa uisarul chuchonhae chushigessumnikka?* (Puu-een-kwah we-sah-ruul chuu-chahn-hay chuu-shee-gay-ssume-nee-kkah?)

H

Haggle *Kapsul kkakta* **(Kahp-sule kahk-tah)**
If you haggle you may get a better price. *Kapsul kkakta tochoun kagyokul odulsu issumnida.* (Kahp-suul kahk-tah tah-choh-uun kah-kyah-kuul ah-duel-suu ee-ssume-nee-dah.) Street vendors expect you to haggle over the price. *Koriui haeng-sangdurun tangshin-i kakyokul kapsul kkakta yesang hago issumnida.* (Kah-ree-we hang-sahng-due-rune tahng-sheen-ee kah-kyah-kuul kahp-suul kahk-tah yeh-sahng-hah-go ee-ssume-nee-dah.)

Hair (on the head) *Morikarak* **(Moe-ree-kah-rahk);** Hairbrush *Pit* (Peet); Haircut *Ibal* (Ee-bahl)
Please set my hair. *Mori-rul sonbwa chushipshio.* (Moe-ree-rule sohn-bwah chuu-sheep-she-oh.) Just a haircut, please. *Ibal-man hae chuseyo.* (Ee-bahl-mahn hay chuu-say-yoe.)

Half *Pan* **(Pahn);** also *Cholban* (Chole-bahn); Half-hour *Pan shigan* (Pahn she-gahn); Half-price *Pan-aek* (Pahn-ache)

Just half of that will be enough. *Kugosui panuro chungbun halgoshimnida.* (Kuu-go-suu-we pahn-uu-roh chuung-buun hahl-gah-sheem-nee-dah.)

Hamburger *Haembogo* (Hame-bah-gah)
Two hamburgers, please. *Haembogo tugae chuseyo.* (Hame-bah-gah tuu-gay chuu-say-yoe.)

Handbag *Haendubaek* (Hane-duu-bake)
I would like to buy a leather handbag. *Kajuk haendubaekul sago shipssumnida.* (Kah-juuk hane-duu-bake-uul sah-goh-sheep-ssume-nee-dah.)

Hand-made *Sonuro mandun* (Soe-nuu-roe mahn-doon)
Is this hand-made? *Igosun sonuro mandungo shimnikka?* (Ee-go-sune soe-nuu-roe mahn-dune-go sheem-nee-kkah?)

Hangover (from drinking) *Sukchwi* (Suke-che-we)
I can't drink much because I have severe hangovers. *Nanun sukchwiga shimhaeso surul mani motamnida.* (Nah-nuun suuk-chwee-gah sheem-hay-sah suu-ruul mahn-ee mah-tahm-nee-dah.)

Harbor (port) *Hanggu* (Hahng-guu)
We arrived at Pusan Harbor. *Pusan Hange tochak haessumnida.* (Puu-sahn Hahng-eh toh-chahk hay-ssume-nee-dah.)

Hat *Moja* (Moe-jah)
Elderly Korean men often wear traditionally styled hats. *Hanguk-ui noindurun jongjong chontongjogin mojarul ssumnida.* (Hahn-gook-we noh-een-due-rune johng-johng chahn-tohng-jahg-een moh-jah-rule ssume-nee-dah.)

Have (possess) *Kajida* (Kah-jee-dah)
Do you have enough money? *Chungbunhan tonul*

kajigo issumnikka? (Chuung-buun-hahn tohn-ule kah-jee-goh ee-ssume-nee-kkah?) Do you have chocolate ice cream? *Chokolleit aisukurimi issumnikka?* (Choh-kahl-leit aye-sue-kuu-reem-ee ee-ssume-nee-kkah?)

Headache *Tutong* **(Tuu-tong);** also *Moriga apunnida* (Mah-ree-gah ah-pune-nee-dah)
I have a headache. *Moriga apumnida.* (Mah-ree-gah ah-pume-nee-dah.)

Health *Kongang* **(Kone-gahng);** Healthy *Konganghan* (Kone-gahng-hahn)
I hope you are in good health. *Konganghashigirul pimnida.* (Kone-gahng-hah-she-ghee-rule peem-nee-dah.) I am very healthy, thank you. *Kamsa hamnida.* (Kahm-sah hahm-nee-dah.) [or] *Nanun kongang hamnida.* (Nah-nune kahn-gahng hahm-nee-dah.)

Heat *Towi* **(Toe-we)**
The heat is unbearable today. *Onurun chamgi oryoulmankum topssumnida.* (Oh-nuu-rune chahm-ghee ah-ryah-uul-mahn-kume tahp-ssume-nee-dah.)

Heater *Chonyolgi* **(Chone-yole-ghee);** also *Hito* (Hee-tah)
We need a heater in the room. *Pange hito-ga pillyo hamnida.* (Pahng-eh hee-tah-gah peel-lyoh hahm-nee-dah.)

Heavy *Mogoun* **(Muu-go-uun)**
Are your bags heavy? *Kabangi mugopssumnikka?* (Kah-bahng-ee muu gahp-ssume-nee-kkah?) Yes, they are very heavy. *Ne, cham mugopssumnida.* (Neh, chahm muu-gahp-ssume-nee-dah.)

Help (aid) *Topta* **(Tope-tah);** Rescue *Kuhada* (Kuu-hah-dah)

May I help you? *Towa turil koshi opsulkkayo?* (Toe-wah tuu-reel koe-she ope-suul-kah-yoe?) [Popular style] *Towa turil kkayo?* (Toh-wah tuu-reel kkah-yoh?) Please help me. *Narul towa chushipshio.* (Nah-rule toh-wah chuu-sheep-shee-oh.)

Her (objective) *Kuyojarul* **(Kuu-yoe-jah-rule);** Genitive case *Kuyojaui* (Kuu-yoe-jah-we) What is her name? *Kuyojaui irumi mwoshimnikka?* (Kuu-yah-jah-we ee-rume-ee mwha-sheem-nee-kkah?) Please give this to her. *Igosul kuyojaege chushipshio.* (Ee-gah-suul kuu-yah-jay-gay chuu-sheep-shee-oh.)

Here (this place) *Yogi* **(Yoe-ghee);** To this place *Yogi-ro* (Yoe-ghee-roe) When did you come here? *Onje yogi wassumnikka?* (Ahn-jay yah-ghee wah-ssume-nee-kkah?) Put my bags here. *Nae kabangul yogie nwachushipshio.* (Nay kah-bahng-ule yah-ghee-eh nwah-chuu-sheep-she-oh.) He's already here. *Kunun imi yogi issumnida.* (Kuu-nune ee-mee yah-ghee ee-ssume-nee-dah.)

High (height) *Nopun* **(Noe-poon)** There are many high buildings in Seoul. *Seoulenun nopun bildingi mansumnida.* (Seoul-eh-nune noh-pune beel-deeng-ee mahn-sume-nee-dah.) Is the mountain very high? *Ku sanun maeu nopsumnikka?* (Kue sah-nune may-uu nohp-sume-nee-kkah?)

Highway (Main Road) *Kosok toro* **(Koh-sohk toh-roh)** This highway goes from Seoul to Pusan. *I kosok toronun Seoul-eso Pusan-kkaji kamnida.* (Ee koh-sohk-toh-roh-nune Seoul-eh-sah Pusan-kkah-jee kahm-nee-dah.)

Hiking *Haiking* **(Hah-ee-keeng)**
Would you like to go hiking in the desert? *Samakuro hiking kashigessumnikka?* (Sah-mahk-uu-roh hah-ee-keeng kah-shee-geh-ssume-nee-kkah?)

Hill *Kogae* **(Koe-gay);** also *Ondok* (Ahn-dahk)
There are several hills within the city limits of Seoul. *Seoul-shi kyonggyeson ane manun chagun sanduri issumnida.* (Seoul-she kyong-gay-soan ahn-eh mah-nune chah-guun sahn-due-ree ee-ssume-nee-dah.)

Him *Kuege* **(Kuu-eh-gay);** also *Kurul* (Kuu-rule)
I gave him the receipt. *Kuege yongsujungul chuossumnida.* (Kuu-eh-gay yahng-suu-jung-ule chuu-ah-ssume-nee-dah.) I've seen him before. *Kurul chone pwassumnida.* (Kuu-rule chahn-eh pwah-ssume-nee-dah.)

History *Yoksa* **(Yoke-sah);** Historical *Yoksajok* (Yoke-sah-joak); Historic place *Sajok* (Sah-joke)
Do you have a history of Korea. *Hanguk yoksarul ashimnikka?* (Hahn-gook yahk-sah-rule ah-sheem-nee-kkah?) Are there any historic places near-by? *Kunchoe sajokjiga issumnikka?* (Kune-chah-eh sah-jahk-jee-gah ee-ssume-nee-kkah?)

Holiday (vacation) *Hyuil* **(Wheel);** National Holiday *Kuk kyongil* (Kuke k'yong-eel)
Tomorrow is a national holiday. *Naeilun kukyongil imnida.* (Nay-eel-uun kuuk-kyahng-eel eem-nee-dah.) I am on vacation. *Hyuga chung imnida.* (Hyuu-gah chuung eem-nee-dah.)

Honeymoon *Mirwol* **(Meer-wole);** Honeymoon trip *Shinhon yohaeng* (Sheen-hoan yoe-hang)
Are all of those couples on honeymoon trips? *Cho ssangdul modu shinhon yohaeng chung imnikka?*

(Chah ssahng-duel moh-duu sheen-hohn yah-
hang chuung eem-nee-kkah?) We are on our
honeymoon. *Wurinun mirwol chung imnida.* (Wuu-
ree-nune meer-wole chuung eem-nee-dah.)

Horse *Mal* (Mahl)
I understand Cheju Island is famous for its
horses. *Chejudonun mari yumyong hangosul algo
issumnida.* (Cheh-juu-doh-nune mah-ree yuu-
myahng-hahn-gah-suul ahl-goh ee-ssume-nee-
dah.) I have never ridden a horse. *Nanun
hanbondo marul tabonjogi opssumnida.* (Nah-nune
hahn-bahn-doh mah-rule tah-bohn-jah-ghee
ahp-ssume-nee-dah.)

Hospital *Pyongwon* (P'yong-won); General hospital *Chonghap pyongwon* (Chong-hahp p'yong-
won)
Where is the nearest hospital? *Kajang kakkaun
pyongwoni odi issumnikka?* (Kah-jahng kah-kkah-
uun pyahng-wahn-ee ah-dee ee-ssume-nee-
kkah? I must go to a hospital. *Pyongwone
kayahamnida.* (Pyahn-wahn-eh kah-yah-hahm-
nee-dah.)

Hospitality *Hwandae* (Hwahn-day); also *Hudae*
(Huu-day); *Houi* (Hoh-we)
Thank you for your hospitality. *Tangshin-ui houie
kamsa hamnida.* (Tahng-sheen-we hoh-we-eh
kahm-sah hahm-nee-dah.)

Host *Chuin* (Chuu-een)
Who is the host? *Nuga chuin ishimnikka?* (Nuu-
gah chuu-een ee-sheem-nee-kkah?)

**Hostess (at dinner party) *Anchuin* (Ahn-chuu-
een);** Night club hostess *Hosutesu* (Hostess)
Would you like to have a hostess? *Hostesurul
teryo olkkayo?* (Hoh-stee-sue-rule tay-ryah ohl-

kkah-yoh?) What is the charge for hostesses? *Hosutesu-e daehan yogumun olma imnikka?* (Hostess-eh day-hahn yoh-gume-uum ahl-mah eemnee-kkah?)

Hot *Toun* (Tah-uun); A hot day *Toun nal* (Tah-uun nahl); Hot water *Toun mul* (Tah-uun-muul) Is it always this hot here in summer? *Yorume yoginun hangsang topssumnikka?* (Yah-rume-eh yahghee-nune hahng-sahng tahp-ssume-nee-kkah?) May I have some hot water, please? *Toun murul chushipshio?* (Tah-uun muu-rule chuusheep-shee-oh?)

Hotel *Hotel* (Hotel); Inn *Yogwan* (Yoag-won) Please take me to the Chosun Hotel. *Chosun Hotel kaji kapshida.* (Chosun Hotel kah-jee kahp-shedah.) What hotel are you staying at? *Onu hotel-e mukko gyeshimnikka?* (Ah-nue hotel-eh muu-kkoh gay-sheem-nee-kkah?)

House *Chip* (Cheep); My house *Ne chip* (Nay cheep); Your house *Tangshin taek* (Tahng-sheen take) I would like to invite you to my house. *Tangshinul uli chipuro chodae hago shipssumnida.* (Tahngsheen-ule uu-lee cheep-uu-roh choh-die hah-goh sheep-ssume-nee-dah.) Is your house far from here? *Tangshin taekun yogieso momnikka?* (Tahngsheen tay-kune yah-ghee-eh-sah mahm-neekkah?)

Humidity *Supki* (Supe-kee); also *Supto* (Supe-toe) The humidity is very high today. *Onul supkiga maeu nopssumnida.* (Oh-nuul supe-kee-gah mayuu nohp-ssume-nee-dah.)

Hungry *Paegopuda* **(Pay-go-puu-dah);** also *Shijanghada* (She-jahng-hah-dah)
Are you hungry? *Shijang hashimnikka?* (Sheejahng hah-sheem-nee-kkah?) [or] *Paego pumnikka?* (Pay-goh pume-nee-kkah?) Yes, I'm very hungry. *Ne, paego pumnida.* (Nay, pay-goh pumenee-dah.) No, I'm not hungry. *Anio, paegopuju anssumnida.* (Ah-nee-oh, pay-goh-puu-juu ahnssume-nee-dah.)

Hurrah! *Manse!* **(Mahn-say)**

Hurry *Soduruda* **(Soe-duu-rue-dah);** Hurry up! *Ppalli* (Pah-lee!)
I am in a hurry. *Nanun sodurugo issumnida.* (Nahnoon soe-duu-rue-go ee-sume-nee-dah.) Please hurry. *Sodurupshio.* (Sah-due-rupe-shee-oh.) [or] *Ppallihaseyo.* (Phahl-lee-hah-say-yoe.)

Husband *Nampyon* **(Nahm-p'yone);** My husband *Chu in* (Chuu een)
This is my husband. *Ibunun che nampyon imnida.* (Ee-buun-uun chay nahm-pyahn eem-nee-dah.) I'll call my husband. *Nampyonege chonwa halgoshimnida.* (Nahm-pyahn-eh-gay chahn-wah hahl-gah-sheem-nee-dah.) Please have your husband sign this. *Igose tangshin nampyon-e somyongi piryohamnida.* (Ee goh-say tahng-sheen nahm-pyahn-eh sah-myahng-ee pee-ryoh-hahm-nee-dah.)

Hygiene *Wisaenghak* **(We-sang-hock);** Public health *Kongjung wisaeng* (Khong-jung we-sang)
It is always best to be careful of hygiene when traveling. *Yohaengshi hangsang wisaenge shingyongssunungoshi cheilimnida.* (Yah-hang-she hahng-sahng wee-sang-eh sheen-yong-ssue-nune-gah-she cheh-eel cem-nee-dah.)

I

I *Na* **(Nah);** When addressing a superior person
Cho (Chah)
I'm Boye De Mente. *Nanun Boye De Mente imnida.*
(Nah-nune Boye De Mente eem-nee-dah.)

Ice *Orum* **(Ah-rume);** Icebox *Naengjanggo*
(Nang-jahng-go)
There is ice on the road. *Kil wie orumi issumnida.*
(Keel wee-eh ah-rume-ee ee-ssume-nee-dah.)
The river has ice on it this morning. *Onul achim
kange orumi issossumnida.* (Oh-nule ah-cheen
kahng-eh ah-rume-ee ee-ssah-ssume-nee-dah.)

Identification *Chungmyongso* **(Chung-m'yong-
soe);** also *Shinbunjung* (Sheen-buun-juung)
Do you have some identification? *Chungmyongso
issumnikka?* (Chung-myahng-sah ee-ssume-nee-
kkah?)

Identification card *Shinbun chungmyong-so*
(Sheen-boon chung-m'yong-soe)
May I see your identification card, please? *Shin-
bun chungmyongsorul poyo chushigessumnikka?*
(Sheen-boon chung-m'yong-soe-rule poe-yoe
chuu-she-gay-ssume-nee-kkah?)

Ill (sick) *Pyongdun* **(P'yong-dune);** also *Apun*
(Ah-puen)
I feel sick, please call a doctor. *Naega apuni, uisarul pullo chushipshio.* (Nay-gah ah-puu-nee, we-
sah-rule puul-lah chuu-sheep-shee-oh.)

Immediately *Chukshi* **(Chuke-she);** also *Kot*
(Kote)
We are leaving immediately. *Urinun kot ttonam-
nida.* (Uu-ree-nune koht ttah-nahm-nee-dah.)   I

would like to have it immediately. *Chukshi kugo-sul kajigo shipssumnida.* (Chuke-shee kuu-gah-sule kah-jee-goh sheep-ssume-nee-dah.)

Impolite (rude) *Porudopnun* (Poe-rue-dope-nuun); also *Muroehan* (Muu-roe-eh-hahn)
That word is rather impolite *Ku marun muroe-hamnida.* (Kuu mah-rune muu-roe-eh-hahm-nee-dah.) Excuse me for being impolite. *Muroehangot yongso haechushipshio.* (Muu-roe-eh-hahn-ght yong-sah hay-chuu-sheep-shee-oh.)

Import *Suiphada* (Sweep-hah-dah); Imported goods *Suippum* (Sweep-pume); Import permit *Suip hoga* (Sweep hoe-gah); Importer *Suipsang* (Sweep-sahng)
Are these imported goods? *Igoturun suippum im-nikka?* (Ee-gah-tuu-rune sweep-puum eem-neek-kkah?) I would like to import some of these. *Igotulchung olmarul suiphago shipssumnida.* (Ee-gah-tule-chuung ahl-mah-rule sweep-hah-goh sheep-ssume-nee-dah.) Are you an importer? *Tangshin-un suipopja imnikka?* (Tahng-sheen-uun sweep-ahp-jah eem-nee-kkah?)

Impossible *Pulganunghan* (Pul-gah-nung-hahn)
I'm sorry but that is impossible. *Mianhamnidaman kugosun pulganunghamnida.* (Mee-ahn-hahm-nee-dah-mahn kuu-gah-sune puul-gah-nuung-hahm-nee-dah.)

Incense *Hyang* (Hyahng); Incense burner *Hyang-no* (Hyahng-no)
I'm looking for a small incense burner. *Jagun hyangnorul chakko issumnida.* (Jah-gune hyahng-noh-rule chah-kkoh ee-ssume-nee-dah.)

Include *Pohamhada* (Poh-hahm-hah-dah)
Does this include everything? *I gosun modungosul*

pohamhago issumnikka? (Ee-gah-sune moh-dune-gah-sule poh-hahm-hah-goh ee-ssume-nee-kkah?)

Income (earnings) *Suip* **(Suu-eep);** also *Soduk* (Soe-duke); Cash income *Hyongum suip* (H'yone-gume suu-eep)
My income is too low. *Nae suipun nomu nassumnida.* (Nay suu-eep-uun nah-muu nah-ssume-nee-dah.)

Indeed (when used for emphasis) *Chonmal!* **(Chong-mahl!);** also *Sasil!* (Sah-sheel!)
Thank you very much indeed. *Chongmal komapsumnida.* (Chong-mahl koe-mahp-sume-nee-dah.) Yes, indeed! *Ne, chomgmal!* (Neh, chong-mahl!)

India *Indo* **(Een-doe);** Indian *Indoe* (Een-doe-eh)
I'm going on to India from here. *Yogieso Indoro kal yejong imnida.* (Yah-ghee-eh-sah Een-doh-roh kahl yeh-jahng eem-nee-dah.)

Indigestion *Sohwa pullyang* **(Soe-whah pool-yahng)**
I ate so much I have indigestion. *Kwashik haeso sohwa pullyangik saenggyossumnida.* (Kwah-sheek hay-sah soh-hwah puul-yahng-eek sang-gyah-ssume-nee-dah.)

Industry *Kongop* **(Kohng-ahp);** also *Sanop* (Sahn-ahp)
Is tourism a major industry in Korea? *Hanguk-eso kwankwangun chuyo sanopimnikka?* (Hahn-gook-eh-sah kwahn-kwahng-uun chuu-yoh sahn-ahp cem-nee-kkah?)

Inexpensive *Kapssan* **(Kahp-sahn)**
This is very inexpensive. *I gosun maeu kapssamnida.* (Ee-gah-sune may-uu kahp-ssahm-nee-

dah.) Do you have any that are inexpensive?
Kupssangoshi issumnikka? (Kahp-ssahn-gah-shee
ee-ssume-nee-kkah?)

Information *Chishik* **(Chee-sheek);** News
Chongbo (Chong-boe); also *Soshik* (Soe-sheek)
Where can I get some information about
Kyongju? *Kyongjue kwanhan annesorul odieso odulsu
issumnikka?* (Kyahng-juu-eh kwahn-hahn ahn-
nay-soh-rule ah-dee-soh ah-dule-sue ee-ssume-
nee-kkah?) I have no information about that.
Kugosegwanhan chishiki opssumnida. (Kuu-gah-seh-
gwahn-hahn chee-sheek-ee ahp-ssume-nee-dah.)

Injection *Chusa* **(Chuu-sah)**
You must have a cholera injection. *Tangshin-un
kollera chusarul majaya hamnida.* (Tahng-sheen-uun
kohl-leh-rah chuu-sah-rule mah-jah-yah hahm-
nee-dah.)

Inn *Yogwan* **(Yah-gwan);** Small hotel *Yoinsuk*
(Yoe-een-suke)
I would like to stay in a Korean inn for a few
nights. *Myochilbam Hanguk yogwaneso chinaego
shipssumnida.* (Myah-cheel-bahm Hahn-gook
yah-gwahn-eh-sah chee-nay-goh sheep-ssume-
nee-dah.)

Inspection *Komsa* **(Kome-sah)**
Everyone must go through baggage inspection.
Nuguna chim komsarul padayahamnida. (Nuu-guu-
nah cheem kome-sah-rule pah-dah-yah-hahm-
nee-dah.)

Insurance *Pohom* **(Poe-home);** Life insurance
Saengmyong pohom (Sang-m'yong poe-home)
Would you like to get some life insurance? *Saengmyong pohome tushigessumnikka?* (Sang-myahng
poe-home-eh tue-shee-geh-ssume-nee-kkah?)

Interesting *Hungmi innun* **(Hung-me een-noon);**
also *Chaemi itnun* (Chaeh-mee eet-noon)
I found it extremely interesting. *Kugoshi maeu
hungmi issumnida.* (Kuu-gah-shee may-uu huung-
mee ee-ssume-nee-dah.)

International *Kukchejogin* **(Kuke-chay-joe-
gheen);** International hotel *Kukche hotel* (Kuke-
chay hotel); International trade *Kukche muyok*
(Kuke-chay muu-yoke)
Seoul is really becoming an international city.
*Seoul-un chongmallo kukchejogin toshiga toeossum-
nida.* (Seoul-uun chahng-mahl-loh kuuk-cheh-
jah-geen toh-shee-gah toeh-ah-ssume-nee-dah.)

Interpreter *Tongyokcha* **(Tong-yoke-chah)**
I would like to hire an interpreter. *Tongyokcharul
koyonghago shipssumnida.* (Tohng-yoke-jah-rule
koh-yohng-hah-goh sheep-ssume-nee-dah.)
Can you find an interpreter for me? *Tongyokcharul
kuhae chushigessumnikka?* (Tohng-yoke-jah-rule
kuu-hay chuu-shee-geh-ssume-nee-kkah?)

Intersection *Kyochachom* **(K'yoe-chah-chome)**
Stop just before the intersection. *Kyochachom
chone paro momchushipshio.* (Kyoh-chah-chahm
chahn-eh pah-roh mahm-chuu-sheep-shee-oh.)

Introduce *Sogaehada* **(Soe-gay-hah-dah)**
Please introduce me to Mr. Kim. *Kim Sonsaeng-
nim-ege narul sogaehae chushipshio.* (Keem Sahn-
sang-neem-eh-geh nah-rule soh-gay-hay chuu-
sheep-shee-oh.) May I introduce you to Mr.
Smith? *Smith Sshi-ege tangshin-ul sogaehalkkayo?*
(Smith Sshe-eh-geh tahng-sheen-ule soh-gay-
hahl-kkah-yoh?)

Introduction (one person to another) *Sogae* **(Soe-
gay);** Letter of introduction *Sogae chang* (Soe-
gay chahng)

An introduction is very important in Korea. *So-gaehanungosun Hanguk-eso maeu chungyo hamnida.* (Soh-gay-hah-nune-gah-sune Hahn-gook-eh-sah may-uu chuung-yoh hahm-nee-dah.)

Invitation *Chodae* **(Choe-day)**
I appreciate your invitation, and accept with plea-sure. *Tangshin-e chodaee kamsahamyo, kippuge ungh-agessumnida.* (Tahng-sheen-eh choh-day-eh kahm-sah-hah-myah, kee-ppue-geh uung-hah-geh-ssume-nee-dah.)

Invite *Chodaehada* **(Choe-day-hah-dah)**
I would like to invite you out for dinner tonight. *Onulbam chongchane tangshinul chodae hagoshipss-umnida.* (Oh-nule-bahm chahng-chahn-eh tahng-sheen-uel choh-day-hah-goh-sheep-ssume-nee-dah.) I have been invited to go sightseeing tomorrow. *Naeil kwangwang chodaerul padassumnida.* (Nay-eel kwahn-gwahng choh-day-rule pah-dah-ssume-nee-dah.)

Invoice *Songchang* **(Song-chahng)**
Please send the invoice to my office. *Nae samu-sillo songchang ponae chushipshio.* (Nay sah-muu-sheel-loh sohng-chahng poh-nay chuu-sheep-shee-oh.)

Irishman *Aelan* **(Aye-lahn)**
Koreans are often compared to the Irish. *Hanguk-indurun kakkum Aelan saram-e pigyodoemnida.* (Hahn-gook-een-due-rune kah-kume Aye-lahn sah-rahm-eh pee-gyoh-dome-nee-dah.)

Island *Som* **(Soam)**; Uninhabited island *Muindo* **(Muu-een-doe)**
There are many small islands off the coast of Ko-rea. *Hanguk haeane manun chagun somduri issum-nida.* (Hahn-gook hay-ahn-eh mah-nune chah-gune sahm-due-ree ee-ssume-nee-dah.)

Italian (person) *Itallia saram* **(Ee-tahl-lee-ah sah-rahm)**

Itinerary (plan of travel) *Yohaeng* **(Yah-hang);**
Written record of destinations *Yohaeng ilgi* (yoe-hang eel-ghee)
May I see your itinerary, please? *Tangshin-ui yohaeng iljongul poyo chushigessumnikka?* (Tahng-sheen-we yah-hang ell-joan-gule chuu-she-geh-ssume-nee-kkah?)

Ivory *Sanga* **(Sahng-ah);** Artificial ivory *Injo sanga* (Een-joe sahng-ah); Ivory chopsticks *Sanga chotkarak* (Sahng-ah chote-kah-rahk)
Ivory chopsticks are too heavy. *Sanga chotkarakun nomu mugopssumnida.* (Sahng-ah chaht-kah-rahk-uun nah-muu muu-gahp-ssume-nee-dah.) May I have wooden chopsticks, please. *Namu chatkarakul chushipshio.* (Nah-muu chaht-kah-rahk-ule chuu-sheep-she-oh.)

J

Jacket *Chaket* **(Chah-keht);** Sportcoat *Undongbok* (Uun-dong-boke)
Should I wear a jacket? *Chaketul iboya hamnikka?* (Chah-keht-ule ee-bah-yah hahm-nee-kkah?) I'd like to have a jacket made. *Kisongbok chaketul kajigo shipssumnida.* (Kee-sahng-bohk chah-keht-ule kah-jee-goh sheep-ssume-nee-dah.)

Jade *Pichwi* **(Pee-chwee)**
Is this genuine jade? *Igosun chinjjha pichwi imnikka?* (Ee-gah-sune cheen-jjah pee-chwee eem-nee-kkah?) I'm looking for a jade necklace. *Pichwi mokorirul chako issumnida.* (Pee-chwee moh-kah-ree-rule chah-koh ee-ssume-nee-dah.)

Jam (food) *Chchaem* **(Chame);** Strawberry jam
Ttalgi chchaem (Tahl-ghee chame); also *Podo
chchaem* (Poe-doe chame)
May I have some jam, please? *Chchaem jom kattachuseyo.* (Chame johm kah-ttah-chuu-say-yoe.)

Japan *Ilbon* **(Eel-bone);** Japanese *Ibonsaram* (Eel-
bone-sah-rahm); Japanese language *Ilbon-o*
(Eel-bone-oh)
Do you speak Japanese? *Ilbono-rul halchul ashimnikka?* (Eel-bone-oh-rule hahl-chuul ah-sheem-
nee-kkah?) Have you been to Japan? *Ilbon-e
kabon chogi issumnikka?* (Eel-bone-eh kah-bohn
chah-ghee ee-ssume-nee-kkah?)

Jazz *Chaeju umak* **(Chay-juu uem-ahk);** Jazz
band *Chaeju aktan* (Chay-juu ahk-tahn)
Is jazz music popular in Korea? *Chaeju umaki
Hanguk-eso inkkiga issumnikka?* (Chay-juu uum-
ahk-ee Hahn-gook-eh-sah een-kee-gah ee-ssume-
nee-kkah?) Are there any American jazz bands
in Seoul? *Seoul-e Miguk chaeju aktuni issumnikka?*
(Seoul-eh Mee-gook chay-juu ahk-tahn-ee ee-
ssume-nee-kkah?)

Jelly *Chelli* **(Chehl-lee)**
Would you like some jelly with your toast? *Toast-
e chelli-rul kyoturo tushigessumnikka?* (Toess-tuu-eh
chehl-lee-rule kyah-tue-rah tue-shee-geh-ssume-
nee-kkah?)

Jellyfish *Haepari* **(Hay-pah-ree)**
Are jellyfish a problem here? *Haepariga yogieso
hanaui munjegori imnikka?* (Hay-pah-ree-gah yah-
ghee-eh-sah hah-nah-we muun-jeh-gah-ree eem-
nee-kkah?) Watch out for jellyfish. *Haeparirul
chosim hashipshio.* (Hay-pah-ree-rule choh-sheem
hah-sheep-shee-oh.)

Jet plane *Chett ugi* **(Cheht-uu-ghee)**

Jewelry *Posok* **(Poe-soak)**; Jeweler *Posoksang* (Poe-soak-sahng)
Is there a jewelry store near here? *I kunchoe posok-sangi issumnikka?* (Ee-kune-chah-eh poh-sahk-sahng-ee ee-ssume-nee-kkah?)

Job (work) *Il* **(Eel)**; Employment *Chigop* (Chee-gahp)
What kind of work do you do? *Chigopi mwo-shimnikka?* (Chee-gah-pee mwah-sheem-nee-kkah?) Are you looking for employment? *Chigopul kuhashimnikka?* (Chee-gah-pule kuu-hah-sheem-nee-kkah?)

Joke *Nongdam* **(Nohng-dahm)**; also *Iksal* (Eek-sahl); Banter *Nollida* (Nohl-lee-dah)
I was just joking. *Nongdam imnida.* (Nohng-dahm eem-nee-dah.)

Juice *Chusu* **(Chuu-sue)**; also *Aek* (Ache); Grape juice *Podo jup* (Poe-doe jupe); Tomato juice *To-mato jup* (Toe-mah-toe jupe)
May I have some orange juice, please. *Orenji chusu chuseyo.* (Oh-rain-jee chuu-sue chuu-say-yoe.)

K

Keep (hold) *Chikida* **(Chee-kee-dah)**; Care for *Tolboda* (Tole-boe-dah)
Please keep this for me until tomorrow. *Naeil kkaji nadaeshin igosul chikyo chushipshio.* (Nay-eel kkah-jee nah-day-sheen ee-gah-sule chee-kyah chuu-sheep-shee-oh.) May I keep this? *Igosul ka-jyodo doemnikka?* (Ee-gah-sule kah-jyah-do dome-nee-kkah?)

Key *Yolsoe* **(Yole-soeh-eh)**
Is this your room key? *Igosun sonsaege pang yolsoe imnikka?* (Ee-gah-sune soan-say-gay pahng yahl-so-eh eem-nec-kkah?) May I have my key, please. *Nae yolsoerul chushipshio.* (Nay yahl-soh-eh-rule chuu-sheep-shee-oh.) I've lost my key. *Yol-soerul punshil haessumnida.* (Yahl-soh-eh-rule puun-sheel hay-ssume-nee-dah.)

Kidney *Shinjang* **(Sheen-jahng);** also *Kongpat* (Kong-paht)
I have a kidney problem and cannot drink very much. *Shinjange munjega issoso surul mani motamnida.* (Sheen-jahng-eh muun-jeh-gah ee-ssah-sah suu-rule mahn-ee moh-tahm-nee-dah.)

Kind (sort) *Chongyu* **(Chong-yuu);** Tender feeings *Chinjolhan* (Cheen-johl-hahn); Kind behavior *Chinjolhan taedo* (Cheen-johl-han tay-doe)
What kind of shoes are you looking for? *Otton chongyu kudurul chakko issumnikka?* (Ah-ttahn chohng-yuu kuu-duu-rule chah-kkoh ee-ssume-nee-kkah?) He is a very kind man. *Kunun maeu chinjolhan saram imnida.* (Kuu-nune may-uu cheen-jahl-hahn sah-rahm eem-nee-dah.)

Kindergarten *Yuchiwon* **(Yuu-chee-won)**
Those children are on their way to kindergarten. *Cho aidurun yuchiwone kanun dochung imnida.* (Chah ah-ee-due-rune yuu-chee-won-eh kah-nune doh-chung eem-nee-dah.)

Kiss *Kisu* **(Kee-sue)**
Kiss me, quick! *Ppalli, kisu haechuseyo!* (Ppahl-lee, kee-sue hay-chuu-say-yoe!)

Kitchen *Puok* **(Puu-ahk);** also *Chubang* (Chuu-bahng)
Is your kitchen Western style? *Puoki soyangshik*

imnikka? (Puu-ahk-ee sah-yahng-sheek eem-nee-kkah?)

Kite *Yon* **(Yone);** Kite-flying *Yon-nalligi* (Yone-nahl-lee-ghee)
I understand kite-flying is very popular in Korea. *Yon-nalligiga Hanguk-eso inkki innun gosul amnida.* (Yone-nahl-lee-gee-gah Hahn-gook-eh-sah een-kee een-nune gah-sule ahm-nee-dah.)

Knee *Murup* **(Muu-rupe)**
I bumped my knee. *Murupul pudichiossumnida.* (Muu-rupe-ule puu-dee-chyah-ssume-nee-dah.)

Knife *Kal* **(Kahl);** also *Naipu* (Nie-puu); Pocket knife *Chumoni-kal* (Chuu-moe-nee-kahl)
Please bring me a steak knife. *Steak naipurul katta chuseyo.* (Steik nie-puu-rule kah-ttah chuu-say-yoe.)

Knock (rap) *Tudurida* **(Tuu-duu-ree-dah);** also *Noku* (Noe-kuu)
Just come on up and knock on the door. *Kot ollawaso noku hashipshio.* (Koht ohl-lah-wah-sah noh-kuu hah-sheep-shee-oh.) Someone is knocking on the door. *Nugungaga munul tudurigo issumnida.* (Nuu-goon-gah-gah muu-nule tuu-duu-ree-go ee-ssume-nee-dah.)

Know (be acquainted with) *(Wa) Anun saida* **(wah) (Ah-noon sah-ee-dah);** Recognize *In-jonghada* (Een-jong-hah-dah); Understand *Alda* (Ahl-dah)
I do not know him. *Nanun kurul morumnida (alji motamnida).* (Nah-nune kuu-rule moh-rume-nee-dah [ahl-jee moh-tahm-nee-dah].) Do you know what time it is? *Myoshi inji ashimnikka?* (Myah-shee een-jee ah-sheem-nee-kkah?) I don't know. *Nanun morumnida.* (Nah-nune moh-rume-nee-dah.)

Korea *Hanguk* **(Hahn-gook);** Republic of Korea *Taehanmin Guk* (Tie-han-meen Gook); North Korea *Pukan* (Puu-kahn)
Are you from Korea? *Hanguk-eso oshin punigunyo?* (Hahn-gook-eh-sah oh-sheen puu-nee-guun-yoe?)

Korean (thing) *Hanguk-e* **(Hahn-gook-eh);** Korean person *Hanguk-in* (Hahn-gook-een); Korean language *Hanguk-o* (Hahn-gook-o); Korean-American *Hanguk-kye-Miguk-in* (Hahn-gook-kay-Me-gook-een)
Are you from Korea? *Hanguk-eso wassumnikka?* (Hahn-guuk-eh-sah wah-ssume-nee-kkah?) I was born in Korea, but I am now an American citizen. *Hangook-eso natchiman, chigum Miguk shimin imnida.* (Hahn-gook-eh-sah nah-tchee-mahn, chee-gume Mee-gook shee-meen eem-nee-dah.) I'm here to study the Korean language. *Hanguk-orul kongbuhagiwihae yogie issumnida.* (Hahn-gook-ah-rule kohng-buu-hah-ghee-wee-hay yah-ghee-eh ee-ssume-nee-dah.)

L

Lacquer *Ot* **(Oat);** also *Raeka* (Ray-kah); Lacquerware *Chilgi* (Cheel-ghee)
I would like to buy a set of lacquered trays. *Chilgi han set-rul sago shipssumnida.* (Cheel-ghee hahn set-rule sah-goh sheep-ssume-nee-dah.)

Lake *Hosu* **(Hoe-sue)**
Are there many lakes in Korea? *Hanguk-e hosuga mani issumnikka?* (Hahn-gook-eh hoh-suu-gah mah-nee ee-ssume-nee-kkah?)

Lane (narrow road) *Chobun kil* **(Choe-boon keel);** Alley *Kolmokkil* (Kole-moak-keel)
Turn right at the first lane after the intersection. *Kyochachom taum chopun kileso uoechon hashipshio.* (Kyoh-chah-chahm tah-uem chah-puun keel-eh-sah uuo-eh-chahn hah-sheep-shee-oh.)

Lantern (paper) *Chedung* **(Chay-duung);** Lantern procession *Chedung haengnyol* (Chay-duung hang-n'yole)
Traditional lanterns are a nostalgic sight in Korea. *Chontong chedungun Hanguk-ul saenggakhage-hanun punggyong imnida.* (Chahn-tohng chay-duung-uun Hahn-gook-ule sahng-gahk-hah-geh-hah-nune puung-gyahng eem-nee-dah.)

Large (big) *Kun* **(Koon);** Spacious *Nolbun* (Nahl-boon); Large number *Manun* (Mah-nune)
This is really a large hotel! *Igosun chongmal kun hotel imnida!* (Ee-gah-sune chahng-mahl kune hoh-tehl eem-nee-dah!) I understand Seoul has a large population. *Nanun Seoul-e manun inguga itnungosul algo issumnida.* (Nah-nune Seoul-eh mah-nune een-guu-gah eet-nune-gah-sule ahl-goh ee-ssume-nee-dah.)

Late *Nujun* **(Nue-juen)**
We are going to be late. *Urinun nujul goshimnida.* (Uu-ree-nune nuu-juul gah-sheem-nee-dah.)
I'm sorry to be late. *Nujo mian hamnida.* (Nue-joe mee-ahn hahm-nee-dah.)

Later *To nujun* **(Tah nuu-june);** also *Huu-eh); Na-junge* (Nah-juung-eh)
I'll call you later. *Najunge chonwha kolgessumnida.* (Nah-juung-eh chone-whah kole-gay-sume-nee-dah.) See you later. *Najunge poepkessumnida.* (*Nah-june-gay pep-kay-sume-nee-dah.*)

Laundry (clothing) *Setangmul* **(Seh-tahng-mul)**
I have some laundry today. *Onul setangmuli is-sumnida.* (Oh-nule say-tahng-muul-ee ee-ssume-nee-dah.) When will my laundry be ready? *Nae setangmuli onje junbi doemnikka?* (Nay seh-tahng-muul-ee ahn-jeh june-bee dome-nee-kkah?)

Lawyer *Pyonhosa* **(P'yone-hoe-sah)**
Can you recommend a good lawyer? *Hul-lyunghan pyonhosarul chuchonhae chushigessum-nikka?* (Huul-lyuung-hahn pyone-hoe-sah-rule chuu-chahn-hay chuu-shee-geh-ssume-nee-kkah?)

Learn *Paeuda* **(Pay-uu-dah)**
Where did you learn Korean? *Odiso Hanguk-ko-rul paewossumnikka?* (Ah-dee-soe Hahn-gook-ko-rule pay-woe-sume-nee-kkah?)

Leather *Kajuk* **(Kah-juke);** Leather bag *Kajuk kabang* (Kah-juuk kah-bahng); Leather gloves *Kujuk changgap* (Kah-juke chahng-gahp)
Are leather goods a bargain in Korea? *Kajuk je-pumi Hunguk-eso ssamnikka?* (Kah-juuk jeh-puum-ee Hahn-gook-eh-sah ssahm-nee-kkah?)

Leave (depart) *Ttonada* **(Toe-nah-dah)**
What time does the train leave? *Kichanun myossie ttonamnikka?* (Kee-chah-nune myah-sshe-eh ttoe-nahm-nee-kkah?) I'm leaving for Tokyo to-morrow. *Naeil Tokyo-ro ttonamnida.* (Nay-eel Tokyo-roh ttoe-nahm-nee-dah.)

Left (direction/side) *Oenjjoge* **(Oehn-joag-eh);**
Left side *Chwachuk* (Chah-chuek); To the left *Oenjjoguro* (Oehn-joag-uu-roh)
Turn left at the next corner. *Taum motungieso oenjjoguro toshio.* (Tah-uum moe-tuung-ee-eh sah oh-ent-joa-guu-roe toe-she-oh.)

Leg *Tari* **(Tah-ree)**
My legs are sore from walking so much. *Nomu mani koroso tariga apumnida.* (Nah-muu mah-nee kah-rah-sah tah-ree-gah ah-pume-nee-dah.)

Leisure *Yoga* **(Yoe-gah);** also *Tum* (Tume)
Do you have any leisure time during the week? *Chu chunge yogaga issumnika?* (Chuu chuung-eh yoe-gah-gah ee-ssume-nee-kkah?)

Lemonade *Remoneidu* **(Ray-moan-a-duu)**
A glass of lemonade, please. *Remonaeidu hachan chuseyo.* (Ray-moan-a-duu hah-chan chuu-say-yoe.)

Length *Kiri* **(Kee-ree);** Lengthen *Kilge hada* (Keel-gay hah-dah)
What is the length of these trousers? *I pachie kirinun olmana toemnikka?* (Ee pah-chee-eh kee-ree-nune ahl-mah-nah toe-em-nee-kkah?) Can you lengthen them? *Pachidulul kilge hae chuseyo?* (Pah-chee-dule-ule keel-gay hay chuu-say-yoe?)

Letter (written message) *Pyonji* **(P'yone-jee);** also *Somyon* (Soam-yone)
Are there any letters for me? *Chohante on pyonchiga opssumnikka?* (Choe-hahn-tay own pyown-jee-gah ope-sume-nee-kkah?) Please mail this letter. *I pyonjiul pucho chushipshipo.* (Ee pyown-jee-ule puu-choe chuu-sheep-she-oh.)

Lettuce *Sangchi* **(Sahng-chee)**
Do you have any fresh lettuce? *Singsinghan sangchuga opssumnikka?* (Sheng-sheng-hahn sahng-chuu-gah ope-sume-nee-kkah?) Would you like lettuce on your sandwich? *Sandwich-e sangchulul noshigetsumnikka?* (Sahn-weechee-eh sahng-chuul-ule no-she-gate-sume-nee-kkah?) A lettuce salad, please. *Sangchu salad chom chushipshio.* (Sahng-chuu salad choam chuu-sheep-she-oh.)

Library *Tosogwan* **(Toh-sah-gwahn);** National Library *Kungnip tosogwan* (Kung-neep toe-soe-gwahn)
I would like to visit the National Library. *Kungnip tosogwanul pangmun hago shipssumnida.* (Kuung-neep toh-sah-gwahn-ule pahng-muun hah-goh sheep-ssume-nee-dah.)

License (authorization) *Myonho* **(Myahn-hah);** Driver's license *Chadongcha unjon myonho* (Chah-dong-chah uun-joan myahn-hah); Temporary license *Imshi myonho* (Eem-shee myahn-hah)
Do you have a driver's license? *Chadongcha unjom myanhojungul kajigo issumnikka?* (Chah-dohng-chah uun-jahm-myahn-hah-juung-ule kah-jee-goh ee-ssume-nee-kkah?) May I see your license, please. *Tangshin-e myonhojungul poyo chushipshio.* (Tahng-sheen-eh myahn-hah-juung-ule poh-yah chuu-sheep-shee-oh.)

Like (be fond of) *Choahada* **(Choe-ah-hah-dah);** Similar to *Pisutan* (Pee-sue-tahn); Alike *Talmun* (Tahl-moon)
I really like this. *Igosul cham choahamnida.* (Ee-gah-sule chahm choh-ah-hahm-nee-dah.) Do you like it? *Kugosul choahashimnikka?* (Kuu-gah-sule choh-ah-hah-sheem-nee-kkah?) Do you have another one like this? *Igot hago pisutan tarungot issumnikka?* (Ee-gaht hah-goh pee-sue-tahn tah-rune-gaht ee-ssume-nee-kkah?)

Line (form a line) *Yorul chitta* **(Yoe-rule cheet-tah);** also *Jurul soda* (Juu-ruel sah-dah)
Please form a single line. *Hanjullo sojushipshio.* (Hahn-juul-loh sah-juu-sheep-shee-oh.) Please wait in that line. *Ku soneso kidaryo chushipshio.* (Kuu sahn-eh-sah kee-dah-rya chuu-sheep-shee-oh.)

Lipstick *Ipsul yonji* **(Eep-sul yoan-jee);** also *Lip-stik* (Leep-steek)
Don't forget your lipstick. *Lipstik-ul itjimaship-shio.* (Leep-steek-ule eet-jee-mah-sheep-shee-oh.)

Liquor (traditional Korean) *Sul* **(Sule);** Foreign liquor *Yangju* (Yahng-juu)
What is the traditional Korean liquor? *Hanguk-e chontongjogin surun mwoshimnikka?* (Hahn-gook-eh chahn-tohng-jah-geen suu-rune mwah-sheem-nee-kkah?) I understand that makkolli is the most traditional Korean liquor. *Makkolliga Hanguk-e kajang chontongjogin sullo nanun algo issumnida.* (Mahk-kahl-lee-gah Hahn-gook-eh kah-jahng chahn-tohng-jah-geen suul-loh nah-nune ahl-goh ee-ssume-nee-dah.)

List (of names) *Myongbu* (M'yong-buu)
Is your name on this list? *Tangshin-e irumi imyongbue issumnikka?* (Tahng-sheen-eh ee-rume-ee ee-myahng-buu-eh ee-ssume-nee-kkah?) I do not have a list of your names yet. *Nanun ajik tangshindur-e myongburul kajigo itchi ansumnida.* (Nah-nune ah-jeek tang-sheen-duur-eh myahng-buu-rule kah-jee-goh eet-chee ahn-ssume-nee-dah.)

Literature *Munhak* **(Moon-hahk);** Modern literature *Hyondae munhak* (H'yone-day moon-hahk); English literature *Yong munhak* (Yahng-moon hahk)
Is the study of literature popular in Korea? *Munhak yonguga Hanguk-eso inkki-ga issumnikka?* (Muun-hahk yahn-guu-gah Hahn-gook-eh-sah een-kee-gah ee-ssume-nee-kkah?) Yes, Korean literature has a long history. *Ne, Hanguk munhakun yoksaga orae doeossumnida.* (Nay, Hahn-gook

muun-hahk-uun yahk-sah-gah oh-ray doe-ah-
ssume-nee-dah.)

Little (small) *Chagun* **(Chah-goon);** Small
amount *Chogun* (Choe-goon); Not much *Chogum* (Choe-gume)
Just give me a little. *Chogumnan chushipshio.*
(Choh-gume-nahn chuu-sheep-shee-oh.) I only
want a little. *Chogumnun chushipshio.* (Choh-
gume-nahn chuu-sheep-she-oh.)

Live (dwell) *Salda* **(Sahl-dah)**
Where do you live? *Odieso sashimnikka?* (Ah-dee-
eh-sah sah-sheem-nee-kkah?) I live in Los Angeles. *L. A.-eso salgo issumnida.* (L. A.-eh-sah sahl-
goh ee-ssume-nee-dah.)

Lobby (hotel) *Lobi* **(Loh-bee)**
I will meet you in the lobby of the Chosun Hotel.
*Chosun Hotel lobi-eso tangshin-ul mannal goshim-
nida.* (Chusun Hoh-tel loh-bee-eh-sah tahng-
sheen-ule mahn-nahl gah-sheem-nee-dah.) Wait
for me in the lobby. *Lobi-eso narul kidaryo chushipshio.* (Loh-bee-eh-sah nah-rule kee-dah-ryo
chuu-sheep-she-oh.)

Lobster *Kajae* **(Kah-jay)**
Lobster is one of my favorite dishes. *Kajaenun
naega cheil choahanun yori-e hana imnida.* (Kah-jay-
nune nay-gah cheh-eel choh-ah-hah-nune yoh-
ree-eh hah-nah em-nee-dah.)

Lock (noun) *Chamulsoe* **(Chah-mule-so-eh) Lock
(verb);** *Chamguda* (Chahm-guu-dah)
Please lock the door. *Munul chamguseyo.* (Muun-
ule chahm-guu-say-yoe.)

Long (lengthy) *Kin* **(Keen);** Duration *Oraen*
(Oh-rain)
Is the Han River very long? *Han Kang-un maeu*

kimnikka? (Hahn Kahng-uun may-uu keem-nee-kkah?) How long will you be gone? *Olmana iges-sumnikka?* (Ahl-mah-nah ee-gay-sume-nee-kkah?)

Lost *Irun* **(Ee-roon);** also *Iroborida* (Ee-rah-bah-ree-dah); *Punshilhada* (Puun-sheel-hah-dah)
I lost my purse. *Nae chigabul iroboryossumnida.* (Nay chee-gah-buul ee-rah-bah-ryo-ssume-nee-dah.) Have you lost something? *Mwosul punshio haessumnikka?* (Mwah-sule puun-she-oh hay-ssume-nee-kkah?)

Loud (not quiet) *Moksoriga kun* **(Moke-soe-ree-gah koon);** Noisy *Shikkuroun* (Sheek-kuu-roe-uun); Conspicuous *Yahan* (Yah-hahn)
The street noise is too loud. *Kori-e soumi nomu kumnida.* (Kah-ree-eh soh-uu-mee nah-muu kume-nee-dah.) The people in the next room are noisy. *Yoppange innun saramduri shikkuropss-umnida.* (Yahp-pahng-eh een-nune sah-rahm-duu-ree shee-kkuu-rahp-ssume-nee-dah.)

Lounge (club or hotel) *Hyugeshil* **(Hue-gay-sheel)**
I'll meet you in the hotel lounge. *Hotel hyugeshi-leso tangshin-ul mannal goshimnida.* (Hoh-tel hue-gay-sheel-eh-sah tahng-sheen-ule mahn-nahl gah-sheem-nee-dah.)

Love (affection) *Sarang* **(Sah-rahng);** Sexual love *Yonae* (Yoe-nay)
I love you. *Tangshin-ul sarang hamnida.* (Tahng-sheen-ule sah-rahng hahm-nee-dah.)

Lovely (beautiful) *Arumdaun* **(Ah-room-dah-uun);** How lovely! *Chongmal arumdawa!* (Chong-mahl ah-room-dah-wah!)
She is lovely. *Kuyojanun arumedapssumnida.* (Kue-yoe-jah-nune ah-rume-dahp-ssume-nee-dah). I

had a lovely time. *Arumdaun shiganul ponaessumnida.* (Ah-rume-dah-uun she-gahn-ule poh-nay-ssume-nee-dah.)

Lover (sweetheart) *Aein* **(Aay-een);** Music lover *Umak aehoga* (Uu-mahk aay-hoe-gah)
This place is popular with lovers. *Ichangsonun aeindurege inkki imnida.* (Ee-chahng-soh-nune aay-een-due-ray-gay een-kee eem-nee-dah.)

Luck (fortune) *Un* **(Uun);** also *Haengun* (Hang-uun)
Good luck! *Haengun-ul pimnida!* (Hang-uun-ule peem-nee-dah!)

Luggage (baggage) *Suhwamul* **(Sue-whah-mul);**
Baggage ticket *Suhamul inhwanpyo* (Sue-hah-mul een-whahn-poe)
Is this your luggage? *Igoshi tangshin-e suhwamul imnikka?* (Eh-gah-shee tahng-sheen-eh suu-hwah-muul eem-nee-kkah?) How many pieces of luggage do you have? *Suhwamuli myokkae imnikka?* (Suu-hwah-muu-ree myah-kkay eem-nee-kkah?)

Lunch *Chomshim* **(Chome-sheem)**
Let's have lunch. *Chomshim mogupshida.* (Chome-sheem-moe-gupe-she-dah.) Can you have lunch with me tomorrow? *Naeil chowa kachi chomshimul hajianketssumikka?* (Nay-eel choe-wah kah-chee choam-sheem-ule hah-jee-ahn-keht-sume-nee-kkah?)

Luncheon party *Ochan hoe* **(Oh-chahn hoe-eh)**
I have to attend a luncheon party today. *Onul ochanhoee chamsok haeya hamnida.* (Oh-nule oh-chahn-hoeh-eh chahm-sahk-hay-yah hahm-nee-dah.)

141

Luxurious *Hohwasuroun* (**Hoh-hwah-sue-rah-uun**); also *Sachisuroun* (Sah-chee-sue-roan) *Sachipum* (Sah-chee-pume)
This hotel is really luxurious. *I hotel-un cham hohwasuropssumnida (sachisuropssumnida).* (Ee-hotel-uun chahm hoh-hwah-sue-rahp-ssume-nee-dah [sah-chee-sue-rahp-ssume-nee-dah].) This is too luxurious for me. *Igosun naege nomu sachisuropssumnida.* (Ee-gah-sune nah-eh-geh nah-muu sah-chee-sue-rahp-ssume-nee-dah.)

M

Made *Mandun* (**Mahn-doon**); also *Che* (Cheh)
Is this made in Korea? *Igosun Hanguk-che imnikka?* (Ee-gah-sune Hahn-gook-cheh eem-nee-kkah?) No, it is made in the U.S. *Anio, Miguk-che imnida.* (Ah-nee-oh, Mee-gook-cheh eem-nee-dah.)

Magazine *Chapchi* (**Chop-chee**); Weekly magazine *Chuganji* (Chuu-gahn-jee); Monthly magazine *Wolganji* (Wole-gahn-jee)
I read about it in a weekly magazine. *Chuganji-eso ilgot sumnida* (Chuu-gahn-jee-eh-sah il-gaht ssume-nee-dah.)

Mahjong *Majak* (**Mah-jahk**)
Do you know how to play mahjong? *Majak nori haljul aseyo?* (Mah-jahk noh-ree hah-juul ah-say-yoe?)

Maid (servant) *Kajongbu* (**Kah-jong-buu**)
The maid will have your room cleaned in just a few minutes. *Kajongbu ga kot pangul chongsohalgo shimnida.* (Kah-jong-buu gah koht pahng-ule chahng-soh hahl-gah-sheem-nee-dah.)

Mail (letters) *Upyonmul* **(Uu-ppyahn-muul);** also *Pyonji* (P'yone-jee); To mail *Usonghada* (Uu-song-hah-dah)
Are there any letters for me? *Naege on pyonji-ga issumnikka?* (Nay-gay own p'yone-jee-gah ee-ssume-neek-kah?) Please mail these for me. *Igol puchigo shipsumnida.* (Ee-gole puu-chee-go sheep-ssume-nee-dah.)

Main *Chuyohan* **(Chuu-yoe-han);** Main street *Pon hwaga* (Pone-whah-gah); Main office *Pon guk* (Pohn-gook)
I'd like to go to the main post office. *Ucheguk ponguke kago shipssumnida.* (Uu-cheh-gook pohn-guuk-eh kah-goh sheep-ssume-nee-dah.)
Where is your main office? *Pon guk samushiri odie issumnikka?* (Pohn-gook sah-muu-shee-ree ah-dee-eh ee-ssume-nee-kkah?) This is the main street in the city. *Yogiga toshi-e ponhwaga imnida.* (Yah-gee-gah toh-shee-eh pahn-hwah-gah eem-nee-dah.)

Make *Mandulda* **(Mahn-dul-dah);** Build *Chitta* (Cheet-tah)
Can you make me a pair of boots in two days? *Itulane kudu hankyollye mandulsu issumnikka?* (Ee-tule-ahn-eh kuu-duu hahn-kyahl-lay mahn-duel-suu ee-ssume-nee-kkah?) Can you make a suit out of this material? *Igosuro yangpok hanbol mandulsu issumnikka?* (Ee-gah-sue-roh yahng-pohk hahn-bahl mahn-duel-suu ee-ssume-nee-kkah?)

Male (man) *Namja* **(Nahm-jah);** Animal *Dong-mul* (Dong-muul)

Man *Ingan* **(Een-gahn);** Person *Saram* (Sah-rahm)
Do you know that man? *Jo saramul ashimnikka?* (Jah sah-rahm-ule ah-sheem-nee-kkah?)

Manager   *Chibaein* **(Chee-bain);**   Hotel manager
Hotel chibaein (Hotel chee-bain);   Business manager   *Yongop pujang* (Yahng-ahp puu-jahng)
I would like to see the manager. *Chibaein-ul mannago shipssumnida.* (Chee-bain-ule mahn-nah-goh
sheep-ssume-nee-dah.)   Please call the manager.
Chibaein-ul pullo chushio. (Chee-bain ule puul-lah
chuu-she-oh.)

Manners   *Taedo* **(Tay-doe);**   also *Yejol* (Yay-jole);
Habits   *Pungsup* (Poong-supe)
Are traditional manners still common in Korea?
Ajik Hanguk-e chontong yejori hunhamnikka? (Ah-
jeek Hahn-gook-eh chahn-tohng yeh-jeh-ree
hune-hahm-nee-kkah?)   Proper etiquette is very
important when meeting older people. *Noinul
mannassulttae chokcholhan yejori maeu chungyo
hamnida.* (Noh-een-ule mahn-nah-ssuul-ttay
chahk-chahl-hahn yeh-jah-ree may-uu chuung-
yoh hahm-nee-dah.)

Mansion   *Kun chotaek* **(Koon choe-take);**   Private
mansion   *Sajo* (Sah-joe)
Mr. Kim lives in a mansion. *Kim Sonsaeng-un
mansion-eso salgo issumnida.* (Keem Sahn-sang-
uun mansion-eh-sah sahl-goh ee-ssume-nee-
dah.)   Whose mansion is that? *Jogosun nugu-e
mansion imnikka?* (Jah-gah-sune nuu-guu-eh mansion eem-nee-kkah?)

Manufacture   *Chejo* **(Chay-joe);   To manufacu-
ture**   *chejohada* (Chay-joe-hah-dah);   Manufactur-
er   *chejoopcha* (Chay-joe-ope-chah)
Was this manufactured in Korea? *Igosun Hanguk-
eso mandun (chejohan) goshimnikka?* (Ee-gah-sune
Hahn-gook-eh-sah mahn-dune [che-joh-hahn]
gah-sheem-nee-kkah?)

Many *Manun* **(Mah-noon);** Numerous *Tasu-e* (Tah-suu-eh); Many things *Manun kot* (Mah-noon-kote); Many people *Manun saram* (Mah-noon sah-rahm)

How many days will you stay here? *Yogieso myochil momulgoshimnikka?* (Yah-gee-eh-sah myah-cheel mah-muul-gah-sheem-nee-kkah?) How many do you want? *Olmana mani wonhashimnikka?* (Ahl-mah-nah mah-nee-wahn-hah-sheem-nee-kkah?) I've been here many times before. *Chone yogie mani wassumnida.* (Chahn-eh yah-gee-eh mah-nee wah-ssume-nee-dah.)

Map *Chido* **(Chee-doe);** Map of Korea *Hanguk chido* (Hahn-gook chee-doe)

Do you have a map of Korea? *Hanguk chido issumnikka?* (Hahn-gook chee-doh ee-ssume-nee-kkah?) Here is a map of Los Angeles. *L. A. chido issumnida.* (L. A. chee-doh ee-ssume-nee-dah.)

Market *Shijang* **(She-jahng);** Fish market *Oshi jang* (Oh-she jahng); Vegetable market *Yachae Shijang* (Yay-chay she-jahng); Market prices *Shijang kagyok* (She-jahng kahg-yoke)

Is there a market near here? *Yogi kunchoe shijangi issumnikka?* (Yah-ghee koon-chah-eh shee-jahng-ee ee-ssume-nee-kkah?) I want to visit one of Seoul's famous markets. *Seoul-e-itnun yumyonghan shijangchung-e hangosul pangmunhago shipssumnida.* (Seoul-eh-eet-nune yuu-myahn-hahn shee-jahng-chuung-eh hahn-goh-suul pahng-muun-hah-goh sheep-ssume-nee-dah.)

Marriage *Kyolhon* **(Kyahl-hone);** Marriage ceremony *Kyolhon shik* (Kyahl-hone sheek); International marriage *Kukche kyolhon* (Kook-chay kyahl-hone)

Are there many international marriages among Koreans? *Hanguk-injunge kukje kyolhoni manssum-nikka?* (Hahn-gook-een-juung-eh kuuk-jeh kyahl-hohn-ee mahn-ssume-nee-kkah?)

Marry (wed) *Kyolhonhada* **(Kyahl-hone-hah-dah)**
Are you married? *Kyolhon hashyossumnikka?* (Kyahl-hohn hah-shyah-ssume-nee-kkah?) When did you get married? *Onje kyolhon haes-suumnikka?* (Own-jay kyahl-hohn hay-ssume-nee-kkah?)

Martini *Matini* **(Mah-tee-nee)**
Two martinis, please. *Matini tuchan chuseyo.* (Mah-tee-nee tuu-chahn chuu-say-yoe.)

Massage *Masaji* **(Mah-sah-jee);** Facial massage *Anmyon masaji* (Ahn-m'yone mah-sah-jee) Would you like to have a massage? *Masaji ha-shigessumnikka?* (Mah-sah-jee hah-shee-geh-ssume-nee-kkah?) How much is a massage? *Masaji kapsun olma imnikka?* (Mah-sah-jee kahp-sune ahl-mah eem-nee-kkah?)

Me *Narul* **(Nah-rule);** also *Naege* (Nay-gay) Let me see it. *Naege poyo chushipshio.* (Nay-gay poh-yah chuu-sheep-shee-oh.) It belongs to me. *Naege sokan goshimnida.* (Nay-gay soh-kahn-gah-sheem-nee-dah.) [or] *Naegoshimnida.* (Nay-gah-sheem-nee-dah.)

Meal *Shiksa* **(Sheek-sah);** Morning meal *Choban* (Choe-bahn); Noon meal *Chomshim* (Chom-sheem); Evening meal *Chonyok shiksa* (Chone-yoke sheek-sah) What time do you eat your evening meal? *Chon-yok shiksahun myoshie hamnikka?* (Chah-nyahk sheek-sah-nune myah-sshe-eh hahm-nee-kkah?) What time is breakfast? *chobanun myoshie*

hamnikka? (Choh-bahn-uun myah-shee-eh
hahm-nee-kkah?)

Measure *Chisu* **(Chee-sue);** also *Chaeda* (Chay-
dah)
Please measure this box. *I box-rul chaeo chushipshio.* (Ee box-rule chay-ah chuu-sheep-shee-
oh.) I need to take your measurements.
Tangshin-e chisurul chaego shipssumnida. (Tahng-
sheen-eh chee-suu-rule chay-goh sheep-ssume-
nee-dah.)

Meat *Kogi* **(Koe-ghee);** Fresh meat *Shing-
shinghan kogi* (Sheeng-sheeng-hahn koe-ghee);
Lean meat *Sal kogi* (Sahl koe-ghee)
I prefer lean meat. *Salkogirul to choahamnida.*
(Sahl-koh-ghee-rule tah choh-ah-hahm-nee-dah.)

Mechanic (auto) *Kigyegong* **(Kee-gay-gong)**
I need a mechanic to fix my car. *Nae charul kochil
kigyegongi piryo hamnida.* (Nay chah-rule koh-
cheel kee-gay-gohng-ee pee-ryah hahm-nee-
dah.)

Medicine *Yak* **(Yahk)**
I need some medicine for an upset stomach. *Ui
kyongryon yakul chushipshio.* (We kyahng-ryahn
yahk-ule chuu-sheep-shee-oh.)

Medium (moderate) *Potong-e* **(Poh-tohng-eh);**
Size *Chunggan-e* (Chung-gahn-eh)
I take a medium size. *Chunggan kugirul kajigo issumnida.* (Chung-gahn kuu-ghee-rule kah-jee-
gah ee-ssume-nee-dah.) How would you like
your steak? *Suteik ottoke kuwo turilkkayo?* (Su-take
oat-toe-kay kuu-woe tuu-reel-kah-yoe?) Medium, please. *Potonguro kuwo chuseyo.* (Poe-tone-
guu-roe kuu-woe chuu-say-yoe.)

Meet *Mannada* **(Mahn-nah-dah);** Welcome *Majunghada* (Mah-jung-hah-dah)
Please meet me in the lobby at noon. *Chongoe lobi-eso mannapshida.* (Chahng-oh-eh loh-bee-eh-sah mahn-nahp-shee-dah.)   Where shall we meet? *Odieso mannal kkayo?* (Ah-dee-eh-sah mahn-nahl-kkah-yoh?)

Meeting *Hoeap* **(Hoe-eh-ahp);** also *Moim* (Moh-eem)
He is in a meeting now. *Kunun chigum hoeapchunge issumnida.* (Kuu-nune chee-gume hoe-eh-ahp-chuung-eh ee-ssume-nee-dah.)   Where is the meeting going to be? *Hoeapun odieso yollimnikka?* (Hoe-eh-ahp-uun ah-dee-eh-sah yahl-leem-nee-kkah?)

Melon *Mellon* **(May-lone);** also *Chamoe* (Chah-moe-eh)
Would you like melon for dessert? *Dijot ro mellonul tushigessumnikka?* (Dee-jot-roe mehl-lohn-ule tuu-shee-geh-ssume-nee-kkah?)

Menu *Menyu* **(Meh-nyuu)**
Menu, please. *Menyurul chushipshio.* (Meh-nyuu-rule chuu-sheep-shee-oh.)

Message *Soshik* **(Soe-sheek);** Verbal *Chongal* (Chone-gahl)
Are there any messages for me? *Naege on soshik issumnikka?* (Nay-gay ohn soh-sheek ee-ssume-nee-kkah?)   May I take a message? *Chonhashil malssumi issushinjiyo.* (Chone-hah-sheel mahl-sue-me ee-sue-sheen-jee-yoe?)   I'd like to leave a message. *Chongalul namgigessumnida.* (Chahn-gahl-ule nahm-ghee-geh-ssume-nee-dah.)

Midnight *Hanbamchung* **(Hahn-bom-chung);** also *Chajong* (Chah-jong)

It's already past midnight. *Koi chajongi chinassumnida.* (Koy chah-jahng-ee chee-nah-ssume-nee-dah.)

Milk *Uyu* **(Uu-yuu);** Bottle of milk *Uyu han pyong* (Uu-yuu hahn p'yong); also *Uyu hanchan* (Uu-yuu hahn-chahn)
Would you like a glass of milk? *Uyu hanchan tushigessumnikka?* (Uu-yuu hahn-chahn tuu-shee-geh ssume-nee-kkah?) A glass of cold milk, please. *Chan uyu hanchan chushipshio.* (Chahn uu-yuu hahn-chahn chuu-sheep-shee-oh.)

Mine (belongs to me) *Naegot* **(Nay-gote)**
It's mine. *Kugosun naegoshimnida.* (Kuu-gah-sune nay-gah-sheem-nee-dah.)

Minute *Pun* **(Poon)**
Just give me five minutes. *Opunman chege chushipshio.* (Oh-puun-mahn chay-gay chuu-sheep-shee-oh.) I'll be ready in one minute. *Ilpunane junbi hagessumnida.* (Eel-puun-ahn-eh june-bee hah-gay-ssume-nee-dah.)

Mirror *Koul* **(Kah-uul)**
May I borrow your mirror? *Koulul pillyo chushipshio?* (Kah-uul-ule peel-lyah chuu-sheep-shee-oh?)

Miss (a train) *Nochida* **(No-chee-dah)**
I missed the train. *Kicha-rul nochyossumnida.* (Kee-chah-rule noh-chyah-ssume-nee-dah.)

Missionary *Songyosa* **(Sone-g'yoe-sah);** Foreign missionary *Oegugin songyosa* (Oeh-goog-een sahn-g'yoe-sah)
Are there still many missionaries in Korea? *Hanguk-e ajik songyosaduri mani issumnikka?* Hahn-gook-eh ah-jeek sahn-gyoh-sah-due-ree mah-nee ee-ssume-nee-kkah?)

Mistake *Chalmot* **(Chahl-mot);** also *Tullim* (Tuul-leem); *Tullida* (Tuul-lee-dah)
I made a mistake. *Shilsu haessumnida.* (Sheel-suu hay-ssume-nee-dah.)   I think you made a mistake. *Tangshin-i chalmot haetago saenggak hamnida.* (Tahng-sheen-ee chahl-mot hay-tah-goh sang-gahk hahm-nee-dah.)

Moment *Sungan* **(Soon-gahn);** A minute *Kot* (Kote)
Just a moment, please. *Kot kagessumnida.* (Kote-kah-gay-sume-nee-dah.)

Money *Ton* **(Tohn);** also *Kumjon* (Kume-joan); Money-changer *Hwan-gumsang* (Hwahn-goom-sahng); also *Hwan-chonsang* (Hwahn-chahn-sahng)
Do you have any money? *Ton kajigo issumnikka?* (Tohn kah-jee-goh ee-ssume-nee-kkah?)   I forgot to bring any money. *Tonul angajyo wassumnida.* (Tohn-ule ahn-gah-jah wah-ssume-nee-dah.)   Is there a money-changer close by? *Kunchoe hwan-chonsangi issumnika?* (Kune-chah-eh hwahn-chahn-sahng-ee ee-ssume-nee-kkah?)

Monsoon *Kyejolpung* **(Kay-jahl-poong)**
Does Korea have a monsoon season? *Hanguk-enun kyejolpung chori issumnikka?* (Hahn-gook-eh-nune kay-jahl-poong chah-ree ee-ssume-nee-kkah?)

Monument *Kinyombi* **(Kee-nyahm-bee);** Ancient monument *Yoksajok kinyommul* (Yoke-sah-joke kee-nyahm-muul)
I want to see some of Korea's most famous monuments. *Hanguk-eso kajang yumyonghan kimyommulul pogo shipssumnida.* (Hahn-gook-eh-sah kah-jahng yuu-myahng-hahn kee-nyahm-muul-ule poh-goh sheep-ssume-nee-dah.)

Moon *Tal* (Tahl); Full moon *Man wol* (Mahn-wole)

Morning *Achim* (Ah-cheem); Before noon *Ojon* (Oh-joan); This morning *Onul achim* (Oh-nul ah-cheem); Tomorrow morning *Naeil achim* (Nay-eel ah-cheem); In the early morning *Irun achim* (Ee-roon ah-cheem)
I'll see you in the morning. *Achime tangshinul mannago shipssumnida.* (Ah-cheem-eh tahng-sheen-ule mann-nah-goh sheep-ssume-nee-dah.) We're leaving tomorrow morning. *Nael achim urinun ttonamnida.* (Nay-eel ah-cheem uu-ree-nuun ttah-nahm-nee-dah.)

Mosquito *Mogi* (Moe-ghee); Mosquito net *Mogi jang* (Moe-ghee jahng)
The mosquitos are bad during the summer. *Yorum tonganenun mogi-ga manayo.* (Yoe-rume tong-ah-nay-nune moe-ghee-gah man-nah-yoe.)

Mother *Omoni* (Ah-mah-nee); also *Mochin* (Moe-cheen); Mother's Day *Omoni nal* (Oh-moe-nee nahl)
I would like to meet your mother. *Tangshin-e mochinul manago shipssumnida.* (Tahng-sheen-eh moh-cheen-ule mah-nah-goh sheep-ssume-nee-dah.)

Motion picture (movie) *Yonghwa* (Yong-whah)
Are motion pictures made in Korea? *Hanguk-eso mandun yonghwaga issumnikka?* (Hahn-gook-eh-sah mahn-dune yahng-hwah-gah ee-ssume-nee-kkah?) Would you like to go see a movie? *Yonghwa poro kashilkkayo?* (Yahng-hwah poh-rah kah-sheel-kkah-yoh?)

Mountain *San* (Sahn)
Are there many mountains in Korea? *Hanguk-e*

sani mani issumnikka? (Hahn-gook-eh sahn-ee
mah-nee ee-ssume-neek-kah?) Yes, Korea is a
mountainous country. *Ne, Hanguk-un sani manun
nara imnida.* (Nay, Hahn-gook-uun sah-nee mah-
nune nah-rah eem-nee-dah.)

Museum *Pangmulgwan* **(Pahng-mul-gwahn)**
What time does the National Museum open?
Kungnip pangmulgwanun myoshie yomnikka?
(Kuung-neep pahng-muul-gwahn-uun myeh-
shee-eh yahm-nee-kkah?)

Mushrooms *Posot* **(Pah-saht)**
Do you like mushrooms? *Posot choahashimnikka?*
(Pah-saht choh-ah-hah-sheem-nee-kkah?)

Music *Umak* **(Uu-mahk); Musician** *Umak-ka*
(Uu-mahk-kah)
What kind of music do you like? *Otton umag-ul
choahashimnikka?* (Aht-tahn uu-mahg-ule choe-
ah-hah-sheem-nee-kkah?) I would like to hear
some Korean music. *Hanguk umakul tukko shipssumnida.* (Hahn-gook uu-mah-kule tuu-kkoh
sheep-ssume-nee-dah.)

Mustard *Kyoja* **(K'yoe-jah)**
Would you like mustard on your sandwich?
Sandwich-e kyojarul noushigessumnikka? (Sandwich-
eh kyah-jah-rule nah-u-shee-gay-ssume-nee-
kkah?)

Mutton *Yang-gogi* **(Yahng-go-ghee)**
I'm sorry, I don't like mutton. *Mianhamnida,
nanun yanggogirul shirohamnida.* (Mee-ahn-hahm-
nee-dah, nah-nune yahng-goh-gee-rule shee-rah-
hahm-nee-dah.)

My *Nae* **(Nay)**
What is my room number? *Nae pangun myopon
imnikka?* (Nay pahng-uun myah-pahn eem-nee-

kkah?) Where is my briefcase? *Nae kabangun odie issumnikka?* (Nay kah-bahng-uun ah-dee-eh ee-ssume nee kkah?) I don't have my passport with me. *Nae yokwoni opssumnida.* (Nay yah-kwahn-ee ahp-ssume-nee-dah.)

N

Name *Irum* **(Ee-rume);** also *Myongching* (M'yong-cheeng); Family name *Song* (Sahng); First name *Irum* (Ee-rume)
What is your name? *Irumi mwoshimnikka?* (Ee-rume-ee mwah-sheem-nee-kkah?) Please write down your name and address. *Tangshin-e irumgwa chusorul sso chushipshio.* (Tahng-sheen-eh ee-rume-gwah chuu-soh-rule ssah chuu-sheep-shee-oh.) How do you spell your last name? *Tangshin-e songul ottoke ssumnikka?* (Tahng-sheen-eh sahng-uel ahttah-keh ssume-nee-kkah?)

Nap (sleep) *Natcham* **(Naht-chahm);** To take a nap *Natcham jada* (Not-chahm jah-dah)
Would you like to take a nap before dinner? *Shiksajone natchamul chumushigetssumnika.* (Sheek-sah-jahn-eh naht-chahm-ule chuu-muu-shee-geh-ssume-nee-kkah?)

Napkin *Naepukin* **(Nahpu-keen)**
Please bring me another napkin. *Tarun naepukinul katta chushipshio.* (Tah-rune nah-pu-keen-ule kah-ttah chuu-sheep-shee-oh.)

National *Kungmin-e* **(Koong-meen-eh);** also *Kukka-e* (Kook-kah-eh); National anthem *Kukka* (Kook-kah); National flag *Kukki* (Kook-kee); National park *Kungnip kongwon* (Koong-neep

Kong-won); National holiday *Kukkyong-il*
(Kuuk-kyahng-eel); National railways *Kugyu
cholto* (Koog-yuu chole-toe)
Tomorrow is a national holiday. *Naeil-un kuk-
kyongil imnida.* (Nay-eel-uun kuuk-kyahng-eel
eem-nee-dah.)

Nausea *Molmi* **(Mahl-mee);** Sea sickness *Pae
molmi* (Paeh mahl-mee)
I feel a little nauseous. *Molmiga chogum namnida.*
(Mahl-mee-gah choh-gume nahm-nee-dah.)

Near *Kakkai* **(Kahk-kie);** Close to *Kunchoe*
(Kune-chah-eh)
It is near the bank. *Kugosun unhaeng kunchoe issumnida.* (Kuu-gah-sune uun-hang kune-chah-eh
ee-ssume-nee-dah.) What is it near? *Ku kunchoe
mwoga issoyo?* (Kuu kune-choe mwha-gah es-soe-
yoe?)

Necklace *Mokkori* **(Moke-koe-ree)**
I'd like to get a jade necklace. *Pichwi mokkorirul
kajigo shipssumnida.* (Pee-chwee mohk-kah-ree-
rule kah-jee-goh sheep-ssume-nee-dah.)

Necktie *Nektai* **(Neck-tie)**
Is it necessary to wear a necktie? *Nektairul haeya
hamnikka?* (Neck-tie-rule hay-yah hahm-nee-
kkah?)

Need *Soyong* **(Soe-yong);** also *Piryo* (Pee-rio)
I need some help. *Toumi piryo hamnida.* (Toh-
uum-ee pee-rio hahm-nee-dah.) Do you need
any help? *Toumi piryo hamnikka?* (Toh-uum-ee
pee-rio hahm-nee-kkah?)

Neighborhood *Kunchoe* **(Kune-choe-eh)**
Is there a market in this neighborhood? *I kunchoe
shijangi issumnikka?* (Ee kune-chah-eh shee-jahng-
ee ee-ssume-nee-kkah?)

Neon signs *Neon sain* **(Neh-own sah-een)**
There are many neon signs in the entertainment
district. *Yuhunggae neon saini mani issumnida.*
(Yuu-huung-gah-eh nay-own sah-een-ee mahn-
ee ee-ssume-nee-dah.)

New *Saeroun* **(Say-roh-uun);** also *Saegot* (Say-
gaht)
Is this new? *Igosun saegot imnikka?* (Ee-gah-sune
say-gaht eem-nee-kkah?) I need a new pair of
shoes. *Saeroun kudu han kyollyega piryohamnida.*
(Say-roh-uun kuu-duu hahn kyahl-lay-gah pee-
ryoh-hahm-nee-dah.)

News (tidings) *Soshik* **(Soe-sheek);** also *Nyus*
(Nyuu-sue)
Have you heard any news this morning? *Onul
achim nyus turossumnikka?* (Oh-nule ah-cheem
nyuu-sue tue-rah-ssume-nee-kkah?)

Newspaper *Shinmun* **(Sheen-moon);** News agen-
cy *Tongshinsa* (Tong-sheen-shah); Newspaper-
man *Shinmun kija* (Sheen-moon kee-jah)
Have you read this morning's newspaper? *Onul
chogan shinmun ilgossumnikka?* (Oh-nule choh-
gahn sheen-muun eel-gah-ssume-nee-kkah?)
Do you carry English language newspapers?
Yongja shinmun paedal hamnikka? (Yahng-jah
sheen-muun pay-dahl hahm-nee-kkah?)

New Year *Sae hae* **(Say-hay);** also *Shin nyon*
(Sheen n'yone); New Year's Eve *Sottal kumum-
nal* (Sote-tahl kuu-muu-nahl); New Year's Day
Solral (Sole-rahl)
Happy New Year! *Sae Hae Pokmani Padushipshio!*
(Say Hay Poke-mah-nee Pah-duu-sheep-she-oh!)

Next *Taum-e* **(Tow-uum-eh);** Neighboring *Yop-e*
(Yope-eh)
We get off at the next station. *Taum yokeso naerim-*

nida. (Tah-uum yahk-eh-sah nay-reem-nee-dah.)
Is Taegu the next station? *Taum yoki Taegu im-nikka?* (Tah-uum yahk-ee Tay-guu eem-nee-kkah?) I'll see you next weekend. *Taum chumale mana poepkessumnida.* (Tah-uum-chuu-mahl-eh mahn-nah pep-keh-ssume-nee-dah.)

Nice (good) *Choun* **(Choe-uun);** Pleasant *Mot-chin* (Mah-cheen); Tasty *Madinnun* (Mah-deen-noon); Nice weather *Choun nalssi* (Choe-uun nahl-she)
The weather is supposed to be nice tomorrow. *Nalssiga naeil choajilgoshimnida.* (Nahl-ssee-gah nay-eel-choh-ah-jeel-gah-sheem-nee-dah.) Have a nice day. *Choun haru ponaeshipshio.* (Choh-uun hah-ruu poh-nay-sheep-shee-oh.)

Nickname *Pyolmyong* **(Pyahl-myong)**
That is my nickname. *Kugosun nae pyolmyong im-nida.* (Kuu-gah-sune nay pyahl-myong eem-nee-dah.) Do you have a nickname? *Pyolmyongi issumnikka?* (Pyahl-myong-ee ee-ssume-nee-kkah?)

Night *Pam* **(Pahm);** Last night *Kanbam* (Kahn-bahm); Night clothes *Chamot* (Chah-mote); Night school *Yagan hakkyo* (Yah-gahn hahk-k'yoe)
How many nights will you be staying? *Myochil pam mugushiryomnikka?* (Myoe-cheel pahm muu-guu-she-re-ohm-nee-kkah?)

Noise *Soum* **(Soe-uum);** Noisy *Shikkuroun* (Sheek-kuu-roan)
It was so noisy last night I couldn't sleep. *Kan-bame namu shikkurowoso chamul mochassumnida.* (Kahn-bahn-eh nah-muu shee-kkue-rah-wah-sah chahm-ule moh-chah-ssume-nee-dah.)

Noon *Chongo* **(Chahng-oh)**
I'll see you at noon. *Chongoe manna poepkessum-nida.* (Chahng-oh-eh mahn-nah pep-keh-ssume-nee-dah.)

North *Puk* **(Pook);** also *Puktchok* (Pook-choke); *Puge* (Poog-eh)
It is just two blocks north of here. *Yogieso tu blok puktchoke issumnida.* (Yah-ghee-eh-sah tuu blohk puuk-choke-eh ee-ssume-nee-dah.) Which way is north? *Onu tchogi puktchogi mnikka?* (Ah-nuu choe-ghee pook-choe-ghee emm-nee-kkah?)

Nose *Ko* **(Koe)**
What is the matter with your nose? *Tangshin-e koe mwoshi nassumnikka?* (Tahng-sheen-eh koh-eh mwah-shee nah-ssume-nee-kkah?)

Not *Animnida* **(Ahn-eem-nee-dah);** also *Anssumnida* (Ahn-sume-nee-dah)
I am not going. *Nanun kaji anssumnida.* (Nah-nune kah-jee ahn-ssume-nee-dah.) She is not going. *Kuyojanun kaji anssumnida.* (Kuu-yah-jah-nune kah-jee ahn-ssume-nee-dah.) This is not right. *Igosun olchi anssumnida.* (Ee-gah-sune ohl-chee ahn-ssume-nee-dah.) Why not? *Wae an doemnikka?* (Way ahn dome-nee-kkah?)

Note *Memo* **(May-moh);** Notebook *Kong-chaek* (Kong-chake)
Please leave me a note. *Memorul namgyo chuship-shio.* (May-moh-rule nahm-gyah chuu-sheep-shee-oh.) Did you get my note? *Nae memorul kajyossumnikka?* (Nay may-moh-rule kah-jyah-ssume-nee-kkah?)

Notify (inform) *Tongjihada* **(Tong-jee-hah-dah);** Announce *Palpyohada* (Pahl-p'yoe-hah-dah); also *Allida* (Ahl-lee-dah)

I will notify you before noon. *Chango chone tang-shinege alyodurigessumnida.* (Chahng-oh chahn-eh tahng-sheen-eh-gay ahl-lyah-due-ree-gay-ssume-nee-dah.) Please announce the departure time again. *Chulbal shiganul tashi allyochushipshio.* (Chuul-bahl shee-gahn-ule tah-shee ahl-lyah-chuu-sheep-shee-oh.)

Novelist *Sosolga* (Soh-sahl-gah)
She wants to be a novelist. *Kuyojanun sosolgaga doegoja hamnida.* (Kuu-yah-jah-nune soh-sahl-gah-gah doe-goh-jah hahm-nee-dah.)

Now *Chigum* (Chee-gume); Right now *Chigum tangjang* (Chee-gume tahng-jahng)
Let's go right now. *Chigum tangjang kapshida.* (Chee-gume tahng-jahng kahp-shee-dah.) The movie is starting right now. *Yonghwaga chigum paro shijak hamnida.* (Yahng-hwah-gah chee-gume pah-roh shee-jahk hahm-nee-dah.)

Nuclear *Wonja-e* (Won-jah-eh); Nuclear energy *Wonja ryok* (Won-jah ryahk)
Please tell me about your nuclear energy program. *Tangshin-e wonjaryok programe daehaeso malhae chushipshio.* (Tahng-sheen-eh wahn-jah-ryahk program-eh day-hay-sah mahl-hay chuu-sheep-shee-oh.)

Number *Saem* (Sah-em); also *Su* (Sue); Numeral *Sucha* (Suu-chah); also *Ponho* (Pone-hoe)
What is your telephone number? *Tangshin-e chonhwa ponhonun mwoshimnikka?* (Tahng-sheen-eh chahn-hwah pone-hoe-nune mwah-sheem-nee-kkah?) What is your room number? *Pang ponhoga olma imnikka?* (Pahng pone-hoe-gah ahl-mah eem-nee-kkah?) My number is . . . . *Nae ponhonun . . . .* (Nay pone-hoe-nune . . . .)

Nurse *Kanhowon* **(Kahn-hoe-won)**
Please call a nurse. *Kanhowonul pullo chushipshio.* (Kahn-hoh-wahn-ule puul-lah-chuu-sheep-shee-oh.)

O

Occupation (business) *Il* **(Eel);** Job *Chigop* (Chee-gahp)
What is your occupation? *Tangshin-e chigopun mwoshimnikka?* (Tahn-sheen-eh chee-gahp-uun mwah-sheem-nee-kkah?) What kind of job do you have? *Musun ilul hashimnikka?* (Muu-sune ee-rule hah-sheem-nee-kkah?)

Ocean *Taeyang* **(Tay-yahng);** Atlantic Ocean *Tae-soyang* (Tay-soe-yang); Pacific Ocean *Taepyong-yang* (Tape-yong-yang)

Octopus *Muno* **(Muu-nah)**
Would you like some octopus? *Munorul tushige-ssumnikka?* (Muu-nah-rule tuu-shee-gay-ssume-nee-kkah?)

Office *Samushil* **(Sah-muu-sheel)**
Where is the manager's office? *Chibaein-e samu-shili odie issumnikka?* (Chee-bay-een-eh sah-muu-sheel-ee ah-dee-eh ee-ssume-nee-kkah?) Please come by my office at ten o'clock. *Yolshie nae sa-mushillo oshipshio.* (Yahl-shee-eh nay sah-muu-sheel-loh oh-sheep-shee-oh.) What time does the office close? *Samushilun myoshie munul da-ssumnikka?* (Sah-muu-shee-rune myah-shee-eh muun-ule dah-ssume-nee-kkah?)

Often *Chongchong* **(Chohn-chohng);** also *Chaju* (Chah-juu)
Do you eat here often? *Yogieso chaju mokssumnikka?* (Yah-gee-eh-sah chah-juu mahk-ssume-nee-kkah?) I hope to see you often from now on. *Chigum ihuro chaju tangshinul mannago shipssumnida.* (Chee-gume ee-huu-roh chah-juu tahng-sheen-ule mahn-nah-goh sheep-ssume-nee-dah.)

Old (aged) *Nulgun* **(Nuel-gune);** Worn *Nalgun* (Nahl-gune); Old man *Noin* (No-een)
We live in a very old house. *Maeu nalgun chipeso salgo issumnida.* (May-uu nahl-gune cheep-eh-sah sahl-goh ee-ssume-nee-dah.)

Olive oil *Ollibuyu* **(Oh-lee-buu-yuu)**
I would like olive oil on my salad. *Salada-e ollibuyurul puo chushipshio.* (Sah-lah-dah-eh ohl-lee-buu-yuu-rule puu-ah chuu-sheep-shee-oh.)

Olympic Games *Kukche ollimpik kyonggi taehoe* **(Kook-chay oh-lim-peek k'yong-ghee tay-hoe-eh);** Olympic Village *Ollimpik Chon* (Oh-lim-peek Chone)
Where is the Olympic Village located? *Olympic Choni odie issumnikka?* (Ohl-leem-peek Chohn-ee ah-dee-eh ee-ssume-nee-kkah?)

Onion *Yangpa* **(Yahng-pah)**
Do you want onions on your hamburger? *Hamburger-e yangparul kyoturishigessumnikka?* (Hame-bah-gah-eh yahng-pah-rule kyah-tuu-ree-shee-geh-ssume-nee-kkah?) Onion soup, please. *Yangpa soupul chushipshio.* (Yahng-pah suup-ule chuu-sheep-shee-oh.)

Open *Yolda* **(Yole-dah);** also *Yollida* (Yole-lee-dah)
What time do the department stores open?

Paekhwajomun myossie yomnikka? (Paehk-hwah-jahm-uun myah-shee-eh yahm-nee-kkah?) Are you open on Sunday? *Ilyoile yomnikka?* (Eel-yoh-eel-eh yahm-nee-kkah?) How late are you open? *Olmana nukke yomnikka?* (Ahl-mah-nah nuu-kkeh yahm-nee-kkah?) Would you open the door for me, please? *Nal weehae munul yoro chushigessumnikka?* (Nahl wee-hay muun-ule yah-rah chuu-shee-geh-ssume-nee-kkah?)

Opener (can) *Kkang tongttagae* **(Kahng-tong-tah-gay)**
I need a can opener. *Kkangtong ttagaerul chuship-shio.* (Kkahng-tohng ttah-gay-rule chuu-sheep-shee-oh.)

Operation (surgical) *Susul* **(Suu-suul)**
You may need an operation. *Susul haeya hamnida.* (Suu-suul hay-yah hahm-nee-dah.)

Orchard *Kwasuwon* **(Kwah-suu-wahn);** Apple orchard *Sagwa Kwasuwon* (Sah-gwah-kwah-suu-wahn)
Are there many orchards in Korea? *Hanguk-e kwasuwoni mani issumnikka?* (Hahn-gook-eh kwah-suu-wahn-ee mah-nee ee-ssume-nee-kkah?)

Orchestra *Okesutura* **(Oh-kess-tuu-rah);** Symphony orchestra *Kyohyangaktan* (K'yoe-h'yahn-gahk-tahn)
Do you enjoy orchestra music? *Okesutura umakul choahashimnikka?* (Oh-keh-sue-trah uu-mah-kuul choh-ah-hah-sheem-nee-kkah?)

Order *Chumunhada* **(Chuu-moon-hah-dah)**
May I take your order? *Chumunul padulkkayo?* (Chuu-muun-ule pah-dule-kah-yoe?) Are you ready to place your order? *Chumun hashigessum-*

nikka? (Chuu-muun hah-shee-gay-ssume-nee-kkah?) We have already ordered. *Wurinun imi chumun haessumnida.* (Wuu-ree-nune ee-mee chuu-muun hay-ssume-nee-dah.)

Orient *Tongyang* **(Tong-yahng);** Oriental person *Tongyang-in* (Tong-yahng-een); Oriental music *Tongyang umak* (Tong-yahng-uu-mahk)
This is my first time in the Orient. *Tongyangun iboni choumimnida.* (Tohng-yahng-uun ee-bahn-ee chah-uum-eem-nee-dah.)

Other *Tarun* **(Tah-roon);** also *Ttan* (Tahn); Other person *Tarun saram* (Tah-roon sah-rahm); Other thing *Tarun kot* (Tah-roon kote)
Have you seen my other bag? *Nae tarun kabangul poassumnikka?* (Nay tah-rune kah-bahng-ule poh-ah-ssume-nee-kkah?)

Our *Uri-e* **(Uu-ree-eh);** Our hotel *Uri hotel* (Uu-ree hotel)
Is this our train? *Igoshi uriga tal kicha imnikka?* (Ee-gah-shee uu-ree-gah tahl kee-chah eem-nee-kkah?) Where are our seats? *Uri chwasogun odie issumnikka?* (Uu-ree chwah-sah-gune ah-dee-eh ee-ssume-nee-kkah?) Please take us back to our hotel. *Uri hotello teryoda chushipshio.* (Uu-ree hoh-tehl-loh tay-ryah-dah chuu-sheep-shee-oh.)

Out-of-date *Naljjaga chinada* **(Nal-jah-gah chee-nah-dah)**
Your visa is out-of-date. *Tangshin-e pija-nun najjaga chinassumnida.* (Tahng-sheen-eh pee-jah-nune nal-jah-gah chee-nah-ssume-nee-dah.)

Overcast *Chanttuk hurin* **(Chahn-tuke huu-reen)**
I'm sorry to say it is overcast today. *Onurun nalshiga chanttuk huryo yugamimnida.* (Oh-nuu-rune

nahl-shee-gah chahn-ttuk huu-ryah yuu-gahm-eem-nee-dah.) Will it be overcast tomorrow? *Naeirun nari hurimnikka?* (Nay-ee-rune nah-ree huu-reem-nee-kkah?)

Overcoat *Oba kotu* (Oh-bah koe-tuu)
Don't forget your overcoat. It's cold today. *Oba kotu-rul ijji mashipshio. Onurul chupssumnida.* (Oh-bah koe-tuu-rule ee-jee mah-sheep-shee-oh. Oh-nuu-rule chuup-ssume-nee-dah.)

Oversleep *Nomu-chada* (Nah-muu-chah-dah)
I overslept this morning. *Onul achim nomu mani chassumnida.* (Oh-nule ah-cheem nah-muu mah-nee chah-ssume-nee-dah.)

Overweight (extra weight) *Chogwa chungyang* (Choag-wah choong-yahng)
I'm sorry. Your bags are overweight. *Mianhamnida. Tangshin-e kabangun chogwa chungyangimnida.* (Mee-ahn-hahm-nee-dah. Tahng-sheen-eh kah-bahng-uun choh-gwah chuung-yahng-eem-nee-dah.)

Owe *Pitchigo itta* (Pee-chee-go ee-tah)
How much do I owe you? *Olma turimyon toejiyo?* (Ole-mah tuu-reem-yone toe-eh-jee-yoe?)

Owner *Imja* (Eem-jah); also *Soyuja* (Soe-yuu-jah); *Chuin* (Chuu-een)
I am the owner. *Naega chuin imnida.* (Nay-gah chuu-een eem-nee-dah.)

Oxygen *Sanso* (Sahn-soe); Oxygen inhaler *Sanso hohupki* (Sahn-soe hoe-huup-kee)
This person needs oxygen. Please hurry! *Isaramun sansoga piryohamnida. Sodurupshio!* (Ee-sah-rahm-uun sahn-soh-gah pee-ryoh-hahm-nee-dah. Sah-duu-rupe-shee-oh!)

Oyster *Kul* **(Kool);** Fried oysters *Kultwigim* (Kool-twee-geem); Raw oysters *Saenggul* (Sang-gule)
Are oysters in season now? *Chigum kuri jechol imnikka?* (Chee-gume kuu-ree jeh-chahl eem-nee-kkah?) Please bring us a plate of raw oysters. *Saenggul han chopshi chushipshio.* (Sang-guul hahn chahp-shee chuu-sheep-shee-oh.)

P

Pacific Ocean *Taepyongyang* **(Tape-yong-yahng)**
Have you crossed the Pacific Ocean before? *Chone Taepyongyangul jinanjogi issumnikka?* (Chahn-eh Tape-yong-yahng-ule jee-nahn-jah-gee ee-ssume-nee-kkah?)

Package (parcel) *Sopo* **(Soe-poe)**
I would like to mail this package. *I soporul puchigo shipssumnida.* (Ee soh-poh-rule puu-chee-goh sheep-ssume-nee-dah.) How much does this package weigh? *I soponun nugega olma imnikka?* (Ee soh-poh-nune nuu-gay-gah ahl-mah-eem-nee-kkah?)

Pagoda *Tap* **(Tahp);** Five-storied pagoda *Ochung tap* (Oh-chung tahp)
Do you know how many pagodas there are in Korea? *Hanguk-ee manun tapi itnungosul ashimnikka?* (Hahn-gook-eh mah-nune tah-bee eet-nune-gah-sule ah-sheem-nee-kkah?)

Pain *Apun* **(Ah-pune)**
Where do you feel pain? *Odiga apushimnikka?* (Oh-dee-gah ah-puu-sheem-nee-kkah?) I have a severe pain in my stomach. *Paega mopshi apumnida.* (Pay-gah mohp-shee ah-pume-nee-dah.)

Pair (two things) *Han ssang* **(Hahn sahng);** Couple (husband and wife) *Bubu* (Buu-buu); Pair of shoes *Kudu han k'yolle* (Kuu-duu hahn k'yole-lay); Pair of trousers *Paji han pol* (Pah-jee hahn pole)
I would like to get a pair of trousers made. *Paji han pol ul machugo shipssumnida.* (Pah-jee hahn-pole-ule mah-chuu-goh Sheep-ssume-nee-dah.)

Pajamas *Chamot* **(Chah-mote)**
Do you sleep in pajamas? *Chamosul ipgo chamnikka?* (Chah-moh-sule eep-goh chahm-nee-kkah?)

Palace *Kungjon* **(Koong-joan);** also *Wanggung* (Wahng-guung)
Are there many palaces in Seoul? *Seoule wanggungi mani issumnikka?* (Seoul-eh wahng-guung-ee mah-nee ee-ssume-nee-kkah?)

Paper *Chongi* **(Chong-gee);** Blank paper *Paekchi* (Pake-chee); Wrapping paper *Pojanji* (Poe-jahng-jee); Paper clip *Chongi chipgye* (Chohng-ee cheep-gyeh)
Do you have any wrapping paper? *Pojangji issumnikka?* (Poh-jahng-jee ee-ssume-nee-kkah?)

Parade (street) *Kadu haengnyol* (Kah-duu hang-n'yole)
There is going to be a parade today. *Onul kadu haengnyoli isumnida.* (Oh-nule kah-duu hang-nyah-lee ee-ssume-nee-dah.)

Parcel (post) *Sopo* **(Soe-poe)**
I would like to send this parcel by registered mail. *I soporul tunggiro ponaego shipssumnida.* (Ee soh-poh-rule tuung-ghee-roh poh-nay-goh sheep-ssume-nee-dah.)

165

Parent *Yangchin* **(Yahng-cheen);** also *Pumo* (Puu-moe)
These are my parents. *Nae pumoimnida.* (Nay puu-moh-eem-nee-dah.)

Park (recreational area) *Kongwon* **(Kong-won)**
Let's take a walk in the park. *Kongwonuro sanchak hapshida.* (Kohng-wahn-uu-roh sahn-chock hahp-shee-dah.)

Party (social gathering) *Pati* **(Pah-tee);** Dinner party *Manchahoe* (Mahn-chah-hoe); Send-off party *Songbyolhoe* (Song-b'yol-hoe)
What time is the party? *Pati-nun myoshie issumnikka?* (Pah-tee-nune myah-shee-eh ee-ssume-nee-kkah?) Where is the party? *Pati-nun odieso yollimnikka?* (Pah-tee-nune ah-dee-eh-sah yahl-leem-nee-kkah?) Thank you for the send-off party. *Songbyolhoerul yorochuoso kamsahamnida.* (Sohng-byahl-hoe-ruel yah-rah-chuu-ah-sah kahm-sah-hahm-nee-dah.)

Passenger (train,bus) *Sunggaek* **(Sung-gake);**
Boat passenger *Son gaek* (Sahn gake); Passenger car *Kaek cha* (Kake-chah); Passenger list *Son-gaek myongbu* (Sahn-gake m'yong-buu)
May I see the passenger list? *Songaek myongburul poyo chushigessumnikka?* (Sahn-gake myahng-buu-rule poh-yah chuu-shee-gay-ssume-nee-kkah?)

Passport *Yokwon* **(Yoe-kwan);** also *Paesupotu* (Pass-poe-tuu); Passport control *Yokwon shimsakwan* (Yoe-kwan sheem-sah-kwahn)
May I see your passport, please? *Yokwonul poyo chushipshio.* (Yoe-kwahn-ule poh-yah chuu-sheep-shee-oh.) Please proceed to Passport Control. *Yokwon Shimsakwanege kashipshio.* (Yoe-kwahn Sheem-sah-kwahn-eh-gay kah-sheep-shee-oh.)

Pay *Chibul* **(Chee-buul);** Salary *Ponggup* (Pong-gupe)
Where do I pay the bill? *Odie chonggusorul chibul hamnikka?* (Ah-dee-eh chahng-guu-sah-rule chee-buul hahm-nee-kkah?) I've already paid the bill. *Imi chibul haessumnida.* (Ee-mee chee-buul hay-ssume-nee-dah.)

Peach *Poksunga* **(Poke-sung-ah)**
Are peaches in season now? *Poksungaga chigum jechol imnikka?* (Pohk-suung-ah-gah chee-gume jay-chohl eem-nee-kkah?)

Peanut butter *Ttang k'ong ppada* **(Ttahng kong ppah-dah);** Peanut butter sandwich *Ttang k'ong ppada ssaenduwichi* (Sahn-du-wee-chee)
A peanut butter sandwich, please. *Ttang k'ong ppada ssaenduwichi, chushipshio.* (Ttahng kong ppah-dah sahn-du-wee-chee chuu-sheep-she-oh.)

Pearl *Chinju* **(Cheen-juu);** Artificial pearl *Injo chinju* (Een-joe cheen-juu); Cultured pearl *Yangshik chinju* (Yahng-sheek cheen-juu)
May I see several pearl necklaces? *Yoro chinju mokorirul poyochuseyo.* (Yah-rah cheen-juu moh-kah-ree-rule poh-yah-chuu-say-yoe.)

Pedestrian *Pohaengja* **(Poe-hang-jah);** Pedestrian crossing *Hoengdan podo* (Hang-dahn poe-doe)
If you are going to drive, be especially careful of pedestrians. *Unjonhashilttae tukhee pohaengjarul choshim hashipshio.* (Uun-jahn-hah-sheel-ttay tuke-hee poe-hang-jah-rule choh-sheem hah-sheep-shee-oh.)

People (individual) *Saram* **(Sah-rahm);** Of a nation *Kungmin* (Koong-meen); Race *Minjok* (Meen-joke); Korean people *Hanguk saram* (Hahn-gook sah-rahm)

How many people are in your group? *Tangshin group-un myosaram imnikka?* (Tahng-sheen group-uun myah-sah-rahm eem-nee-kkah?)

Perfume *Hyangsu* **(H'yahng-sue)**
I like your perfume. *Hyangsu naemsaega chokunyo.* (Hyahn-suu name-say-gah choh-kuun-yoh.)

Permission *Hoga* **(Hah-gah);** Permit (allow) *Hogahada* (Hah-gah-hah-dah)
You must have a special permit to visit Panmunjom. *Panmunjom pangmunun tukpyol hogarul padaya hamnida.* (Pahn-muun-jahm pahng-muu-nune tuke-ryahl hah-gah-rule pah-dah-yah hahm-nee-dah.)   Where do I get permission to go to Panmunjom? *Panmunjome kallyomyon odieso hogarul padaya hamnikka?* (Pahn-muun-jahm-eh kahl-yome-yone ah-dee-eh-so hoe-gah-rule pah-dah-yah hahm-nee-kkah?)

Persimmon *Kam* **(Kahm);** Dried persimmon *Kotkam* (Kote-kahm)
Are persimmons a popular fruit in Korea? *Hanguk-e kami hunhamnikka?* (Hahn-gook-eh kahm-ee huun-hahm-nee-kkah?)

Personal *Kaeinui* **(Kay-een-we)**
I recommend that you take a personal taxi. *Kaein taxirul taseyo.* (Kay-een tack-see-rul tah-say-yoe.)

Pharmacist *Yakchesa* **(Yahk-chay-sah);** Pharmacy *Yakkuk* (Yahk-kuke)
Is there a pharmacy nearby? *Kunchoe yakkugi issumnikka?* (Kune-chah-eh yahk-kuug-ee ee-ssume-nee-kkah?)

Pheasant *Kkwong* **(K'kwong)**
Pheasant hunting is very popular on the island of Cheju. *Kkwong sanyangun Chejudo-eso maeu*

inkki imnida. (Kkwahng sah-nyahng-uun Cheh-juu-doh-eh-sah may-uu een-kee eem-nee-dah.)

Photograph *Sajin* **(Sah-jeen);** Photographer *Sajinsa* (Sah-jeen-sah)
Would you please take our photograph? *Sajin jom chchigo chushigessumnikka?* (Sah-jeen johm cchee-gah chuu-shee-gay-ssume-nee-kkah?)

Pickpocket *Somaechigi* **(Soe-may-chee-ghee)**
Watch out for pickpockets. *Somechigi choshim.* (Soe-may-chee-ghee choe-sheem.)

Picnic *Sopung* **(Soe-puung);** also *Pikunik* (Pee-kuu-neek)
The hotel has a picnic every Saturday for all of its guests. *Hoteleso modun sonnimul wihae maeju toyoire sopungul ganda.* (Hotel-eh-sah moh-dune sohn-neem-ule we-hay may-juu toh-yoh-ee-reh soh-puung-ule gahn-dah.)

Pie *Pai* **(Pie)**
What kind of pie do you like? *Otton pai-rul choahashimnikka?* (Ah-ttahn pie-rule choh-ah-hah-sheem-nee-kkah?) What kind of pie do you have? *Otton pai-rul tushigessumnikka?* (Ah-ttahn pie-rule tuu-shee-gay-ssume-nee-kkah?)

Pill (medical) *Hwanyak* **(Hwahn-yahk);** Vitamin pill *Pitamin je* (Bee-tah-meen jay)
What are these pills? *I hwanyagun mwoshimnikka?* (Ee hwahn-yah-gune mwah-sheem-nee-kkah?) They are vitamin pills. *Pitamin yagimnida.* (Pee-tah-meen yah-gheem-nee-dah.)

Pillow *Begae* **(Bay-gay)**
I never use a pillow. *Pegaerul ssuji anssumnida.* (Pay-gay-rule ssue-jee ahn-ssume-nee-dah.) Would you like another pillow? *Tarun pegaerul ha-*

shigessumnikka? (Tah-rune pay-gay-rule hah-shee-gay-ssume-nee-kkah?)

Pilot (airplane) *Chojongsa* **(Choe-jong-sah);** also *Pihaenggi chojongsa* (Pee-hang-ghee choe-jong-sah)
This is your pilot speaking. *Nanun yorobun-e chojongsa imnida.* (Nah-nune yah-rah-buun-eh choh-johng-sah eem-nee-dah.)

Pineapple *Painaepul* **(Pie-nap-puul)**
Do you have fresh pineapple? *Shinsonhan painaepul issumnikka?* (Sheen-sahn-hahn pine-ahh-puul ee-ssume-nee-kkah?)

Ping-pong *Takku* **(Tah-kuu);** also *Pingpong* (Ping-pong)
Do you play ping-pong? *Takku chiljul amnikka?* (Tahk-kuu cheel-juul ahm-nee-kkah?) Does the hotel have ping-pong tables? *Hotele takkudaega issumnikka?* (Hotel-eh tahk-kuu-day-gah ee-ssume-nee-kkah?)

Platform (at train station) *Pullaetpom* **(Puu-lat-pome)**
Is this the platform for the Pusan train? *I pullaetpom Pusan haeng yolchayong imnikka?* (Ee puu-lat-pome Pusan hang yahl-chah-yohng eem-nee-kkah?)

Police *Kyongchal* **(K'yong-chahl);** Policeman *Kyonggwan* (K'yong-gwahn); Police box *Pachulso* (Pah-chuul-soe); Police station *Kyongchalso* (K'yong-chahl-soe)
Please call the police. *Kyongchal-ul pullo chuseyo.* (Kyong-chahl-uul puul-lah chuu-say-yoc.)
Where is the nearest police box? *Kajang kakkawun pachulsoga odie issumnikka?* (Kah-jahng kah-kkah-wuun pah-chuul-soh-gah ah-dee-eh ee-ssume-nee-kkah?)

Popular *Taejunge* **(Tay-juung-eh)**
What is the most popular food in Korea? *Han-guk-eso kajang taejungjogin umshigun mwoshim-nikka?* (Hahn-gook-eh-sah kah-jahng tay-juung-jah-geen uum-shee-gune mwah-sheem-nee-kkah?) Is baseball popular in Korea? *Yagu-ga Hanguk-eso inkiissumnikka?* (Yah-guu-gah Hahn-gook-eh-sah een-kee-ee-ssume-nee-kkah?)

Porcelain *Chagi* **(Chah-ghee)**; also *Sagi kurut* (Sah-ghee kuu-ruut)
I'd like to visit a porcelain shop. *Chagisangjomul pangmun hago shipssumnida.* (Chah-ghee-sahng-joe-muul pahng-muun hah-goh sheep-ssume-nee-dah.)

Pork *Tweajigogi* **(Tway-jee-go-ghee)**
Let's also have a pork dish. *Tweajigogi yorido tup-shida.* (Tway-jee-go-ghee yoh-ree-doh tupe-shee-dah.)

Porter (train station) *Poto* **(Poe-toe)**; also *Chim-kkun* (Cheem-kuun)
Please have a porter carry my bags. *Nae kabangul chimkkunege unbanhage haechuseyo.* (Nay kah-bahng-ule cheem-kkuun-eh-gay wuun-bahn-hah-gay hay-chuu-say-yoe.)

Postage *Upyon yogeum* **(Uu-pyone yoe-gay-um)**;
Postage stamp *Upyo* (Uu-pyoe)
Where can I get postage stamps? *Upyorul odieso ossumnikka?* (Uu-pyoh-rule ah-dee-eh-sah ah-ssume-nee-kkah?)

Postcard *Upyon yopso* **(Uup-yone yope-soe)**
How much does it cost to send a postcard air-mail? *Upyon yopso hanggong yogumi olma imnikka?* (Uu-pyahn yahp-sah hahng-gohng yoh-gume-ee ahl-mah eem-nee-kkah?)

Postpone *Yongihada* **(Yone-ghee-hah-dah)**
Our departure has been postponed for two
hours. *Chulbari tushigan yongidoeo ssumnida.*
(Chuul-bah-ree tuu-shee-gahn yahn-ghee-doe-ah
ssume-nee-dah.)

Potato *Kamja* **(Kahm-jah)**; Boiled potatoes *Sal-
mun kamja* (Sahl-muun kahm-jah); Fried potatoes *Twigin kamja* (Twee-gheen kahm-jah);
Mashed potatoes *Chinnigin kamja* (Cheen-nee-
gheen kahm-jah)
Mashed potatoes, please. *Chinnigin kamja, chushipshio.* (Cheen-nee-gheen kahm-jah chuu-
sheep-she-oh.)

Pottery (ceramics) *Tojagi* **(Toe-jah-ghee)**
I want to buy two or three pieces of good pottery. *Choun tajagi tul hogun sejomul sago shipssumnida.* (Choh-uun toh-jah-ghee tuul hoh-gune say-
jahm-ule sah-goh sheep-ssume-nee-dah.)

Pound *Paundu* **(Poun-duu)**
How many pounds does this weigh? *I muge-ga
myot pound imnikka?* (Ee muu-gay-gah myaht
pound eem-nee-kkah?) What is the cost per
pound to mail it to the U.S.? *Miguk kkaji ponaenunde pound-dang olma imnikka?* (Mee-gook kkah-
jee poh-nay-nune-day pound-dahng ahl-mah
eem-nee-kkah?)

Prepare *Chonbihada* **(Chone-bee-hah-dah)**
My wife is preparing breakfast. *Nae anaega achi-
mul junbi hamnida.* (Nay ah-nay-gah ah-cheem-ule
june-bee-hahm-nee-dah.) We have prepared a
snack for you. *Tangshin-ege jul kanshigul junbi
haessumnida.* (Tahng-sheen-eh-geh juul kahn-
shee-gule june-bee hay-ssume-nee-dah.)

Present (gift) *Sunmul* **(Sune-muul)**
Please accept this as a gift. *Igosul sonmullo pada chushipshio.* (Ee-gah-sule sahn-muul-loh pah-dah chuu-sheep-shee-oh.)

President (of a company) *Sajang* **(Sah-jahng);** Of a country *Taetongnyong* (Tay-tong-n'yong)
Which one is the president of the company? *Onupuni hoesa sajangnim imnikka?* (Ah-nuu-puun-ee hoeh-sah sah-jahng-neem eem-nee-kkah?)

Price *Kap* **(Kahp);** also *Kagyok* (Kahg-yoke); *Taekka* (Tay-kah); Wholesale price *Tomae kagyok* (Toe-may kah-gyoke)
What is the price of this? *I kagyogi olma imnikka?* (Ee kah-gyah-ghee ahl-mah eem-nee-kkah?) Will you sell it to me at a wholesale price? *Tomae kagyoge pashige ssumnikka?* (Toh-may kah-gyah-gay pah-shee-gay ssume-nee-kkah?) That price is too high. *Ku kagyogun nomu nopssumnida.* (Kuu kah-gyah-gune nah-muu nohp-ssume-nee-dah.)

Prime Minister *Kungmu chongni* **(Kuung-muu chohng-nee);** also *Susang* (Sue-sahng)
Who is the present prime minister? *Nuga hyonje kungmu chongni imnikka?* (Nuu-gah hyahn-jay kuung-muu chohng-nee eem-nee-kkah?)

Printing *Inse* **(Een-say);** Printed matter *Inse mul* (Een-say muul)
Please print five copies of this. *Igosul tasotchang inswae haechuseyo.* (Ee-gah-sule tah-sah-chahng een-sway hay-chuu-say-yoe.) How much does it cost to send printed matter airmail? *Inswaemurul hanggonguro ponaenunde olma imnikka?* (Een-sway-muu-rule hahng-gohng-uu-roh poh-nay-nune-day ahl-mah eem-nee-kkah?)

Product *Mulgun* **(Muul-goon)**
Do you know who makes this product? *I saeng-sanpumul nuga mandununji ashimnikka?* (Ee sang-sahn-puum-ule nuu-gah mahn-due-nune-jee ah-sheem-nee-kkah?) Is this product made in Korea? *I saengsanpumun Hanguk-je imnikka?* (Ee sang-sahn-puum-uun Hahn-gook-jay eem-nee-kkah?)

Profession *Chigop* **(Chee-gahp)**
What is your profession? *Chigobi mwoshimnikka?* (Chee-gah-bee mwah-sheem-nee-kkah?)

Professor *Kyosu* **(K'yoe-sue);** Associate professor *Pu kyosu* (Puu k'yoe-sue); Assistant professor *Cho gyosu* (Choe g'yoe-sue)
My wife is a professor at Arizona State University. *Nae anaenun Arizona Churip Taehakyo kyosu imnida.* (Nay an-nay-nune Ah-ree-zoe-nah Chuu-reep Tay-hah-kyoh kyoh-suu eem-nee-dah.)

Prohibit *Kumhada* **(Kuum-hah-dah)**
Smoking here is prohibited by law. *Igoseso smoking-un paburo kumjidoeo issumnida.* (Ee-goh-say-soe smoking-uun pah-bue-roh kume-jee-doe-ah ee-ssume-nee-dah.)

Promise *Yaksok* **(Yahk-soak)**
I promise you the weather will be good tomorrow. *Naeil nalssiga choachilgoshirago yaksok hamnida.* (Nay-eel nahl-she-gah choh-ah-cheel-gah-shee-rah-goh yahk-sohk hahm-nee-dah.)

Promissory note *Yaksok oum* **(Yahk-soak oh-uum)**
I cannot accept a promissory note. *Nanun yaksok oumul patchi anssumnida.* (Nah-nune yahk-soak ah-mule pah-chee ahn-ssume-nee-dah.)

Protest *Hangi* **(Hahng-ee);** To lodge a protest *Hangihada* (Hahng-ee-hah-dah)

What is the protest about? *Mwose tahayo hangi hamnikka?* (Mwah-say tah-hah-yah hahng-ee hahm-nee-kkah?) I want to lodge a protest. *Hangi hago shipssumnida.* (Hahng-ee hah-goh sheep-ssume-nee-dah.)

Province (prefecture/state) *Do* (Doe)

How many prefectures are there in Korea? *Han-guk-enun myot kae-e do-ga issumnikka?* (Hahn-gook-eh-nuun m'yote kay-eh doe-gah ee-ssume-nee-kkah?)

Prune *Oyat* (Oh-yaht)

I'd like a dish of prunes, please. *Oyat han chopshi chuseyo.* (Oh-yaht hahn chahp-she chuu-say-yoe.)

Pub *Sonsul jip* (Sahn-suul jeep)

Are there any British-style pubs in Seoul? *Seoul-e Yonggukshik sonsul chipi issumnikka?* (Seoul-eh Yahng-gook-sheek sahn-suul chee-bee ee-ssume-nee-kkah?)

Public *Konggong-e* (Kong-gong-eh); Public telephone *Kongjung chonhwa* (Kong-juung chone-whah); Community *Sahoe* (Sah-hoe)

Pumpkin *Hobak* (Hoe-bahk)

Do you have any pumpkin pie? *Hobak pie issumnikka?* (Hoh-bahk pie ee-ssume-nee-kkah?)

Punctual *Shiganul omsuhanun* (She-gahn-ule ahm-suu-hah-nuun)

Please be punctual. *Shiganul omsuhashipshio.* (Shee-gahn-ule ahm-suu-hah-sheep-she-oh.)

Puncture *Ppangkku* (Pahng-kuu)

This tire has a puncture. *I tio-nun ppangkku-ga nassumnida.* (Ee tee-oh-nune pahng-kuu-gah nah-ssume-nee-dah.)

Purse *Chigap* **(Chee-gahp);** Leather purse *Kajuk chigap* (Kah-juuk chee-gahp)
Don't forget your purse. *Chigabul itchimashipshio.* (Chee-gah-buul ee-tchee-mah-sheep-she-oh.)
Hold onto your purse. *Chigabul chal dulko kyeshipshio.* **(Chee-gah-buul chahl duul-koh kay-sheep-she-oh.)**

Put (place) *Tuda* **(Tuu-dah);** also *Nota* (No-tah)
Put my suitcase on the bed. *Chimdae-e naui otkabangul tushipshio.* (Cheem-day-eh nah-we oht-kah-bahng-ule tuu-sheep-she-oh.) Where did you put your passport? *Yokwonul odie tuossumnikka?* (Yah-kwahn-ule ah-dee-eh tuu-ah-ssume-nee-kkah?)

Q

Quality *Pumjil* **(Puum-jeel);** also *Yangjil* (Yahng-jeel)
The quality is not very good. *Pumjili chochi anssumnida.* (Puum-jee-lee choh-chee ahn-ssume-nee-dah.) Is this the best quality that you have? *Igosun yogie innungochunge kajangchoun pumjil imnikka?* (Ee-gah-sune yah-ghee-eh een-nune-gah-chuung-eh kah-jahng-choh-uun puum-jeel eem-nee-kkah?)

Quantity *Pullyang* **(Puul-yahng);** also *Suryang* (Suur-yahng); Large amount *Taeryang* (Tayr-yahng)
What quantities do you have? *Suryangi olma imnikka?* (Suu-ryahng-ee ahl-mah eem-nee-kkah?)
What numbers are you talking about? *Olma-ui pullyangul malhashimnikka?* (Ahl-mah-we puul-lyahng-ule mahl-hah-sheem-nee-kkah?)

Quarantine *Komyok* **(Kome-yoke);** Ship quarantine *Komyok chongson* (Kome-yoke choong-sone) That ship is quarantined because of cholera. *Cho paenun kollera komyokul padassumnida.* (Chah pay-nune kohl-leh-rah kahm-yahk-ule pah-dah-ssume-nee-dah.)

Question *Chilmun* **(Cheel-muun);** Problem *Munje* (Muun-jay); To ask a question *Shimmunhada* (Sheem-muun-hah-dah) If you have any questions, please ask. *Chilmuni issumyon, muroposeyo.* (Cheel-muun-ee ee-ssue-myahn, muu-rah-poh-say-yoe.) What is your problem? *Mujega mwoshimnikka?* (Muun-jay-gah mwah-sheem-nee-kkah?)

Questionnaire *Chiruiso* **(Chee-rue-ee-sah);** also *Chilmunji* (Cheel-muun-jee); *Angketu* (Ahng-ke-tuu) Please fill out this questionnaire. *I chilmunjie taphaechuseyo.* (Ee cheel-muun-jee-eh tahp-hay-chuu-say-yoe.)

Quick *Pparun* **(Pah-ruun);** also *Nallaen* (Nahl-laen); Quickly *Ppalli* (Pahl-lee) Quick! Call a doctor! *Ppalli, uisarul pullo chuseyo!* (Ppahl-lee, we-sah-rule puul-lah chuu-say-yoe!) He always walks quickly. *Kunun hangsang ppali konnunda.* (Kuu-nune hahng-sahng ppahl-lee kahn-nune-dah.)

Quiet *Choyonghan* **(Choe-yong-hahn)** This is a very quiet place. *Yoginun maeu choyonghan chongso imnida.* (Yah-ghee-nune may-uu choh-yohng-hahn chahng-soh eem-nee-dah.) Do you have a quieter room? *Choyonghan pang issumnikka?* (Choh-yohng-hahn pahng ee-ssume-nee-kkah?)

177

Quit (give up) *Pogihada* **(Poe-ghee-hah-dah);**
also *Kumanduda* (Kuu-mahn-duu-dah)
You should quit smoking. *Tambae piwonungosul kumandushipshio.* (Tahm-bay pee-woo-nune-gah-suul kuu-mahn-duu-sheep-shee-oh.)

Quota (share) *Mok* **(Moke);** Proportion *Haltang-nyang* (Hahl-tahng-n'yang)
What is your quota? *Tangshim-e moksun mwoshim-nikka?* (Tahng-sheen-eh mohk-sune mwah-sheem-nee-kkah?) I have already used up my quota. *Nae moksul imi da ssoboryossumnida.* (Nay moke-suul ee-mee dah ssah-bah-ryah-ssume-nee-dah.)

Quotation (price) *Shise* **(She-say);** also *Shika* (She-kah); Foreign exchange quotation *Hwan yul shise* (Hwahn yuul she-say)
What is today's exchange quotation? *Onul hwan-yul shisenun olma imnikka?* (Oh-nuul hwahn-yuul shee-say-nune ahl-mah eem-nee-kkah?)

R

Rabbit *Tokki* **(Toh-kkee);** Rabbit hunting *Tokki sanyang* (Toke-kee sah-nyahng)
Is rabbit hunting common in Korea? *Tokki san-yangi Hanguk-eso hunhamnikka?* (Toh-kkee sahn-yahng-ee Hahn-gook-eh-sah hune-hahm-nee-kkah?)

Race (competition) *Kyongju* **(K'yong-juu);** Horse race *Kyong ma* (K'yong mah); Marathon race *Maraton kyongju* (Mah-rah-tone k'yong-juu); Ko-rean race *Hanguk minjok* (Hahn-gook meen-

joke);   Racial prejudice   *Injonjok pyon-gyon* (Een-joeng-joke p'yone-g'yone)
Where is the race going to be? *Kyongju-ga odieso yollimnikka?* (Kyahng-juu-gah ah-dee-eh-sah yahl-leem-nee-kkah?)   Do you want to see the race? *Kyong juhanbungot poshigessumnikka?* (Kyahng-juu-hah-nune-gaht poh-shee-gay-ssume-nee-kkah?)

Radiator (heat) *Naenggakki* **(Naehng-gahk-kee)**
My car radiator has a leak. *Nae cha-e naenggakkiga saemnida.* (Nay-chah-eh naehng-gahk-kee-gah same-nee-dah.)

Radio   *Radio* *(Rah-dee-oh);*   Portable radio   *Hyudaeyong radio* (Hew-day-yong rah-dee-oh)
Shall I turn the radio on? *Radio-rul tulkkayo?* (Rah-dee-oh-rule tuul-kah-yoe?)   Does the car have a radio? *Ku chae radio-ga issumnikka?* (Kuu chah-eh rah-dee-oh-gah ee-ssume-nee-kkah?)

Radish   *Muu* **(Mu-uu);**   Pickled radish   *Muu gimchi* (Muu geem-chee)
Do you have fresh radishes? *Shinsonhan muu issumnikka?* (Sheen-sahn-hahn muu ee-ssume-nee-kkah?)

Railroad (railway)   *Cholto* **(Chahl-toh);**   Railway company   *Cholto hoesa* (Chole-toe hoe-eh-sah);   Railroad station   *Kicha yok* (Kee-chah yoke)
Please take me to the railroad station. *Kicha yok guro narul teryoda chushipshio.* (Kee-chah yoke guu-roe nah-ruul tay-ryoh-dah chuu-sheep-she-oh.)

Rain   *Pi* **(Pee);**   also *Piga oda* (Pee-gah oh-dah);   Hard rain   *Pogu* (Poe-guu);   Rainbow   *Mujigae* (Muu-jee-gay);   Rainy   *Piga onun* (Pee-gah oh-nuun);   Rainy day   *Pi onun nal* (Pee oh-nuun nahl)

It looks like it's going to rain. *Piga olgot kassum-nida.* (Pee-gah ohl-gaht kah-ssume-nee-dah.) Do you think it will rain all day? *Harujongil piga orira saenggakhamnikka?* (Hah-ruu johng-eel pee-gah oh-ree-rah sang-gahk-hahm-nee-kkah?) Is it supposed to rain tomorrow? *Naeil piga olkkayo?* (Nay-eel pee-gah ohl-kkah-yoh?)

Raincoat *Piot* (Pee-oat); also *Reinkotu* (Rein-koe-tuu)
Don't forget your raincoat. *Piosul itji mashipshio.* (Pee-oh-suul eet-jee mah-sheep-shee-oh.)

Rare (scarce) *Tumun* (Tuu-muun); also *Chingwi-han* (Cheen-gwee-hahn); Undercooked *Sori-gun* (Soe-ree-guun)
I would like my steak rare, please. *Naegosun salt-chak ikkyo chuseyo.* (Nay-go-sune sahl-chahk eek-yoe chuu-say-yoe.)

Rate (price) *Shise* (She-say); Charge *Yogum* (Yoe-guum); Ratio *Piyul* (Pee-yuul)
Do you have an advertising rate card? *Kwanggo yogum kadrul kajigo issumnikka?* (Kwahng-goh yoh-gume kahd-ruul kah-jee-goh ee-ssume-nee-kkah?)

Raw (uncooked) *Nalgos-e* (Nahl-gos-eh)
Would you like to try some raw fish? *Saengson-hoerul tushigessumnikka?* (Sang-sahn-hoe-rule tuu-shee-geh-ssume-nee-kkah?)

Razor *Myondokal* (M'yone-doe-kahl); also *Myondogi* (Myahn-doh-gee); Safety razor *Anjon myondokal* (Ahn-joan m'yone-doe-kahl)
I forgot to bring my razor. *Myondogi kajoonungo-sul ijossumnida.* (Myahn-doh-gee kah-jah-oh-nune-gah-suul ee-jah-ssume-nee-dah.)

Read *Ikta* **(Eek-ttah)**
I cannot read Korean. *Hanguk-o-rul ilguljul morumnida.* (Hahn-gook-ah-rule eel-guul-juul mohrume-nee-dah.) Can you read English? *Yong-o-rul ilguljul ashimnikka?* (Yahng-ah-rule eel-guul-juul ah-sheem-nee-kkah?)

Ready (prepared) *Junbidoen* **(June-bee-doe-een)**
Are you ready? *Junbinun toeossumnikka?* (June-bee-nuun toc-eh-oh-sume-nee-kkah?)

Ready-made *Kisong-pume* **(Kee-song pume-eh);**
Ready-made shoes *Kisong-hwa* (Kee-song-hwah)
Do you have a ready-made suit that would fit me? *Naege mannun kisongpogi issumnikka?* (Nay-gay mahn-nune kee-sahng-poh-ghee ee-ssume-nee-kkah?)

Reason (cause) *Iyu* **(Ee-yuu);** Motive *Tonggi* (Tong-ghee)
What is your purpose in coming to the U.S.? *Miguk-e onun mokjogi mwoshimnikka?* (Mee-gook-eh oh-nune mohk-joe-gee mwah-sheem-nee-kkah?)

Receipt *Yongsujung* **(Yong-suu-juung)**
May I have a receipt, please? *Yongsujung chuseyo.* (Yong-suu-juung chuu-say-yoe.)

Reception (welcome) *Hwanyong* **(Hwahn-yong)**
Thank you very much for the wonderful reception. *Motjin hwanyonge kamsahamnida.* (Maht-jeen hwahn-yahng-eh kahm-sah-hahm-nee-dah.)

Recommend *Chuchonhada* **(Chuu-chone-hah-dah)**
Can you recommend a good Korean-style restaurant? *Choun Hanguk shiktangul chuchonhae chushigessumnikka?* (Choh-uun Hahn-gook sheek-tahng-ule chuu-chahn-hay chuu-shee-geh-ssume-nee-kkah?) Which hotel do you

181

recommend? *Onu hotel-ul chuchon hamnikka?* (Ah-nuu hoh-tel-ule chuu-chahn hahm-nee-kkah?)

Red *Ppalgan* **(Pahl-gahn)**
Do you have any red dresses? *Ppalgan oshi issumnikka?* (Ppahl-gahn oh-she ee-ssume-nee-kkah?)

Refreshment (light snack) *Kandanhan shiksa* **(Kahn-dahn-hahn sheek-sah);** also *Kanshik* (Kahn-sheek)
Would you like some refreshments? *Kanshikul tushigessumnikka?* (Kahn-she-kuul tuu-shee-gay ssume-nee-kkah?)

Refrigerator *Naengjanggo* **(Nang-jahng-go)**
There is beer in the refrigerator. *Naengjanggo ane maekjuga issumnida.* (Nang-jahng-goh ahn-eh make-juu-gah ee-ssume-nee-dah.)

Register (at hotel) *Tungnokada* **(Tuung-no-kah-day);** Register a letter *Tunggiro puchida* (Tuung-ghee-roe puu-chee-dah)
I would like to register this letter. *I pyonjirul tunggiro puchigo shipsumnida.* (Ee pyone-jee-ruul tuung-ghee-roe puu-chee-go sheep-sume-nee-dah.)

Religion *Chonggyo* **(Choong-g'yoe);** Buddhist religion *Pulgyo* (Puul-g'yoe); Christian religion *Kidokkyo* (Kee-doke-k'yoe); Religious *Chonggyo-e* (Choong-g'yoe-eh)
Is Buddhism still a popular religion in Korea? *Pulgyonun ajikdo Hanguk-e taejungjok chonggyoimnikka?* (Puul-gyo-nune ah-jeek-do Hahn-gook-eh tay-juung-jahk chohng-gyoh eem-nee-kkah?)

Remain (stay) *Momuruda* **(Moe-muu-rue-dah)**
Please remain seated until the bus stops. *Posu-ga momchulttae kkaji charie momurupshio.* (Pah-sue-

gah mahm-chuul-tay-kkah-jee chah-ree-eh mah-muu-rupe-shee-oh.)

Remember   *Kiokhada* **(Kee-ahk-hah-dah)**
I don't remember the name of the restaurant. *Ku shiktang irumul kiokmotamnida.* (Kuu sheek-tahng ee-rume-ule kee-ahk-moh-tahm-nee-dah.)   Do you remember where we were last night? *Chinanpam uriga odie issonnunji kiokhashimnikka?* (Chee-nahn-pahm uu-ree-gah ah-dee-eh ee-ssahn-nune-jee kee-ahk hah-sheem-nee-kkah?)

Rent (a car)   *Pillida* **(Peel-lee-dah)**
I want to rent a car. *Charul pilligo shipsumnida.* (Chah-ruul peel-lee-go sheep-sume-nee-dah.)

Repair (mend)   *Kochida* **(Koe-chee-dah);**   also *Surihada* (Suu-ree-hah-dah)
Can you repair this? *Igosul gochilsu issumnikka?* (Ee-gah-suul goh-cheel-suu ee-ssume-nee-kkah?)   Please fix this. *Kugosul surihae chushipshio.* (Kuu-gah-sule sue-ree-hay chuu-sheep-shee-oh.)

Repeat (say again)   *Toepuri malhada* **(Toe-eh-puu-ree mahl-hah-dah);**   also *Panbokhada* (Pahn-bohk-hah-dah);   Do again   *Toepurihada* (Toe-eh-puu-ree-hah-dah)
Please repeat that. *Kugosul panbokhae chushipshio.* (Kuu-gah-suul pahn-bohk-hay chuu-sheep-shee-oh.)

Reputation   *Pyongpan* **(P'yong-pahn)**
This shop has a good reputation. *I sangjomun pyongpani chosumnida.* (Ee-sahng-jahm-uun pyahng-pahn-ee choh-ssume-nee-dah.)

Reservation   *Yeyak* **(Yay-yahk)**
I would like to make reservations for two please. *Tu sarambunul yeyak hago shipssumnida.* (Tuu sah-

rahm-buun-uel yeh-yahk hah-goh sheep-ssume-
nee-dah.) Do you have reservations? *Yeyak
hashyossumnikka?* (Yeh-yahk hah-shyah-ssume-
nee-kkah?) I'm sorry, we do not have your reservation. *Mianhamnida, tangshin-e daehaesonun
yeyak haji anassumnida.* (Mee-ahn-hahm-nee-dah,
tahng-sheen-eh day-hay-sah-nune yeh-yahk hah-
jee ahn-ah-ssume-nee-dah.)

Resort (recreational) *Yuwonji* **(Yuu-won-jee);**
Summer resort *Pisoji* (Pee-soe-jee); Health re-
sort *Hyuyangji* (Hyu-yahng-jee)
Are there many hot-spring resorts in Korea?
Hanguk-e onchoni mani issumnikka? (Hahn-gook-eh
ohn-chahn-ee mahn-ee ee-ssume-nee-kkah?)

Rest (repose) *Hyushik* **(Hyuu-sheek);** also *Chada*
(Chah-dah); Stop work *Shwida* (Sh-wee-dah)
Let's take a rest. *Chom shwipshida.* (Chome
shweep-she-dah.) You look like you need a rest.
Tangshin-un hyushiki piryo hamnida. (Tahng-sheen-
uun hyuu-shee-kee pee-ryoh hahm-nee-dah.)

Restaurant *Shiktang* **(Sheek-ttahng);** also *Um-
shikchom* (Uum-sheek-chome)
Yes, there are several Korean restaurants in Chicago. *Chicago-e Hanguk shiktangi mani issumnida.*
(Chicago-eh Hahn-gook sheek-tahng-ee mahn-ee
ee-ssume-nee-dah.)

Restroom (at a theater or station) *Pyonso* **(P'yone-
soe);** also *Hwajangshil* (Hwah-jahn-sheel)
Is there a restroom here? *Yogie hwajangshiri issumnikka?* (Yah-gee-eh hwah-jahng-shee-ree ee-
ssume-nee-kkah?)

Rice (cooked) *Pap* **(Pahp)**
Would you like rice or bread? *Pab-ul tushigessum-*

nikka? Ppang-ul tushigessumnikka? (Pahb-ule tuu-shee-gay-ssume-nee-kkah? Ppahng-ule tuu-shee-gay-ssume-nee-kkah?)

Ring (for finger) *Panji* **(Pahn-jee)**
Rings are a bargain in Korea. *Panjinun Hanguk-eso Kap i ssamnida.* (Pahn-jee-nune Hahn-gook-eh-sah kahp-i ssahm-nee-dah.) I want to buy a ring for myself. *Narul wihan panjirul sago shipssumnida.* (Nah-rule wee-hahn pahn-jee-rule sah-goh sheep-ssume-nee-dàh.)

Ripe (mature) *Igun* **(Ee-guun)**
These apples are not ripe. *I sagwanun an igossumnida.* (Ee sah-gwah-nune ahn ee-gah-ssume-nee-dah.)

River *Nae* **(Nay);** also *Kang* (Kahng)
What is the name of that river? *Jo kang-e irumun mwoshimnikka?* (Jah kahng-eh ee-rume-uun mwah-sheem-nee-kkah?) Is that the famous Han River? *Jo kangi yumyonghan Han Kang imnikka?* (Jah kahng-ee yuu-myahng-hahn Hahn Kahng eem-nee-kkah?)

Road (highway) *Toro* **(Toe-roe);** Roadway *Kil* (Keel)
Is this the highway to Pusan? *Igoshi Pusan haeng kosok toro imnikka?* (Ee gah-shee Pusan hang koh-sohk toh-roh eem-nee-kkah?)

Roast beef *Pulgogi* **(Puul-go-ghee);** Roast pork *Twaeji pulgogi* (Tway-jee puul-go-ghee)
Which do you prefer, roast beef or roast pork? *Pulgogi wa twaeji pulgogi chungeso onugosul to choahashimnikka?* (Puul-goh-gee-wah twaeh-jee puul-goh-gee chuung-eh-sah ah-nue-gah-suul tah choh-ah-hah-sheem-nee-kkah?)

185

Room *Pang* **(Pahng);** also *Shil* (Sheel)
A single room for five nights, please. *Oilgan mugul ilinyong pang-ul chuseyo.* (Oh-eel-gahn muuguul eel-een-yohng pahng-ule chuu-say-yoe.)
How much is the room charge? *Sukpakyonun olma imnikka?* (Suuk-pahk-yoh-nune ahl-mah eemnee-kkah?)

Rotary (traffic circle) *Rotori* **(Roe-toe-ree);** also *Kyocharo* (K'yoe-chah-roe); Rotary Club *Rotori kullop* (Roe-toe-ree kuul-lope)
There are many rotaries in Seoul. *Seoul-e Kyocharoga mani issumnida.* (Seoul-eh kyoh-chah-roh-gah mahn-ee ee-ssume-nee dah.)

Ruby *Rubi* **(Ruu-bee);** also *Hongok* (Hohn-gohk)

Rush (in a hurry) *Punju* **(Puun-juu);** Rush-hour traffic *Roshi auwoe kyotong* (Roe-she ah-wah k'yoe-tong)
I'm in a big rush. *Nanun maeu pappumnida.* (Nahnune may-uu pah-ppume-nee-dah.) We were caught in rush-hour traffic. *Urinun roshi-auwoe kyotonge kollyossumnida.* (Uu-ree-nune rah-sheeah-wah kyoh-tohng-eh kahl-lyah-ssume-needah.)

Russia *Roshia* **(Roe-she-ah);** Russian (person) *Roshiain* (Roe-she-ah-een); Russian language *Roshia-o* (Roe-she-ah-oh); Russian (thing) *Roshia-ui* (Roe-she-ah-we)

Rye *Homil* **(Hoe-meel);** Rye bread *Homil ppang* (Hoe-meel-pahng)
Rye bread toast, please. *Homil ppang tostu chuseyo.* (Hoh-meel-ppahng toh-stuu chuu-say-yoe.)

S

Safe (secure) *Anjonhan* **(Ahn-joan-hahn)**
Is it safe to go swimming here? *Yogieso suyong-hanungosun anjonhamnikka?* (Yah-ghee-eh-sah suu-yahng-hah-nune-gah-sune ahn-jahn-hahm-nee-kkah?)

Safety belt *Kumyongdae* **(Kuum-yong-day);** also *Anjon belt* (Ahn-jahn behlt)
Please fasten your safety belts. *Anjon beltrul mae-shipshio.* (Ahn-jahn belt-rule may-sheep-shee-oh.)

Salad *Ssalladu* **(Sah-lah-duu);** Fruit salad *Kwail ssalladu* (Kwah-eel sah-lah-duu); Vegetable salad *Yachae ssaladu* (Yah-chay sah-lah-duu)
Would you like salad or soup? *Ssalladu na soup tushigessumnikka?* (Sah-lah-duu nah suup tue-shee-geh-ssume-nee-kkah?)

Sale *Pammae* **(Pahm-may);** Bargain sale *Yomga pammae* (Yahm-gah pahm-may); Sales tax *Pammae se* (Pahm-may-say)
Are you having a sale now? *Chigum pammae hamnikka?* (Chee-gume pahm-may hahm-nee-kkah?) We have a sales tax in the U.S. *Urinun Miguk-e pammae serul naego issumnida.* (Uu-ree-nune Mee-gook-eh pahn-may say-rule nay-goh ee-ssume-nee-dah)

Salmon *Yono* **(Yahn-ah)**
I'd like a salmon steak, please. *Yono steik-rul chu-shipshio.* (Yahn-ah steik-rule chuu-sheep-shee-oh.)

Salt *Sogum* **(Soe-guum);** Salty *Tchan* **(Chahn)**
May I have some salt, please? *Sogum chuseyo.*

(Soe-guum chuu-say-yoe.)   This soup is too salty.
Isoupun nomu tchamnida. (Ee-suup-unn nah-muu
tcham-nee-dah.)

Same (identical) *Katun* (Kah-tuun); Similar *Pi-sutan* (Pee-suu-tahn)
Let me have two of the same, please. *Katungot
tugaerul kajigo shipssumnida.* (Kah-tune-gaht tuu-gay-rule kah-jee-goh sheep-ssume-nee-dah.)

Sample *Kyonbon* (K'yone-bone); Sample copy
Kyonbon chaek (K'yone-bone chake);   Trade (busi-ness) sample *Sangpum kyonbon* (Sahng-puum
k'yone-bone)
Let me see a sample. *Kyonbon-ul poyo chushio.*
(K'yone-bone-uul poe-yoe chuu-she-oh.)

Sardines *Chongori* (Chahng-ah-ree); Canned sar-dines *Chongori tongjorim* (Chahng-ah-ree tong-joe-reem)

Satisfactory *Chungbunhan* (Chuung-buun-han)
Is everything satisfactory? *Moduga chungbun
hamnikka?* (Moh-duu-gah chuung-buun hahm-nee-kkah?)

Sauce *Sosu* (Soe-suu); Korean-style sauce *Kan-jang* (Kahn-jahng)
May I have some sauce, please? *Sosu jom chu-shipshio.* (Soh-sue johm chuu-sheep-shee-oh.)

Say (speak) *Malhada* (Mahl-hah-dah); Polite
form *Malssumhashida* (Mahl-sume-hah-she-dah)
How do you say this in Korean? *Igosul Hanguk-o-ro mworago malhamnikka?* (Ee-go-sule Hahn-gook-oh-ro mwah-rah-go mahl-hahm-nee-kkah?)
What did you say? *Mworago malssumehashyos-sumnikka?* (Mwah-rah-goh mahl-ssume-hah-shyah-ssume-nee-kkah?)

Scarf *Sukapu* **(Suu-kah-puu)**
It's cold today, so you need a scarf. *Onurun chuwoso sukapu-ga piryo hamnida.* (Oh-nuu-rune chuu-wah-sah suu-kah-puu-gah pee-ryoh hahm-nee-dah.)

Scenery *Punggyong* **(Puung-g'yoong);** also *Kyongchi* (Kyahng-chee)
The scenery is fantastic. *Kyongchiga hullyung hamnida.* Kyahng-chee-gah huul-yuung hahm-nee-dah.)

Schedule (program) *Yejong* **(Yay-jong);** also *Iljong* (Eel-jahng)
What is your schedule today? *Onul iljongi mwoshimnikka?* (Oh-nule eel-jahng-ee mwah-sheem-nee-kkah?) I am scheduled to leave for Cheju Island tomorrow. *Naeil Chejudo-ro ttonal yejong imnida.* (Nay-eel Cheh-juu-doh-roh ttah-nahl yeh-jahng eem-nee-dah.)

School *Hakkyo* **(Hahk-y'oe);** Primary school *Kungmin hakkyo* (Kuung-meen hahk-k'yoe); High school *Kodung hakkyo* (Koe-duung hahk-k'yoe); Public school *Kongnip hakkyo* (Kong-neep hahk-k'yoe)
Are you still in school? *Ajik hakkyo tanimnikka?* (Ah-jeek hahk-kyoh tah-neem-nee-kkah?) When do you have school vacation? *Hakkyo panghagi onje imnikka?* (Hahk-kyoh pahng-hah-ghee ahn-jeh eem-nee-kkah?)

Science *Kwahak* **(Kwah-hahk);** Scientist *Kwahakcha* (Kwah-hahk-chah); Social Science *Sahoe kwahak* (Sah-hoe-eh kwah-hahk); Ministry of Science and Technology *Kwahak kisulcho* (Kwah-hahk kee-suul-choe)
Is science a popular subject in Korean schools?

Kwahaki Hanguk hakkyoeso inkki itnun kwamog im-nikka? (Kwah-hahkee Hahn-gook hahk-kyo-eh-sah een-kee it-nune kwah-mohg eem-nee-kkah?)

Scissors *Kawi* **(Kah-we);** Pair of scissors *Kawi han charu* (Kah-we hahn chah-ruu)
I need to borrow a pair of scissors. *Kawi pillyo chushipshio.* (Kah-wee peel-lyah chuu-sheep-shee-oh.)

Score (points) *Tukchom* **(Tuuk-chome);** also *Chomsu* (Chahm-suu)
What is the score? *Chomsu-ga olma imnikka?* (Chahm-suu-gah ahl-mah eem-nee-kkah?)

Scotch whisky *Sukotullandusan wisuki* **(Suu-ko-tuul-lahn-duu-sahn wee-suu-kee);** also *Skachi wisuki* (Skah-chee wee-suu-kee)
A Scotch and soda, please. *Sodasu sokkun skachi hajan chushipshio.* (Soh-dah-suu sahk-kune skah-chee hahn-jahn chuu-sheep-shee-oh.)

Screen (partition) *Kanmagi* **(Kahn-mah-ghee);**
Folding screen Pyongpung (P'yong-puung);
Movie pictures Yonghwa (Yahng-hwah)
I'm looking for a large folding screen. *Kun pyong-pungul chakko issumnida.* (Kune pyahng-puung-ule chah-kkoh ee-ssume-nee-dah.)

Sculptor *Chogakka* **(Choe-gahk-kah);** Sculpture *Chogak* (Choe-gahk)
I appreciate the sculptures in front of many buildings in Seoul. *(Seoul-e innun manun konmul appe chogakul kamsang haessumnida.* (Seoul-eh een-nune mah-nune kahn-muul ahp-eh choh-gahk-ule kahm-sahng hay-ssume-nee-dah.)

Sea *Pada* **(Pah-dah);** By sea (ship) *Paero* (Pay-roe); Seacoast *Hae byon* (Hay b'yone); Sea shore *Haean* (Hay-ahn); Seaport *Hanggu*

(Hahng-guu); Sea level *Haemyon* (Hame-yone)
How far is Seoul from the sea? *Padaeso Seoul kkaji
olmana momnikka?* (Pah-dah-eh-sah Seoul kkah-
jee ahl-mah-nah mahm-nee-kkah?) Do you live
near the seacoast? *Haebyon kakkai sashimnikka?*
(Hay-byahn kah-kkie sah-sheem-nee-kkah?)

Seasickness *Paemolmi* (**Pay-mahl-mee**)
I am seasick. Do you have some medicine I can
take? *Paemolmiga namnida. Yak jom odulsu issumnikka?* (Pay-mahl-mee-gah nahm-nee-dah. Yahk
johm ah-duul-suu ee-ssume-nee-kkah?)

Search *Chosa* (**Choe-sah**); also *Chatta* (Chaht-tah)
What are you searching for? *Mwosul chatko issumnikka?* (Mwah-suul chaht-koe ee-sume-nee-
kkah?)

Season *Kyejol* (**Kay-jole**); also *Chol* (chole); Four
seasons *Sa chol* (Sah chole); Rainy season
Changma chol (Chang-mah chole); Out of season *Chori chinan* (Choe-ree chee-nahn); To season (flavor) *Matturida* (Maht-tuu-ree-dah);
Seasoning *Chomiryo* (Choe-mee-rio)
Is it always this hot during the summer season?
Yorum cholenun hangsang topssumnikka? (Yah-rume
chah-leh-nune hahng-sahng tahp-ssume-nee-
kkah?) How is the weather during the spring
season? *Pomcholenun nalshiga ottossumnikka?*
(Pohm-chah-leh-nune nahl-shee-gah attah-
ssume-nee-kkah?)

Seat (to sit on) *Chwasok* (**Chwah-soak**); Chair
Uija (We-jah); Bench *Penchi* (Pen-chee)
Please have a seat. *Charie anjushipshio.* (Chah-ree-
eh ahn-juu-sheep-shee-oh.) Are there any seats
available? *Anjul chariga issumnikka?* (Ahn-juul
chah-ree-gah ee-ssume-nee-kkah?) This is your

seat. *Igoshi tangshin chwasok imnida.* (Ee-gah-shee
tahng-sheen chwah-sahk eem-nee-dah.)

Second (thing) *Cheie* **(Cheh-ee-eh);** also *Tultchaee*
(Tuult-chay-eh); Second (time) *Cho* (Choe)
This is my second time in Seoul. *Seoul-un iboni
tubontchae imnida.* (Seoul-uun ee-bahn-ee tuu-
bahn-chay eem-nee-dah.) Pusan is Korea's second largest city. *Pusanun Hanguk-e cheie kun toshi
imnida.* (Pusan-uun Hahn-gook-eh cheh-ee-eh
kune toh-shee-eem-nee-dah.)

Secretary *Sogi* **(Soe-ghee);** Private secretary *Pi
so* (Pee sah)
Are you Mr. Kim's secretary? *Tangshini Kim Son-
saengnim-e piso imnikka?* (Tahng-sheen-ee Keem
Sahn-sang-neem-eh pee-sah eem-nee-kkah?)
No, I am Mr. Lee's secretary. *Anio, nanun Lee
Sonsaengnimui piso imnida.* (Ah-nyoh, nah-nune
Lee Sahn-sang-neem-we pee-sah eem-nee-dah.)

See (look at) *Poda* **(Poe-dah);** Meet *Mannada*
(Mahn-nah-dah)
I would like to see some shoes. *Kudurul pogo
shipssumnida.* (Kuu-duu-rule poh-goh sheep-
ssume-nee-dah.) I am here to see Mr. Cho. *Cho
Sonsaengnim-ul manaro yogie wassumnida.* (Choh
Sahn-sang-neem-ule mahn-nah-rah yah-ghee-eh
wah-ssume-nee-dah.) I see. *Arassoyo.* (Ah-rah-
soe-yoe). Let me see. *Popshida.* (Pohp-shee-
dah). See you later. *Najunge poepkessumnida.*
(Nah-juun-gay pep-kay-ssume-nee-dah.)

Sell *Palda* **(Pahl-dah)**
Will you sell me this at a discount? *Igosul harin-
haeso naege palgessumnikka?* (Ee-gah-suul hah-
reen-hay-sah nay-gay pahl-gay-sume-nee-

kkah?) What will you sell it for? *Musun iyuro kugosul pamnikka?* (Muu-sune ee-yuu-roh kuu-gah-suul pahm-nee-kkah?)

Semester *Ilhakki* **(Eel-hahk-kee);** also *Han hakki* (Hahn hahk-kee)
We are just starting the spring semester. *Urinun pomhakkie shijak hamnida.* (Uu-ree-nune pohm-hahk-kee-eh shee-jahk hahm-nee-dah.)

Senate *Sangwon* **(Sang-won)**

Send (by post) *Puchida* **(Puu-chee-dah);** also *Ponaeda* (Poe-nay-dah)
I want to mail this. *Igosul upyonuro puchigo ship-ssumnida.* (Ee-gah-suul uu-pyahn-uu-roh puu-chee-goh sheep-ssume-nee-dah.) Please send a bellboy to get my bags. *Nae kabangul kajigool boirul ponae chushipshio.* (Nay kah-bahng-ule kah-jee-goh-ohl boh-ee-rule poh-nay chuu-sheep-shee-oh.)

Senior (in rank) *Sanggub-e* **(Sahng-gube-eh);**
Older *Sonwie* (Sone-we-eh); In age *Yonjangja* (Yone-jahng-jah)
In Korea it is very important to know who is senior in age and rank. *Hanguk-eso yonjangjarul anungosun maeu chungyohamnida.* (Hahn-gook-eh-sah yahn-jahg-jah-rule ah-nune-gah-sune may-uu chuung-yoh-hahm-nee-dah.)

Serious (grave) *Shimgakan* **(Sheem-gah-kahn);**
Important *Chungdaehan* (Chuung-day-hahn)
Is it very serious (grave)? *Kugosun maeu shimga-kamnikka?* (Kuu-gah-sune may-uu sheem-gah-kahm-nee-kkah?) This is a serious mistake. *Igosun chungdaehan shilsu imnida.* (Ee-gah-sune chuung-day-hahn sheel-suu eem-nee-dah.)

Service (expert help) *Sobisu* **(Sah-bee-sue);** To
serve Pongsa (Pong-sah); also *Ssobisu ryo* (Sah-
bee-suu rio)
The service is very good here. *Yoginun sobisuga
maeu chosumnida.* (Yoh-gee-nune sah-bee-sue-gah
may-uu choe-sume-nee-dah.) How much is
your service charge? *Pongsaryoga olma imnikka?*
(Pohng-sah-ryoh-gah ahl-mah eem-nee-kkah?)

Several *Yorosue* **(Yoe-roe-suu-eh);** Several people *Yoro saram* (Yoe-roe sah-rahm)
I have been here several times. *Nanun yogie yoro-
bon wassumnida.* (Nah-nune yah-ghee-eh yah-rah
bahn wah-ssume-nee-dah.) I'll take several.
Nanun yorogaerul kajil goshimnida. (Nah-nune yah-
rah-gay-rule kah-jeel gah-sheem-nee-dah.)

Sex *Song* **(Song);** Male sex *Nam song* (Nahm
song); Female sex *Yo song* (Yoe-song); Sex appeal *Songchok maeryok* (Song-choke maeh-ryahk)
She has extraordinary sex appeal. *Kuyojanun
songchok maeryoki ttwionamnida.* (Kuu-yah-jah-
nune sahng-chahk may-ryahk-ee ttwee-ah-nahm-
nee-dah.)

Shark *Sango* **(Sahng-ah)**
Are there any sharks in this area? *I chiyoke san-
goga issumnika?* (Ee chee-yahk-eh sahng-ah-gah
ee-ssume-nee-kkah?)

Shave *Myondo* **(M'yone-doe);** Shaver *Myondogi*
(M'yone-doe-ghee); Electric shaver *Chongi
myondogi* (Chone-ghee m'yone-doe-ghee)
Just a shave, please. *Paro myondo haechuseyo.*
(Pah-roh myone-doh hay-chuu-say-yoe.)

She *Kuyojanun* **(Kuu-yoe-jah-nuun);** Honorific
Kubunun (Kuu-kuu-nuun)
Who is she? *Kuyojanun nuguimnikka?* (Kuu-yah-

jah-nune nuu-guu-eem-nee-kkah?)   Is she coming? *Kuyojaga omnikka?* (Kuu-yah-jah-gah ohm-nee-kkah?)

Sheep   *Yang* **(Yahng)**
There are not many sheep in Korea. *Hanguk-enun yangi manchi ansumnida.* (Hahn-gook-eh-nune yahng-ee mahn-chee ahn-ssume-nee-dah.)

Sheet (bedding)   *Shitu* **(She-tuu);**   Sheet of paper *Han chang* (Hahn chahng)
May I change your sheets, please? *Shitu-rul pakkulkkayo?* (Sheet-rule pahk-kuul-kkah-yoh?)

Shine (shoes)   *Kwangnaeda* **(Kwang-nay-dah);**
also *Takta* (Tahk-tah)
Please have my shoes shined. *Nae kudu-rul takka chushipshio.* (Nay kuu-duu-rule tahk-kah chuu-sheep-shee-oh.)

Ship   *Pae* **(Pay);**   Send by ship *Paero susonghada* (Pay-roe suu-song-hah-dah); Sailing ship *Totan pae* (Toe-tahn pay)
Please ship these boxes to the U.S. *I sangjarul Miguk kkaji paero omgyo chushipshio.* (Ee sahng-jah-rule Mee-gook kkah-jee pay-roe ohm-gyah chuu-sheep-shee-oh.)   I want to go to Japan by ship. *Ilbone paero kago shipssumnida.* (Eel-bohn-eh pay-roh kah-goh sheep-ssume-nee-dah.)

Shirt   *Syassu* **(Shah-suu);**   White shirt *Wai syassu* (Wie shah-suu)
Is this your shirt? *Igosun tangshin syassu imnikka?* (Ee-gah-sune tahng-sheen shah-ssue eem-nee-kkah?)   Can you make me another shirt like this one? *Igotgwa katun syassurul manduro chushigessumnikka?* (Ee-gaht-gwah kah-tune shah-ssue-rule mahn-duu-roe chuu-shee-geh-ssume-nee-kkah?)

Shoe *Kudu* **(Kuu-duu);** also *Shin* (Sheen); Shoe horn *Kudu chugok* (Kuu-duu chuu-goke); Shoe polish *Kudo yak* (Kuu-duu yahk)
Do I take my shoes off? *Kudu-rul posodo doemnikka?* (Kuu-duu-rule pah-sah-doh dome-nee-kkah?) Please keep your shoes on. *Kudunun an posodo chossumnida.* (Kuu-duu-nuun ahn poe-soe-doe choe-ssume-nee-dah.)

Shop (store) *Sangjom* **(Sahng-joam)**
What is the name of the shop? *Sangjom irumi mwoshimnikka?* (Sahng-joam ee-rume-ee mwah-sheem-nee-kkah?) At what shop did you buy these? *Onu sangjomeso igosul sassumnikka?* (Oh-nuu sahng-joam-eh-sah ee-gah-suul sha-ssume-nee-kkah?)

Shopping *Mulgonsagi* **(Muul-gahn-sah-ghee);** also *Syoping* (Show-peeng); Shopping bag *Chang paguni* (Chahng pah-guu-nee)
I want to go shopping tomorrow. *Naeil syoping gagoja hamnida.* (Nay-eel show-peeng gah-goh-jah hahm-nee-dah.) Have you already been shopping? *Imi changul pwassumnikka?* (Ee-mee chahng-ule pwah-ssume-nee-kkah?)

Short (not long) *Tchalbun* **(Chal-buen);** Shorten *Tchalke hada* (Chal-kay hah-dah)
This dress is too short. *Iosun nomu tchalssumnida.* (Ee-oh-sune nah-muu tchahl-ssume-nee-dah.) Don't cut my hair too short. *Nae morirul nomu tchalke hajimashipshio.* (Nay mah-ree-rule nomuu tchahl-kay hah-jee-mah-sheep-shee-oh.)

Show (make visible) *Pvida* **(Poh-ee-dah);** Point out *Karikida* (Kah-ree-kee-dah); Guide *Annaehada* (Ahn-nay-hah-dah); Exhibit *Chollamhoe* (Choel-lahm hoe-eh)
Please show me your boarding pass. *Tapsung*

pyorul poyo chushipshio. (Tahp-sung-pyoh-rule poh-yah chuu-sheep-shee-oh.) Show me another one, please. *Tarungosul naege poyo chushipshio.* (Tah-rune-gah-suul nay-gay poh-yah chuu-sheep-shee-oh.) I will be very happy to show you around. *Kikkoi boyo durigetsumnida.* (Khee-kko-ee boh-yoe duu-ree-geh-sume-nee-dah.)

Shower (bath) *Syawo* **(Sha-wah);** Rain *Sonagi* (Soe-nah-ghee)
A room with a shower, please. *Shyawo shiri innun pang-ul chushipshio.* (Sha-wah-shee-ree een-nune pahng-ule chuu-sheep-shee-oh.)

Shrimp *Saeu* **(Say-uu);** Fried shrimp *Saeu twigim* (Say-uu twee-gheem)
Do you like shrimp? *Saeu choahashimnikka?* (Say-uu choh-ah hah-sheem-nee-kkah.) I love shrimp. *Saeu-rul maeu choahamnida.* (Say-uu-rule may-uu choh-ah-hahm-nee-dah.)

Shut (close) *Tatta* **(Tah-tah);** also *Tachida* (Tah-chee-dah)
Please shut the door. *Munul tadu shipshio.* (Muu-nuul tah-duu sheep-she-oh.) I can't shut my suitcase. *Ot kabangul tatulsu opssumnida.* (Oht-kah-bahng-ule tah-tuul-suu ahp-ssume-nee-dah.)

Shy *Pukkurowohanun* **(Puuk-kuu-roe-woe-han-nuun)**
Are Korean children shy? *Hanguk orinidurun pukkurowohamnikka?* (Hahn-gook ah-reen-ee-due-rune puuk-kuu-rah-wah-hahm-nee-kkah?)

Sick *Pyongnan* **(P'yong-nahn);** Car-sick *Chamolmihanun* (Chah-mohl-mee-hah-noon)
I feel sick. *Momi apumnida.* (Mohm-ee ah-pume-nee-dah.) I'm going to be sick (vomit). *Tohol kot kassumnida.* (Toe-hahl kaht kah-sume-nee-dah.)

Side (direction) *Tchok* **(Choke);** Left side *Oen
tchok* (Oh-en choke); Right side *Orun tchok*
(Oh-ruun choke); Back side *Twi-tchok* (Twee-
choke); Front side *Ap-tchok* (Ahp-choke)
It is on the right side of the street. *Kugosun ku
toroe orun tchoke issumnida.* (Kuu-gah-sune kuu
toh-roh-eh oh-rune-choke-eh ee-ssume-nee-
dah.). Please sit on the left side. *Oen tchoke anjushipshio.* (Ahn choke-eh ahn-juu-sheep-shee-
oh.)

Sightseeing *Kwangwang* **(Kwahn-gwahng)**
We have three days for sightseeing. *Urinun sa-
milgan kwangwang hamnida.* (Uu-ree-nune sahm-
eel-gahn kwahn-kwahng hahm-nee-dah.)

Sign (signboard) *Kanpan* **(Kahn-pahn);** Sign
(traffic signal) *Shinho* (Sheen-hoe); Sign one's
name *Somyonghada* (Sah-myahng-hah-dah)
The shop has a big sign. *Sangjome kun kanpani issumnida.* (Sahng jahm-eh kune kahn-pahn-ee
ee-ssume-nee-dah.) Turn right at the first stop
sign. *Choum chongji shinhoeso uhoechon hashipshio.*
(Chah-uum chahng-jee sheen-hoh-eh-sah uu-
hoe-chahn hah-sheep-shee-oh.)

Signature *Somyong* **(Sah-myahng)**
I need your signature right here, please. *Yogi
oruntchoge tangshin-e somyongi piryo hamnida.* (Yah-
ghee oh-rune-tcho-geh tahng-sheen-eh sah-
myahng-ee pee-ryoh hahm-nee-dah.)

Silk *Pidan* **(Pee-dahn);** also *Myongju* (M'yong-
juu); Silk apparel *Pidan ot* (Pee-dahn oat);
Raw silk *Saengsa* (Sang-sah)
I would like to buy a silk shirt/dress. *Pidan osul
sago shipssumnida.* (Pee-dahn oh-suul sah-goh
sheep-ssume-nee-dah.)

Silver *Un* **(Uun);** Silver coins *Unhwa* (Uun-hwah); Silverware *Ungurut* (Uun-guu-ruut) Please show me some silverware. *Unguru-sul poyo chushipshio.* (Uun-guu-rue-sule pah-yah chuu-sheep-shee-oh.)

Sing *Noraehada* **(No-ray-hah-dah);** Singer *Kasu* (Kah-suu)
In Korea everyone is expected to sing at parties. *Hanguk-esonun patieso moduga noraepurul chunbirul haeyahamnida.* (Hahn-gook-eh-sah-nune pah-tee-eh-sah moh-duu-gah no-ray-puu-rule chuun-bee-rule hay-yah-hahm-nee-dah.) How about singing a Korean song? *Hanguk noraerul puru-shigessoyo?* (Hahn-gook no-ray-rule puu-rue-she-gay-ssah-yoh?)

Single (room) *Tokpang* **(Toak-pahng);** Single ticket *Pyondo chapyo* (P'yone-doe chah-pyoe); Single (not married) *Tokshinui* (Toke-sheen-we)
Are you still single? *Ajik tokshin ishimnikka?* (Ah-jeek tohk-sheen ee-sheem-nee-kkah?) I'd like a single room with a shower for tonight, please. *Harubam chal shawo shiri innun tokpang chushipshio.* (Hah-ruu-bahm chahl shah-wah-shee-ree een-nune tohk-pahng chuu-sheep-shee-oh.)

Sister *Chamae* **(Chah-may);** Older sister *Nunim* (Nuu-neem); Your older sister *Tangshin-e nunim* (Tahng-sheen-eh nuu-neem)
Do you have any sisters? *Chamae-ga issumnikka?* (Chah-may-gah ee-ssume-nee-kkah?)

Sit *Anta* **(Ahn-tah)**
Please sit down. *Anju shipshio.* (Ahn-juu sheep-shee-oh.)

Size *Kugi* **(Kuu-ghee);** Measurement *Chisu* (Chee-suu); also *Saiju* (Sie-juu)

I wear a size nine dress. *Nanun saiju kuu osul ips-sumnida.* (Nah-nune sie-juu kuu-eh oh-sule eep-ssume-nee-dah.)   What size shoes do you wear? *Tangshin kudue saijunun olmaimnikka?* (Tahng-sheen kuu-duu-eh sie-juu-nune alh-mah-eem-nee-kkah?)

Ski *Suki* **(Su-kee);** Skiing *Sukitagi* (Su-kee-tah-ghee)
Skiing is very popular in Korea. *Ski-ga Hanguk-eso maeu inkki gaissumnida.* (Sukee-gah Han-gook-eh-sah may-uu een-kee gah-ee-ssume-nee-dah.) Would you like to go skiing? *Ski-taro gashiges-sumnikka?* (Sukee-tah-rah gah-shee-gay-ssume-nee-kkah?)

Skirt *Sukoto* **(Sue-kah-tue);** also *Chima* (Chee-mah)
Is it all right if I wear a skirt today? *Onul chi-marul ipodo choul kkayo?* (Oh-nuul chee-mah-rule eep-ah-doh choh-uul-kkah-yoh?)

Sky *Hanul* **(Hah-nuel);** Clear sky *Malgun hanul* (Mahl-guun hah-nuel); Cloudy sky *Hurin hanul* (Huu-reen hahn-uul)
We may have cloudy skies for several days. *Myo-chilgan hanuri hurigessumnida.* (Myah-cheel-gahn hah-nuu-ree huu-ree-gay-ssume-nee-dah.)

Skyscraper *Machollu* **(Mah-chahl-luu)**
Seoul is famous for its skyscrapers. *Seoul-un ma-cholluro yumyonghamnida.* (Seoul-un mah-chahl-luu-roh yuum-yahng hahm-nee-dah.)

Sleep *Cham* **(Chahm);** Also *Sumyon* (Sume-yone); Fall asleep *Chada* (Chah-dah); Sleepy *Chollinun* (Chol-lee-nuun)
I went to sleep early last night. *Jinan pam iltchik chassumnida.* (Jee-nahn-pahm eel-tcheek chah-

ssume-nee-dah.) I did not get enough sleep last night. *Jinan pam chamul chungbuni chajimotaessumnida.* (Jee-nahn pahm chahm-ule chuung-buun-ee chah-jee-moh-tay-ssume-nee-dah.)

Slippers *Sullipo* **(Suul-leep-ah)**
Please take your shoes off and put these slippers on. *Kudu-rul posushigo sulliporul shinushipshio.* (Kuu-duu-ruul pah-sue-shee-goh suul-lee-pah-rule sheen-uu-sheep-shee-oh.)

Slow *Nurin* **(Nuu-reen);** Late *Nujun* (Nuu-juun); Slowly *Chonchoni* (Chone-chone-ee)
Please drive more slowly. *Jomdo chonchoni unjonhaseyo.* (Johm-dah chahn-chahn-ee uun-jahn-hah-say-yoe.) Please speak more slowly. *Jomdo chonchoni malhaseyo.* (Johm-dah chahn-chahn-ee mahl-hah-say-yoe.)

Small (size) *Chagun* **(Chah-guun);** Quantity *Chogun* (Choe-guun)
This room is too small. *Ipangun nomu chagssumnida.* (Ee-pahng-uun nah-muu chahg-ssume-nee-dah.) These gloves are too small. *Ichanggabun nomu chagssumnida.* (Ee-chahng-gah-bune nah-muu chahg-ssume-nee-dah.)

Smallpox *Chonyondu* **(Chone-yone-duu)**
Have you been vaccinated for smallpox? *Chonyondu chopchongul padassumnikka?* (Chahn-yahn-duu chahp-chohng-ule pah-dah-ssume-nee-kkah?)

Smile *Miso* **(Mee-soe);** also *Misohada* (Mee-soe-hah-dah); *Utda* (Uut-dah)
Smile, please. *Ususeyo.* (Uu-suu-sey-yoe.)

Snack *Kabyoun shiksa* **(Kah-byah-uun sheek-sah);** Snack bar *Kani shiktang* (Kah-nee sheek-tahng)

Would you like an afternoon snack? *Ohu kanshikul tushigessoyo?* (Oh-huu kahn-shee-kuul tuu-shee-gay-ssah-yoh?)

Snow *Nun* **(Nuun);** Snowman *Nunsaram* (Nuun-sah-rahm); Snow storm *Nun bora* (Nuun boe-rah)
The weather bureau says it will snow tonight. *Kisangdaega onulpam nuni ogetago malhamnida.* (Kee-sahng-day-gah oh-nuul pahm nuun-ee oh-gay-tah-goh mahl-hahm-nee-day. It's still snowing. *Nuni kyesok naerimnida.* (Nuun-ee kay-sohk nay-reem-nee-dah.)

Soap *Pinu* **(Pee-nuu);** Toilet soap; *Sesu pinu* (Say-suu pee-nuu); Laundry soap *Setak pinu* (Say-tahk pee-nuu)
Did you bring any soap? *Pinu kajo wassumnikka?* (Pee-nuu kah-jah wah-ssume-nee-kkah?) Ask the maid to bring some soap. *Hanyoege pinu kajyo orago malhaseyo.* (Hah-nyah-eh-gay pee-nuu kah-jah oh-rah-goh mahl-hah-say-yoe.)

Socks *Yangmal* **(Yahng-mahl)**
Are these your socks? *Igosun tangshin yangmal imnikka?* (Ee-gah-sune tahng-sheen yahng-mahl eem-nee-kkah?) One of my socks didn't come back. *Yangmal hantchagi oji anassumnida.* (Yahng-mahl-hahn-tchah-ghee oh-jee ahn-ah-ssume-nee-dah.)

Soda *Soda* **(Soe-dah);** Soda water *Soda su* (Soe-dah suu)
Bring me a glass of soda water, please. *Sodasu hanjan kajyo oseyo.* (Soh-dah-suu hahn-jahn kah-jyah oh-say-yoe.)

Sometimes *Ttaettaero* **(Tate-tay-roe);** also *Kakkum* (Kah-kkuum)

I sometimes hear from friends in Korea. *Kakkum Hanguk chingudulegeso soshik tussumnida.* (Kahkkume Hahn-gook cheen-guu-duul-eh-geh-sah soh-sheek tuu-ssume-nee-dah.)

Song *Norae* **(No-ray);** Folksong *Minyo* (Meenyoe); Children's song *Tongyo* (Tong-yoe)
Folk songs are very popular in Korea. *Minyo-ga Hanguk-eso maeu inkki imnida.* (Meen-yoh-gah Hahn-gook-eh-sah may-uu een-kee eem-needah.)

Soon *Kot* **(Koat);** also *Inae* (Ee-nay)
Are we leaving soon? *Urinun kot ttonamnikka?* (Uu-ree-nune koht ttah-nahm-nee-kkah?)
Please come back as soon as possible. *Kanunghan han kot tora oshipshio.* (Kah-nung-hahn hahn koht-toh-rah oh-sheep-shee-oh.)

Soup *Supu* **(Suu-puu);** also *Kuk* (Kuuk); Chicken soup *Takkogi supu* (Tahk-koe-ghee suu-puu)
We have several kinds of soup. *Yoro chongnyue kuki issumnida.* (Yah-rah chohng-nyuu-eh kuukee ee-ssume-nee-dah.) What kind of soup would you like? *Otton supurul tushigessumnikka?* (Ah-ttahn suu-puu-rule tuu-she-gay-ssume-neekkah?)

South *Namtchok* **(Nahm-chock);** also *Nambu* (Nahm-buu); Southeast *Namdong* (Nahmdong); Southwest *Namso* (Nahm-soe); South Korea *Nam han* (Nahm hahn)
It's about thirty minutes south of Seoul. *Seoul-eso namtchakulo yak samshibun gorie issumnida.* (Seouleh-soe nahm-chock-uu-lo yahk sahm-she-bune go-ree-eh es-ssume-nee-dah.)

Souvenir *Kinyompum* **(Kee-nyome-pume);** Gift *Sonmul* (Sone-muul)

Would you like to buy a souvenir? *Kinyompumul sashigessumnikka?* (Kee-nyahm-puum-ule sah-she-gay-ssume-nee-kkah?) This would make a good souvenir. *Igosun choun kinyompumi doegessumnida.* (Ee-gah-sune choh-uun kee-nyahm-puum-ee doe-gay-ssume-nee-dah.)

Soy beans *Kong* **(Kohng)**
Are soy beans raised in Korea? *Kongi Hanguk-eso chabaedoemnikka?* (Kohng-ee Hahn-gook-eh-sah chah-bay-dome-nee-kkah?)

Space *Uju* **(Uu-juu);** Space ship *Uju son* (Uu-juu soan); Space travel *Uju yohaeng* (Uu-juu yoe-hang)
Korea is also interested in space technology. *Hanguk-indo uju kwahake kwanshim issumnida.* (Hahn-gook-een-doh uu-juu kwah-hahk-eh kwahn-sheem ee-ssume-nee-dah.)

Spain *Supein* **(Suu-pain);** Spanish *Supein saram* (Suu-pain sah-rahm); Spanish language *Supeino* (Suu-pain-oh)
Do many Spanish people come to Korea? *Manun Supein sarami Hanguk-e omnikka?* (Mah-nune Suu-pain sah-rahm-ee Hahn-gook-eh ohm-nee-kkah?)

Speak (say) *Malhada* **(Mal-hah-dah)/** Make a speech *Yonsolhada* (Yone-sole-hah-dah.)
Do you speak Korean? *Hangung marul hal chul ashimnikka?* (Hahn-guung mah-ruul hahl chuul ah-sheem-nee-kah?) I speak it a little. *Chugum hal chul amnida.* (Choe-guum hahl chuul ahm-nee-dah.) Please speak a little more slowly. *Chom chonchonhi malssumhae chushipshio.* (Chome chone-chone-hee mahl-sume-hay chuu-sheep-shee-oh.)

Specialty product *Tuksan mul* **(Tuuk-sahn muul)**
Ginseng is a specialty product of Korea. *Insamun Hanguk-e tuksanmurimnida.* (Een-sah-muun Hahn-gook-eh tuuk-sahn-muu-reem-nee-dah.) What are some of the other specialty products of Korea? *Hanguk-e tto darun tuksan murun mwoshimnikka?* (Hahn-gook-eh ttoh dah-rune tuke-sahn muu-rune mwah-sheem-nee-kkah?)

Speed (swiftness) *Shinsok* **(Sheen-soak);** Velocity *Sokto* (Soak-toe); Speed limit *Sokto chehan* (Soak-toe chay-hahn)
What is the speed limit in Korea? *Hanguk-eso sokto chehanun olmakkaji imnikka?* (Hahn-gook-eh-sah sohk-toh cheh-hahn-nune ahl-ma-kkah-jee eem-nee-kkah?)

Spend (money) *Sobihada* **(Soe-bee-hah-dah);** also *Ssuda* (Ssue-dah)
How much do you want to spend? *Olmamankum ssugo shipssumnikka?* (Ahl-mah-mahn-kume ssue-goh sheep-ssume-nee-kkah?) I have already spent too much. *Polsso nomu mani sobihaessumnida.* (Pahl-ssah nah-muu mah-nee soh-bee-hay-ssume-nee-dah.)

Spinach *Shigumchi* **(She-guum-chee)**
Is spinach a popular dish in Korea? *Shigumchi-rul Hanguk-eso mani moksumnikka?* (Shee-gume-chee-rule Hahn-gook-eh-sah mah-nee moke-sume-nee-kkah?)

Spoon *Sukkarak* **(Suuk-kah-rahk);** Tea spoon *Chat sukkarak* (Chaht suuk-kah-rahk); Table spoon *Papsukkarak* (Pap-suuk-kah-rahk)
May I have a tea spoon, please? *Chat sukkarak chushipshio.* (Chaht suuk-kah-rahk chuu-sheep-she-oh.)

Stadium *Kyonggijang* **(K'yoong-ghee-jahng)**
Please take me to the Olympic Stadium. *Ollimpic Kyonggijange teryoda chushipshio.* (Ohl-leemp-peck kyahng-ghee-jahng-eh tay-ryah-dah chuu-sheep-she-oh.)

Stamp (postage) *Upyo* **(Uu-pyoe);** Rubber stamp *Komu in* (Koe-muu een); Name seal *Tojang* (Toe-jahng)
Do you sell postage stamps here? *Yogieso upyo-ul pamnikka?* (Yah-ghee-eh-sah uu-pyoh-ule pahm-nee-kkah?) How much postage do I need for this? *Yogie olmatchari upyoga piryohamnikka?* (Yah-ghee-eh ahl-mah-tchah-ree uu-pyoh-gah pee-ryoh-hahm-nee-kkah?)

Start (beginning) *Shijak* **(She-jahk)**
What time does it start? *Myoshie shijak hamnikka?* (Myah-she-eh shee-jahk hahm-nee-kkah?) What time do we start? *Myoshie shijak hamnikka?* (Myah-she-eh she-jahk hahm-nee-kkah?)

Station (railway) *Yok* **(Yahk)**
Where is the nearest railway station? *Kajang kakkaun yokun odie issumnikka?* (Kah-jahng kah-kkah-uun yahk-uun ah-dee-eh ee-ssume-nee-kkah?) I want to go to Seoul Station. *Seoul yok kago shipssumnida.* (Seoul-yahk-eh kah-goh sheep-ssume-nee-dah.)

Stationery *Munbanggu* **(Muun-bahng-guu)**
Is there a stationery store near here? *I kunchoe munbangguga issumnikka?* (Ee kune-chah-eh muun-bahng guu-gah ee-ssume-nee-kkah?)

Statue *Chosang* **(Choe-sahng)**
You must see the beautiful statues in Washington, D.C. *Washington-e sonun arumdaun chosangul polsu issumnida.* (Washington-eh-sah-nune ah-

rume-dah-uun choh-sahng-ule pohl-suu ee-
ssume-nee-dah.)

Steak *Suteiku* **(Suu-tay-kuu);** Beef steak *Sogogi
suteiku* (Soh-goh-ghee suu-tay-kuu)
I'll have a filet mignon steak, medium well. *Filei
minyong suteiku-ul potonguro kuwoso chushipshio.*
(Fee-lay mee-nyohng sue-take-ule poh-tohng-uu-
roh kuu-wah-sah chuu-sheep-shee-oh.)

Stewardess (airline) *Sutyuodisu* **(Stu-wah-dee-
suu)**
How long have you been a stewardess? *Sutyuodisu-ro olmatongan issossumnikka?* (Stu-wah-dee-
suu-roh ahl-mah-tohng-ahn ee-ssah-ssume-nee-
kkah?) Do you like working as a stewardess?
Sutyuodisu-ro ilhanungosul choahashimnikka? (Stu-
wah-dee-suu-roh eel-hah-nune-gah-suul choh-
ah-hah-sheem-nee-kkah?)

Stockings *Yangmal* **(Yahng-mahl);** Nylon stockings *Naillon yangmal* (Nie-loan yahng-mahl);
Silk stockings *Shilku yangmal* (Sheel-kuu yahng-
mahl)
I am missing a pair of stockings. *Yangmal han
kyollyeruli ropuryo ssumnida.* (Yahng-mahl hahn-
kyahl-layh-rule ee-roe-puu-ryo ssume-nee-dah.)

Stomachache *Wi-tong* **(We-tong);** Stomach
cramps *Wi gyongnyon* (We-g'yong-n'yone)
I have a stomachache. *Paega apumnida* (Pay-gah
ah-pume-nee-dah.)

Stop (pause) *Chongji* **(Chahng-jee);** Stay *Mo-
muruda* (Moe-muu-rue-dah)
Does this train stop at Kwangju? *I kichanun
Kwangjue momurumnikka?* (Ee-kee-chah-nune
Kwahng-juu-eh mah-muu-rume-nee-kkah?) We
are stopping in Taegu for two nights. *Urinun itul*

pam Taegue momurumnida. (Uu-ree-nune ee-tuul-pahm Taegu-eh mah-muu-rume-nee-dah.)

Stopover *Tojung hacha* **(Toe-juung hah-chah)**
I will have only a one-day stopover in Seoul.
Seoul-eso haruman tojunghacha halgoshimnida.
(Seoul-eh-sah hah-ruu-mahn toe-juung-hah-chah
hahl-gah-sheem-nee-dah.)

Store (shop) *Kage* **(Kah-gay);** also *Sangjom*
(Sahng-joam)
Let's try this store. *I sanjhome kapopshida.* (Ee
sahng-joam-eh kah-pohp-shee-dah.)

Storm (wind) *Pokpung* **(Poak-puung);** Rain
storm *Pokpungu* (poak-pung-uu); Snowstorm
Nunbora (nuun-boe-rah)
There's going to be a storm tonight. *Onulpam
pokpungi olgoshimnida.* (Oh-nuul-pahm pohk-
puung-ee ohl-gah-sheem-nee-dah.) Does Seoul
often have snowstorms? *Seoulenun chongchong
nunboraga chimnikka?* (Seoul-eh-nune chohng-
chohng nuun-boh-rah-gah cheem-nee-kkah?)

Straight (direction) *Ttokparun* **(Toke-pah-ruun);**
also *Kotparo* (Koht-pah-roh)
Please go straight ahead. *Ttokparo kashipshio.*
(Toke-pah-roe kah-sheep-she-oh.)

Strawberry *Ttalgi* **(Tahl-ghee)**
Strawberries are in season now. Would you like
some? *Ttalgiga chigum checholimnida. Jom tushigessumnikka?* (Ttahl-ghee-gah chee-gume chay-
chole eem-nee-dah. Johm tuu-shee-gay ssume-
nee-kkah?)

Street *Kori* **(Koe-ree);** also *Karo* (Kah-roe)
The post office is on this street. *Uchegugi ikorie issumnida.* (Uu-chay-guu-ghee ee-koe-ree-eh ee-
ssume-nee-dah.) Please turn right at the next

street. *Taum korieso uhoechon hashipshio.* (Tah-uum koh-ree-eh-sah uu-hoe-chahn hah-sheep-shee-oh.)

String *Jul* **(Juul)**
I need some string to tie this box. *Nanun i sangja-ul mael juli pilyo hamnida.* (Nah-nune ee song-jah-ule mail juul-ee peel-yoe hahm-nee-dah.)

Student *Haksaeng* **(Hahk-sang);** Graduate student *Tae hagwonsaeng* (Tay hah-g'won-sang)
Are you still a student? *Ajigdo haksaeng imnikka?* (Ah-jeeg-doe hahk-sang eem-nee-kkah?) What school are those students from? *I haksaengdurun onuu hakyo chulshin imnikka?* (Ee hahk-sang-duu-rune oh-nuu hah-kyo chuul-sheen eem-nee-kkah?)

Subway *Chihachul* **(Chee-hah-chule);** Under-pass *Chihado* (Chee-hah-doe)
Shall we take the subway? *Chihachul-eul talgayo?* (Chee-hah-chuul uul tahl-gah-yoe?) Does the subway go to Seoul Station? *I chihachul-i Seoul yoke gamnikka?* (Ee Chee-hah-chule-ee Seoul yoe-kay gahm-nee-kkah?)

Sugar *Soltang* **(Sole-tang);** White sugar *Paek soltang* (Pake sole-tang)
Would you like sugar in your coffee? *Kopi-e sultang-ul talkayo?* (Koe-pee-eh suul-tahng-uul tahl-kah-yoe?) May I have some more sugar, please? *Sultang du chuseyo.* (Sule-tahng duu chu-say-yoe.)

Suit (apparel) *Yangbok* **(Yahng-boak);** Casual suit *Undongbok* (Uun-dong-boak)
Please have this suit cleaned. *I yangbok setak he chuseyo.* (Ee yahng-boak say-tock hay chu-say-yoe.) Should I wear a suit? *Yangbok-ul ibuya hamnikka?* (Yahng-bock-ule ee-buu-yah hahm-nee-kkah?)

Suitcase *Yuheng kabang* **(Yuu-hang kah-bahng);**
also *Suutsu keisu* (Suu-tsuu kay-e-suu)
How many suitcases do you have? *Yuheng kabang-i myotke isumnikka?* (Yuu-hang kah-bahng-ee myot-kay ee-sume-nee-kkah?) I'm missing a suitcase. *Kabang-ul iroporyosumnida.* (Kah-bahng-ule ee-roe-poe-ryo-ssume-nee-dah.)

Summer *Yorum* **(Yoe-ruum);** Summer vacation *Yorum hyuga* (Yoe-ruum hyuu-gah); Summer resort *Piso ji* (Pee-soe jee)
Is this your summer vacation? *Yorum hyuga imnikka?* (Yoe-rume hyu-gah eem-nee-kkah?) Is summer a good time to go to Korea? *Yorum-eun Hanguk-e kanungoshi chosumnikka?* (Yoe-rume-eh-uun Hahn-gook-eh kanune-go-she choe-ssume-nee-kkah?)

Sun *Hae* **(Hay);** Sunshine *Haetpit* (Hate-peet); Sunbathe *Ilgwangyok* (Eel-gwahn-yoak); Sunrise *haedoji* (Hay-doe-jee); Sunset *Haegorum* (Hay-go-ruum)
Do you think the sun will shine tomorrow? *Naeil haega nalggaya?* (Nay-eel hay-gah nahl-gah-yah?) Let's sit out in the sunshine. *Haetbyote nagabshida.* (Hate-byo-tay nah-gahb-she-dah)

Sunburn *Haetbyote tan* **(Hate-byo-tay tahn)**
Be careful about sunburn. *Haetbyote tajianke joshimhaseyo.* (Hate-byo-tay tah-jhee-ahn-kay joe-sheem hah-say-yoe.) It looks like you are sunburned. *Haetbyote tangut kasumnida.* (Hate-byo-tay tahn-got kah-ssume-nee-dah.)

Supper *Chonyok* **(Chone-yoke);** also *Shiksa* (Sheek-sah)
Where would you like to go for supper? *Odieso chonyok-ul mogul kkayo?* (Ah-dee-eh-suh chone-yoke-ule moe-guul kkah-yoe?) How about Japa-

nese food for supper? *Chonyok-eun Ilbon umshik-ul
mogul kkayo?* (Chone-yoke-eh-uun Eel-bone
umm-sheek-ule moe-guul kkah-yoe?)

Sweat *Ttam* **(Tahm);** also *Ttami nada* (Tah-mee
nah-dah); *Ttamul* (Tah-muul)
Boy! I'm really sweating! *Uhyo! Ttame chojotne!*
(Uu-hyoe! Ttah-may choe-joat-nay!)

Sweater *Seta* **(Say-tah)**
You had better bring a sweater. *Seta-rul kajiko
kanunge chosumnida.* (Say-tah-rule kah-jee-koe
kah-nune-gay choe-sume-nee-dah.)   Will I really
need a sweater? *Seta-ga chongmal piryo hamnikka?*
(Say-tah-gah choong-mahl pee-ryo hahm-nee-
kkah?)

Sweet (sugary) *Tan* **(Tahn)**
This soup is too sweet. *I supnun nomu tamnida.*
(Ee supe-nune no-muu tahm-nee-dah.)

Sweetheart *Aein* **(Ay-een);** also *Yonin* (Yone-een)
Those two are sweethearts. *Chodulrun yonin imnida.* (Choe-duul-rune yone-neen eem-nee-
dah.)   Do you have a sweetheart? *Aeini
isumnikka?* (Ay-ee-nee ee-ssume-nee-kkah?)

Swim *Suyong* **(Sue-yong);** also *Suyonghada* (Suu-
yong-hah-dah)
Do you know how to swim? *Suyong haljol ashimnikka?* (Sue-yoong hahl-johl ah-sheem-nee-
kkah?)   I cannot swim. *Nanun suyong haljol
Morumnida.* (Nah-nuun sue-yoong hahl-johl
moe-rume-nee-dah.)   Would you like to go
swimming? *Suyong haro kashigessoyo?* (Sue-yong
hah-roe kah-she-gay-sso-yoe?)

Symptoms (medical) *Chungse* **(Chuung-say)**
What are your symptoms? *Chungse-ga otto sumnikka?* (Chuung-say-gah aht-tah sume-nee-
kkah?)

Synagogue *Yuttae kyohoe* **(Yuut-tay k'yoe-hoe-eh)**
Are there any synagogues in Seoul? *Seoul-e Yutaein kyohoega issumnikka?* (Seoul-eh Yuu-tay-een kyo-hoe-eh-gah es-sume-nee-kkah?)

T

Table *Teibul* **(Tay-buul);** also *Takcha* (Tahk-chah)
A table for three, please. *Saminyong teibul-rul chushipshio.* (Sahm-een-yohng tay-buul-rule chuu-sheep-shee-oh.) Will this table be all right? *I teibul-i masumnikka?* (Ee tay-buul-ee mah-ssume-nee-kkah?)

Tag (label) *Kkoripyo* **(Koe-reep-yoe);** Price tag *Kagyokpyo* (Kah-g'yoak-p'yoe)
I can't find the price tag. *Kagyokpyorul mot chatgessumnida.* (Kahg-yoke-pyo-rule mot chaht-gay-ssume-nee-dah.)

Tailor *Chaebongsa* **(Chay-bong-sah);** also *Yangbokchom* (Yahng-boak-choam)
Do you know a good tailor? *Hulryunghan chaebongsarul ashimnikka?* (Huul-ryung-hahn chay-bohng-sah-rule ah-sheem-nee-kkah?) This tailor has a very good reputation. *I yangbokchomun pyongpani chossumnida.* (Ee yahng-bohk-chahm-uun pyahng-pahn-ee choh-ssume-nee-dah.)

Take (carry) *Katko kada* **(Kaht-koe kah-dah)**
Should I take an umbrella? *Usanul katko kayahamnikka?* (Uu-sahn-ule kaht-koh kah-yah-hahm-nee-kkah?) Will you take me with you? *Narul teryo kachushigessumnikka?* (Nah-rule tay-ryah kah-chu-she-gay-ssume-nee-kkah?) Please take my bags to my room. *Nae kabangul nae pange*

katta chuseyo. (Nay kah-bahng-ule nay pahng-eh kah-ttah chu-say-yoe.)

Takeoff *Chulbal* **(Chuul-bahl)**
What time is your takeoff? *Myoshie chulbal hamnikka?* (Myah-shee-eh chuul-bahl hahm-nee-kkah?)

Tall (height) *Nopun* **(No-puun)**; Stature *Ki kun* (Kee-kuun)
How tall are you? *Kiga olma imnikka?* (Kee-gah ahl-mah eem-nee-kkah?) Is that the tallest building in Seoul? *Jogosun Seouleso cheil kun kohmulimnikka?* (Jah-gah-sune Seoul-eh-sah chay-eel-kune kah-muul-eem-nee-kkah?)

Tangerine *Kyul* **(Kyuul)**; also *Orenji* (Oh-rane-jee)
Can we buy tangerines on the train platform? *Kicha platform-eso kyulul salsu issumnikka?* (Kee-chah platform-eh-sah kyuu-rule sahl-suu ee-ssume-nee-kkah?)

Taste (flavor) *Mat* **(Maht)**; also *Matpoda* (Mahtpoe-dah); Tasty *Mat choun* (Maht choe-uun)
How does it taste? *Mashi ottossumnikka?* (Mahshe aht-toe-sume-nee-kkah?) It tastes good. *Mashi chossumnida.* (Mah-shee choh-ssume-nee-dah.)

Tax *Segum* **(Say-gume)**; also *Kwasehada* (Kwahsay-hah-dah); Tax-free goods *Myon-sepum* (M'yone-say-puum); Business tax *Yongop se* (Yahng-ahp-seh)
Does that include tax? *Segumi pohamdoeossumnikka?* (Say-gume-ee poh-hahm-doe-ah-ssume-nee-kkah?) No, the tax is separate. *Animnida, segumun ttaro imnida.* (Ah-neem-nee-dah say-gume-uun tah-roh eem-nee-dah.)

Taxi *Taekshi* **(Tack-she)**
Let's go by taxi. *Taekshiro kapshida.* (Tack-she-roh kahp-shee-dah.) Where is the best place to catch a taxi? *Odiga taekshi chapgie kajang chossumnikka?* (Ah-dee-gah tack-she chahp-ghee-eh kah-jahng choh-ssume-nee-kkah?)

Tea *Cha* **(Chah);** Black tea *Hong cha* (Hong-chah); Tea cup *Cha chan* (Chah-chahn)
Would you like tea or coffee? *Cha na kopi tushigessumnikka?* (Chah-nah koh-pee tuu-she-gay-ssume-nee-kkah?) I'll have tea, thank you. *Charul chushipshio.* (Chah-rule chuu-sheep-shee-oh.)

Teacher *Kyosa* **(K'yoe-sah);** also *Sonsaengnim* (Soan-sang-neem)
My oldest daughter is a teacher. *Nae changnyonun kyosa imnida.* (Nay chahng-nyah-nune kyoh-sah eem-nee-dah.)

Team *Tim* **(Teem);** Baseball team *Yagu tim* (Yah-guu teem); Football team *Chukku tim* (Chuke-kuu teem)
Which baseball team do you like? *Onu yagu timul choahamnikka?* (Ah-nuu yah-guu-teem-ule choh-ah-hahm-nee-kkah?)

Telegram *Chonbo* **(Chone-boe);** Telegraph *Chonshin* (Chone-sheen)
I need to send a telegram. *Chonborul ponaego shipssumnida.* (Chahn-boh-rule poh-nay-go sheep-ssume-nee-dah.) Where is the telegraph office? *Chonshingugi odie issumnikka?* (Chahn-sheen-guug-ee ah-dee-eh ee-ssume-nee-kkah?)

Telephone *Chonwha* **(Chone-whah)**
Please telephone me. *Naege chonhwa hashipshio.* (Nay-gay chahn-hwah hah-sheep-shee-oh.) I

will telephone you. *Tangshin-ege chonhwa golges-sumnida.* (Tahng-sheen-eh gay chah-hwah gahl-gay-ssume-nee-dah.) Here is my telephone number. *Igosun nae chonhwa ponho imnida.* (Ee-gah-sune nay chahn-hwah pahn-hoh eem-nee-dah.) What is your telephone number? *Tangshin-e chonhwa ponhonun olmaimnikka?* (Tahng-sheen-eh chahn-hwah pahn-hoh-nune ahl-mah-eem-nee-kkah?)

Television *Tellebijon* **(Tay-lay-bee-joan)**; Television set *Tellebijon susanggi* (Tay-lay-bee-joan suu-sahng-ghee)
Does the room have a television set? *Kupange T.V. susanggiga issumnikka?* (Kuu-pahng-eh TV suu-sahng-ghee-gah ee-ssume-nee-kkah?) I watched television last night. *Chinan pam T.V. rul poassumnida.* (Chee-nahn-pahm T.V. rule poh-ah-ssume-nee-dah.)

Temperature (air) *Ondo* **(Own-doe)**; Body temperature *Che on* (Chay own); Air temperature *Ki on* (Kee own)
What is the temperature this morning? *Oneul achim myudo imnikka?* (Oh-nule ah-cheem myu-doe eem-nee-kkah?) I'll take your temperature. *Yorul chaeo pogessumnida.* (Yoe-ruul chay-oh poe-gay-ssume-nee-dah.)

Temple (Buddhist) *Chol* **(Chole)**; also *Sadang* (Sah-dahng)
Why are there so many famous temples in Korea? *Hanguk-neun ochchaesu yoyunghan chuli sumnikka?* (Hahn-gook-nay-uun ah-chay-sue yoe-yuung-hahn chuu-lee ssume-nee-kkah?) Which is the most famous temple in Seoul? *Unu chuli Seoul-esu gajang yomyung hapnikka?* (Uu-nuu chuu-lee Seoul-eh-sue gah-jahng yome-yuung hahp-nee-kkah?)

215

Tennis *Tenisu* **(Tay-nee-suu);** also *Jongku* (Joong-kuu)
Do you play tennis? *Jongku chishipnikka?* (Joong-kuu chee-sheep-nee-kkah?) Is there a tennis court nearby? *I kunchoe jongku jangi isumnikka?* (Ee kune-cho-eh joong-kuu jahn-ghee ee-ssume-nee-kkah?)

Thank you *Komapsumnida* **(Koe-mop-ssume-nee-dah)**

Thanksgiving Day *Chosugamsajul* **(Choe-sue-gahm-sah-jule)**
Since tomorrow is Thanksgiving Day it is a national holiday. *Neil-un Choso kamsajul inika, kukyongil imnida.* (Nail-uun choe-soe kahm-sah-jule ee-nee-kah, kook-gyon-gheel eem-nee-dah.)

That *Ku* **(Kuu);** also *Cho* (Choe); *Kugot* (Kuu-got); *Chogot* (Choe-got)
What is that? *Kugotsi mwoshimnikka?* (Kuu-got-she mwah-sheem-nee-kkah?) Who is that? *Kupunun nuguijiyo?* (Kuu-puu-nune nuug-we-jee-yoe?) That's right. *Chossumnida* (Choe-ssume-nee-dah.) also *Kurossumnida.* (Kuu-roe-ssume-nee-dah.) Is that so? *Ku raeyo?* (Kuu ray-yoe?)

Theater *Kukchang* **(Kuuk-chahng)**
I'd like to go to the theater tonight. *Nanum onul bame kukchang-e gagirul wonhamnida.* (Nah-nume oh-nule bah-may kuuk-chahng-eh gah-ghee-rule wohn-hahm-nee-dah.) What is playing at the theater? *Kukchang-esor mwoshi sangyong toemnikka?* (Kuuk-chahng-eh-sor mwah-she sahng-yoong tome-nee-kkah?)

Thermometer (weather) *Ondogye* **(Own-doe-gay);** Clinical thermometer *Cheon-gye* (Chay-own-gay); Centigrade thermometer *Sopssi*

ondogye (Sope-she own-doe-gay);   Fahrenheit
thermometer   *Hwassi ondogye* (Hwah-shee own-
doe-gay)

Do you have a thermometer? *Tangshin-un ondo-
gyerul gajigo isumnikka?* (Tahng-sheen-uun own-
doe-gay-rule gah-jee-go ee-ssume-nee-kkah?)

These   *I(gut)dul* (Ee-(gote)-dull)
I'll take both of these. *Nanun igosul dulda kajil-
gopminda.* (Nah-nune ee-go-sule duul-dah kah-
jeel-gope-mee-dah.)   Are these the ones you
wanted to see? *I goshi (tangshini) pogirul wonhan
gushimnikka?* (Ee go-she (tahng-sheen-ee) poe-
ghee-rule wahn-hahn guu-sheem-nee-kkah?)

**They (person)   *Kudul* (Kuu-duul);   People   *Saram-
dul* (Sah-rahm-duul);   Thing   *Kugutul* (Kuu-
gute-tuul)**
Are they going with us? *Kudulun woriwa kachi
kamnika?* (Kuu-duul woe-ree-wah kah-chee
kahm-nee-kkah?)   They said they didn't want to
go. *Kudulun ganeun guteul wonhaji annundago mal-
hasumnida.* (Kuu-duul-uun gah-nuun guu-tay-
ule wohn-hah-jee ahn-nuun-dah-go mahl-hah-
ssume-nee-dah.)

**Thing (object)   *Mulgon* (Muul-goan);   also *Sang-
pum* (Sang-puum);   Immaterial things   *Kot*
(Kote);   Belongings   *Sojipum* (Soc-jee-puum)**
What are these things? *I mulgundulun mwoshimnikka?* (Ee muul-goon-duul-uun mwah-sheem-
nee-kkah?)   Please take my things to my room.
Ne mulgunul ne pange gattu juseyo. (Nay muul-
guu-nuul nay pahn-gay got-tah juu-say-yoe.)

Think   *Saenggakhada* (Sang-gahk-hah-dah)
I think it is going to rain. *Piga olgut katago saenggakhamnida.* (Pee-gah ole-goot gah-tah-go sang-
gahk-hahm-nee-dah.)   What do you think?

217

Mwosul saenggakhamnikka? (Mwah-sule sang-gahk hahm-nee-kkah?)

Thirsty *Mokmarun* **(Moak-mah-ruun)**; also *Kalchung* (Kahl-chuung)
I'm thirsty. *Nanum mogi marumnida.* (Nay-nuum moe-ghee mah-rume-nee-dah.) Are you thirsty? *Mogi marumnikka?* (Moe-ghee mah-rume-nee-kkah?)

This *Igut* **(Ee-gute)**; also *Kum* (Kuum)
This belongs to me. *Igutsun nagushimnida.* (Ee-gute-suun nah-guu-sheem-nee-dah.) Is this yours? *Igutsun tangshin-e gushimnika?* (Ee-gute-suun tahng-sheen-eh guu-sheem-nee-kkah?)

Throat *Mokkumong* **(Moke-kuu-moang)**
My throat is sore. *Nae mogi apumnida.* (Nay moe-ghee ah-pume-nee-dah.)

Ticket *Pyo* **(P'yoe)**; also *Kwon* (K'won); Admission ticket *Ipchang kwon* (Eep-chang k'won); Return ticket *Wangbok chapyo* (Wahng-boak chah-p'yoe); Ticket office *Maepyoso* (May-p'yoe-soe)
Two first-class tickets to Pusan. *Pusan-haeng ildung pyotujang.* (Puu-sahn-hang eel-dung pyoe-tuu-jahng.) Two second-class tickets to Pusan. *Pusan-haeng idung pyotujang.* (Puu-sahn-hang ee-dung pyoe-tuu-jahng.)

Tip (gratuity) *Tip* **(Teep)**; To tip *Tibul chuda* (Tee-buul chuu-dah)
Should I leave a tip? *Tip-ul naya hamnikka?* (Tip-ule nah-yah hahm-nee-kkah?) No, the tip is added to your bill in hotel restaurants. *Anio, i hotel-esunun tibi kyesansoe poham toemnida.* (Ah-nee-yoe, ee hotel-eh-suu-nuun tee-bee kay-sahn-soe-eh poe-hahm tome-nee-dah.)

Tissue paper *Hwajanggi* **(Hwah-jahn-ghee)**
Do you have any tissue paper? *Hwajanggi-ga isumnika?* (Hwah-jahn-ghee-gah ee-ssume-nee-kkah?)

Toast (bread) *Tost* **(Tost);** Salutation *Chukba* (Chuke-bah)
Just coffee and toast, please. *Kopi wa tost chuseyo.* (Koe-pee wah tost chu-say-yoe.)

Today *Onul* **(Oh-nuul)**
What day of the week is today? *Onul musun yoi-limnika?* (Oh-nuul muu-suun yoe-eel eem-nee-kkah?) I'm leaving today for Tokyo. *Onul Tokyo-ro gamnida.* (Oh-nuul Tokyo-roe gahm-nee-dah.)

Together *Hamkke* **(Hahm-kay);** also *Takachi* (Tah-kah-chee); *Modu* (Moe-duu)
Are you all together? *Tangshin-dulun moduga il-hangimnikka?* (Tahng-sheen-duu-luun moe-duu-gah eel-hahng-eem-nee-kkah?) We are together. *Ilhang imnida.* (Eel-hahng eem-nee-dah.)

Toilet *Pyonso* **(P'yone-soe);** Toilet paper *Hyuji* (Hew-jee); Flush toilet *Suseshik pyonso* (Suu-say-sheek p'yone-soe)
Where is the toilet? *Pyonso ga odi imnikka?* (P'yone-soe gah ah-dee eem-nee-kkah?)

Toll road *Yuryo doro* **(Yue-rio doe-roe)**
It is a toll road, so have some money ready. *Yuryo doro imnida, tonul junbi haseyo.* (Yuu-rio doe-roe eem-nee-dah, toe-nuul june-bee hah-say-yoe)

Tomb (grave) *Myo* **(M'yoe)**
Why are there so many tombs in Korea? *Ochchaso Hanguk-enun myoga manumnika?* (Oh-chah-soe, Hahn-gook-eh-nuun myoe-gah mah-nuum-nee-kkah?) They are mostly the tombs of kings or other famous people. *Kudul tabubunun wangkwa*

tarun yumyonghan saram-dul myoimnida. (Kuu-duul tah-buu-buu-nune wahng-kwa tah-rune yume-yoong-hahn sah-rahm-duul myo-eem-nee-dah.)

Tomorrow *Naeil* **(Nay-eel);** Tomorrow morning *Naeil achim* (Nay-eel ah-cheem); Tomorrow evening *Naeil chonyok* (Nay-eel chone-yoke) I am leaving the day after tomorrow. *Nanun naeil more chulbal hamnida.* (Nah-nuun nay-eel moe-ray chuul-gahl hahm-nee-dah.)

Tonight *Onul pam* **(Oh-nuul pahm);** also *Onul chonyok* (Oh-nuul chone yoke) What are your plans for tonight? *Onul pam gye-hoieki mwoshimnikka?* (Oh-nuul pahm gay-hoe-ee-eh-kee mwah-sheem-nee-kkah?) I'd like to see a movie tonight. *Onul pame yonghwa-ul boryugo hamnida.* (Oh-nuul pah-may yong-hwa-ule boe-ryo-go hahm-nee-dah.)

Toothache *Chitong* **(Chee-tong);** Toothbrush *Chissol* (Chee-sole); Toothpaste *Chiyak* (Chee-yahk); Toothpick *Issoshigae* (Ee-soe-she-gay) I have a toothache. *Nanun chitongi itsumnida.* (Nah-nuun chee-tong-ghee eet-ssume-nee-dah.) A toothpick, please. *Isoshigae nana chuseyo.* (Ee-soe-she-gay hah-nah chu-say-yoe.)

Tour *Yuram* **(Yuu-rahm);** Round trip *Kwan-gwang yohang* (Kwahn-gwahng yoe-hang) We want to take a night tour of Seoul. *Urinun Seoul yagyongul pogo shipseumnida.* (Uu-ree-nuun Seoul yah-gyong-ule poe-go sheep-ssume-nee-dah.)

Tourist *Gwangwanggaek* **(Gwahn-gwahng-gake);** Tourist visa *Gwan-gwang pija* (Kwahn-gwhang pee-jah); also *Sachung* (Sah-chuung) Where do we get a tourist visa? *Odiso kwangwang* *pija-rul patseumnika?* (Ah-dee-sah gwahn-gwahng pee-jah-ruul paht-ssume-nee-kkah?) May I see your visa, please? *Pija-rul poyo chuseyo.* (Pee-jah-ruul poe-yoe chu-say-yoe.)

Towel *Tawol* **(Tah-ole);** also *Sogun* (Soe-guun) Please bring some more towels. *Sogun-ul to chuseyo.* (Soe-guun-ule toe chu-say-yoe.)

Traffic (vehicular) *Kyotong* (K'yoe-tong); Traffic signal *Kyotong shinho* (K'yoe-tong sheen-hoe); Traffic accident *Kyotong sago* (K'yoe-tong sah-go) The traffic today is terrible. *Onul kyotongi honja-phamnida.* (Oh-nuul kyo-tong-ghee hoan-jop-hahm-nee-dah.) Be careful of the traffic. *Kyotong choshim haseyo.* (Kyo-tong choe-sheem hah-say-yoe.)

Train *Yolcha* **(Yole-chah);** also *Kicha* (Kee-chah); Express train *Kupaeng yolcha* (Kuu-pang yole-chah)
We want to go to Pusan by train. *Urinun kicharo Pusan-e guryogo hamnida.* (Uu-ree-nuun kee-chah-roe Pusan-eh gah-ryo-go hahm-nee-dah.) Is the train much more expensive than the bus? *Kicha-ga posu-boda to pissamnika?* (Kee-chah-gah pah-suu-boe-dah toe pees-sahm-nee-kkah?)

Transfer (subway, bus or train) *Karatada* **(Kah-rah-tah-dah)**
Do I have to transfer to get to Seoul Station? *Seoul yoge karyomyon karataya hamnika?* (Seoul yoe-gay kah-ryom-yon kah-rah-tah-yah hahm-nee-kkah?) Where do I transfer to go to the Chosun Hotel? *Chosun Hotel-eh karyomon odieso karataya hamnika?* (Choe-suun Hoe-tel-eh kah-ryom-yoan ah-dee-sue kah-rah-tah-yah hahm-nee-kkah?)

Translate *Bonyokhada* **(Bone-yaak-hah-dah);**
Translation *Bonyok* (Bone-yak)
Can you translate this for me? *Igosul bonyok hae chushipshiyo?* (Ee-go-suul bone-yak hay chu-sheep-she-yoe?) How much would you charge to translate this? *Bonyok ryonun olmana toegessumnikka?* (Bone-yak ryo-nuun alh-mah-nah toe-gay-ssume-nee-kkah?)

Travel *Yohaeng* **(Yoe-hang);** To travel *Yohaenghada* (Yoe-hang-hah-dah); Traveler *Yohaengja* (Yoe-hang-jah); Travel bag *Yohaeng kabang* (Yoe-hang kah-bahng); Travel expenses *Yobi* (Yoe-bee)
Are you traveling together? *Kachi yohaeng hamnika?* (Kah-chee yoe-hang hahm-nee-kkah?)
Have you traveled overseas before? *Chone haeoee yohaeng hashin chogi isumnika?* (Choe-nay hay-oh-eh yoe-hang hah-sheen choe-ghee ee-sume-nee-kkah?)

Tree *Namu* **(Nah-muu);** Tree-lined streets *Karosu kil* (Kah-roe-suu keel)
What kind of trees are those? *Igodurun musan namu imnika?* (Ee-go-duu-ruun muu-sune nah-muu eem-nee-kkah?)

Trip *Yohaeng* **(Yoe-hang)**
See travel.

Trousers *Baji* **(Bah-jee)**
Do you want your trousers pressed or cleaned? *Baji-rul tarilkkayo ppalkkayo?* (Bah-jee-rule tah-reel-kah-yoe ppahl-kah-yoe?) The trousers are too long. *Baji-ga nomu kimnida.* (Bah-jee-gah no-muu keem-nee-dah.)

Trout (fish) *Songuh* **(Song-oh)**
Do you have fresh trout? *Singsonhan songo issum-*

nikka? (Sheeng-soan-hahn song-oh ee-ssume-nee-kkah?)

Truck *Turok* **(Tuu-ruk)**
If you are going to drive, be careful of trucks.
Unjonn haltte truck-ul choshim haseyo. (Uun-joan hahl-tay truck-ule choe-sheem hah-say-yoe.)

Tub (for bathing) *Mogyok* **(Moag-yoke)**; Bath-tub *Mogyoktong* (Moag-yoke-tong)
Please fill the bathtub for me. *Mogyok murul pa-duseyo.* (Moag-yoke muu-rule pah-duu-say-yoe.)

Tunnel *Tonol* **(Tu-nole)**
Yes, Korea is very hilly so there are many tun-nels. *Ne, Hanguk-enun ondogi manaso tunnel-i manssumnida.* (Nay, Hahn-gook-eh-nunn own-doe-ghee mah-nah-soe tunnel-ee mahn-ssume-nee-dah.)

Turkey (fowl) *Chilmyonjo* **(Cheel-m'yone-joe)**;
Turkey (country) *Toki* (Toe-kee)
I'd like a turkey sandwich, please. *Turkey sand-wich chuseyo.* (Turkey sandwich chuu-say-yoe.)

Turn (change direction) *Tolda* **(Tole-dah)**
Please turn right at the next corner. *Taum konoeso uhoejun haseyo.* (Tah-uum koe-no-eh-so uu-ho-eh-juun hah-say-yoe.)

Type (write) *Tajahada* **(Tah-jah-hah-dah)**; also *Taipuchida* (Tie-puu-chee-dah); Typewriter *Ta-jagi* (Tah-jah-ghee); also *Taipuraito* (Tie-puu-rie-tah); Typist *Tajasu* (Tah-jah-suu); also *Taipisutu* (Tie-pees-tuu)
Do you know how to type? *Tajachiljul ashimnika?* (Tah-jah-cheel-juul ah-sheem-nee-kkah?) Will you type this for me, please? *Tahal-ul cho chuseyo?* (Tah-jah-ule choe-chu-say-yoe?)

Typhoon   *Taepung* **(Tay-puung)**
Yes, typhoons sometimes strike the southern areas of Korea. *Ne, taepung-un kakkum Hanguk namchokul gangta hamnida.* (Nay, tay-poong-uun kahk-kume Hahn-gook nahm-cho-kuul gahng-tah hahm-nee-dah.)   When is the typhoon season in Korea? *Onjega Hanguk-e-nun taepung-chol imnika?* (Own-jay-gah Hahn-gook-eh-nuun tay-poong-chole eem-nee-kkah?)

U

Ulcer (stomach)   *Wikweyang* **(We-kway-yahng)**
I have a stomach ulcer, so I cannot drink. *Wikweyang ttaemune surul mashilsu opssumnida.* (Wee-kway-yahng ttay-muun-eh suu-rule mah-sheel-suu ahp-ssume-nee-dah.)

Umbrella (for rain)   *Usan* **(Uu-sahn)**
Do you have an umbrella? *Usan issumnikka?* (Uu-sahn ee-ssume-nee-kkah?)   Where can I buy an umbrella? *Odieso usanul salsu issumnikka?* (Ah-dee-eh-sah uu-sahn-ule sahl-suu ee-ssume-nee-kkah?)

Under (beneath)   *Mite* **(Meet-eh)**
My ticket was under your purse. *Nae pyoga tangshin chigap mite issumnida.* (Nay pyoh-gah tahng-sheen chee-gahp meet-eh ee-ssume-nee-dah.)

Underwear   *Sogot* **(Soe-got);**   Undershirt   *Naeui* **(Nay-we)**
I need to buy some more underwear. *Sogotul saya gessumenida.* (Soh-got-ule sah-yah geh-ssume-nee-dah.)

Understand *Alda* **(Ahl-dah);** also *Ihaehada* (Ee-hay-hah-dah)
Do you understand English? *Yongorul ashimnikka?* (Yahng-ah-rule ah-sheem-nee-kkah?) Did you understand me? *Naemarul ihaehasyossumnikka?* (Nay-mah-rule ee-hay-hah-shah-ssume-nee-kkah?) I didn't understand you. *Tangshin-ul ihaehalsu opssumnida.* (Tahng-sheen-ule ee-hay-hahl-suu ap-ssume-nee-dah.) Yes, I understood. *Ne, ihaehamnida.* (Neh, ee-hay-hahm-nee-dah.)

Unique (sole) *Yuirhan* **(Yuu-eer-hahn)**
Is that custom unique to Korea? *Ku pungsupun Hanguk-eso yuilhamnikka?* (Kuu puung-supe-uun Hahn-gook-eh-sah yuu-eel-hahm-nee-kkah?)

United States of America *Amerika Hapchungguk* **(Ah-may-ree-kah Hahp-chuung-gook);** also *Miguk* (Mee-guuk)
Were you born in the United States of America? *Tangshinum Miguk-eso taeonassumnikka?* (Tahng-sheen-uun Mee-gook-eh-sah tay-ah-nah-ssume-nee-kkah?) [or] *Tangshinun Amerika Hapchungguk-eso taeonassumnikka?* (Tahng-sheen-uun Ah-meh-ree-kah Hahp-chuung-gook-eh sah tay-ah-nah-ssume-nee-kkah?)

University *Taehakkyo* **(Tay-hahk-yoe);** University hospital *Taehak pyongwon* (Tay-hahk p'yong-won)
Are you still attending the university? *Ajik Taehakkyoe tanishimnikka?* (Ah-jeek tah-hahk-kyoh-eh tah-nee-sheem-nee-kkah?) What university do you go to? *Onu taehakkyoe tanishimnikka?* (Ah-nuu tay-hahk-kyoh-eh tah-nee-sheem-nee-kkah?) I attended a state university. *Churip taehakkyoe tanimnida.* (Chuu-reep tay-hahk-kyoh-eh tahn-eem-nee-dah.)

Unpack *Pulda* **(Puul-dah)**
I haven't unpacked yet. *Nanun ajik mot purossum-nida.* (Nah-nune ah-jeek moht puu-rah-ssume-nee-dah.)

Unpaved *Pojanghaji anun* **(Poh-jahng-hah-jee ah-nuun);** also *Pipojang* (Pee-poh-jahng)
The street is unpaved. *Ku toronun pojangdoeji an-assumnida.* (Kuu toh-roh-nune poh-jahng-doe-jee ahn-ah-ssume-nee-dah.)

Unsafe *Wihomhan* **(We-home-hahn)**
Walking around at night is unsafe in some areas. *Otton chiyokesonun yagan sanchaegi wihomhamnida.* (Ah-ttahn chee-yak-eh-sah-nune yah-gahn sahn-chay-ghee wee-hahm-hahm-nee-dah.)

Usher (theater, etc.) *Annaein* **(Ahn-nay-een)**
The usher will show you to your seats. *Annaeini tangshinui chwasogul annaehalgoshimnida.* (Ahn-nay-een-ee tahng-sheen-we chwah-sah-guul ahn-nay-hahl-gah-sheem-nee-dah.)

V

Vacancy (unoccupied room) *Pinbang* **(Peen-bahng)**
Do you have any vacancies? *Pinbangi issumnikka?* (Peen-bahng-ee ee-sume-nee-kkah?)

Vacation *Hyuga* **(Hew-gah)**
Are you on vacation now? *Chigum hyugachung imnikka?* (Chee-gume hew-gah chuung eem-nee-kkah?) Where did you go for vacation last year? *Chaknyone hyugachung odie kassossumnikka?* (Chahk-nyahn-ah hew-gah-chuung ah-dee-eh kah-ssah-ssume-nee-kkah?)

Vaccination *Chongdu* **(Chong-duu);** Vaccination certificate *Chongdu chopchong* (Chong-duu chop-choeng)
Do you have a vaccination certificate? *Chongdu chopchong chungmyongso issumnikka?* (Chohng-duu chahp-chohng chung-mayahng-sah ee-ssume-nee-kkah?) May I see your vaccination certificate, please? *Chongdu chopchong chungmyongsorul poyo chushio?* (Chong-duu chop-choeng chuung-m'yong-soe-ruul poe-yoe chuu-she-oh?)

Valid (good for) *Yuhyohan* **(Yuu-h'yoe-hahn)**
This visa is valid for three months. *I pijanun sam kaewolgan yuhyohamnida.* (Ee pee-jah-nune sahm kay-wole-gahn yuu-h'yoe-hahm-nee-dah.)

Valuables *Kwijungpum* **(Kwee-juung-puum);**
also *Kachiinnun* (Kah-chee-een-nune)
Please put your valuables in the hotel safe. *Kwijungpumun hotel kumgoe pokwan hashipshio.* (Kwee-juung-puum-uun hoh-tel kume-goh-eh poh-kwahn hah-sheep-shee-oh.)

Value (worth) *Kachi* **(Kah-chee);** Price *Kap* (Kahp)
What is the value of this brass bed? *I kumsok chimdae-e kachinun mwoshimnikka?* (Ee kume-soak cheem-day-ee kah-chee-nune mwah-sheem-nee-kkah?)

Vase *Pyong* **(P'yong);** Flower vase *Kkot pyong* (Kote p'yong)
I am looking for a small flower vase. *Chagun kkotpyongul chakko issumnida.* (Chah-gune kote-pyong-ule chah-kkoh ee-ssume-nee-dah.)

Veal *Songaji kogi* **(Sohng-ah-jee koh-gee)**
I'll have veal, please. *Songaji kogirul chushipshio.* (Sohng-ah-jee koh-ghee-rule chuu-sheep-shee-oh.)

Vegetables *Chaeso* **(Chay-soe);** also *yachae* (Yah-chay); Green vegetables *Pusonggi* (Puu-song-ghee); Vegetable dish *Yachae yori* (Yah-chay yoe-ree)
Let's have a vegetable dish and some noodles. *Yachae yoriwa myonjom chushipshio.* (Yah-chay yoh-ree-wah myahn-johm chuu-sheep-shee-oh.)

Vegetarian *Chaeshikchuuija* **(Chay-sheek-chuu-we-jah)**
I am a vegetarian. *Nanun chaeshik chuuija imnida.* (Nah-nune chay-sheek-chuu-we-jah eem-nee-dah.) Please bring me vegetarian dishes. *Yachae yorirul chushipshio. (Yah-chay-yoh-ree-rule chuu-sheep-shee-oh.)*

Vending machine *Chadong panmaegi* **(Chah-dong pahn-may-ghee)**
There are soft drink vending machines on all floors. *Modun chungmada umnyosu chadong panmaegiga issumnida.* (Moh-dune chung-mah-dah uum-nyoh-suu chah-dong pahn-may-ghee-gah ee-ssume-nee-da.)

Veranda *Peranda* **(Pay-rahn-dah)**
All rooms have verandas. *Modun pange perandaga issumnida.* (Moh-dune pahng-eh pay-rahn-dah-gah ee-ssume-nee-dah.)

Very much *Maeu* **(May-uu);** Very little *Aju chogun* (Ah-juu choe-guun); Very good *Taedani* (Tay-dahn-ee)
I like it very much. *Nanun kugosul maeu choahamnida.* (Nah-nune kuu-gah-sule may-uu choh-ah-hahm-nee-dah.)

Vest (waistcoat) *Chokki* **(Tchoke-kee)**
You look very good in a vest. *Chokkiga oullimnida.* (Choke-kee-gah ah-uul-leem-nee-dah.)

Via Tokyo *Tokyo-rul kyongyuhayo* (Tokyo-ruul k'yong-yuu-hah-yoe)
I am returning via Honolulu. *Honolulurul kyongyuhayo toragamnida.* (Honolulu-rule kyahng-yuu-hah-yah toh-rah-gahm-nee-dah.)

Vicinity *Kuncho* (Kuun-choe)
Is there a theater in this vicinity? *I kunchoe kukchangi issumnidda?* (Ee-kune-choe-eh kook-chahng-ee ee-ssume-nee-kkah?)

View (scenery) *Kyongchi* (K'yong-chee); Sight *Chonmang* (Chone-mahng)
The view from here is fantastic. *Yogi Kyongchiga hullyunghamnida.* (Yah-ghee kyahng-chee-gah huul-lyuung-hahm-nee-dah.) Do the hotel rooms have a view? *Hotel pangun kyongchiga issumnikka?* (Hoh-tel pahng-uun kyahng-chee-ga ee-ssume-nee-kkah?)

Village *Maul* (Mah-ule); Villagers *Maul saram* (Mah-ule sah-rahm)
I was born in a mountain village. *Nanun sanchoneso taeonassumnida.* (Nah-nune sahn-chohn-eh-sah tay-ah-nah-ssume-nee-dah.) We will pass through several villages. *Urinun yoro maulul tonggwahamnida.* (Uu-ree-nune yah-rah mah-ule-ule tohng-gwah-hahm-nee-dah.)

Vinegar *Cho* (Choe); also *Shikcho* (Sheek-choe)
I'd like vinegar on my salad. *Sarada-e shikchorul chojuseyo.* (Sah-rah-dah-eh sheek-choh-rule chah-juu-say-yoe.)

Visa *Sachung* (Sah-chuung); also *Pija* (Pee-jah); Entry visa *Ipkuk sachung* (Eep-kook sah-chuung); Exit visa *Chulguk sachung* (Chule-gook sah-chuung)
May I see your visa, please? *Pijarul poyojushil-*

kkayo? (Pee-jah-rule poh-yoe-juu-sheel-kkah-yoe?)   Where do I go to get my visa extended? *Odiso pija yungireul hamnika?* (Ah-dee-soe pee-jah yuung-ee-rule hahm-nee-kkah?)

Vocabulary (words known)   *Ohwi* **(Oh-wee)**
My vocabulary of Korean words is small. *Nae Hanguk ohwiga pujok hamnida.* (Nay Hahn-gook oh-we-gah puu-joak hahm-nee-dah.)

Volcano   *Hwasan* **(Whah-sahn)**
Are there many active volcanoes in Korea? *Hanguk-e-neun hwal hwasani manseumnika?* (Hahn-gook-eh-nay-uun hwahl-hwah-sahn-ee mahn-sume-nee-kkah?)

Vomit   *Tohada* **(Toe-hah-da);**   also *Kuto* (Kuu-tah)
I vomited last night and this morning. *Oje pamkwa onul achime tohaesumnida.* (Uu-jay bahm-kwah oh-nule ah-chee-may toe-hay-sume-nee-dah.)

Voyage   *Hanghae* **(Hahng-hay)**
Are you on a round-the-world voyage? *Segye hanghae-ul hashimnika?* (Say-gay hahng-hay-ule hah-sheem-nee-kkah?)

W

Wages   *Imgum* **(Eem-guum);**   Basic wages   *Kibon imgum* (Kee-bone eem-guum); Pay   *Kumnyo* (Kuum-n'yoe)
Do you receive a raise in wages every year? *Maenyon insangtoen imgumul passumnikka?* (May-nyahn een-sahng-toe-een eem-gume-ule pah-ssume-nee-kkah?)

Wait *Kidarida* **(Kee-dah-ree-dah)**
Please wait a minute. *Chamshi kidarryo chuship-shio.* (Chahm-she kee-dah-ryo chuu sheep-she-oh.) Please wait here. *Yogiso kidari shipshio.* (Yoe-ghee-soe kee-dah-ree sheep-she-oh.) I'm waiting for Mr. Lee. *Lee Sonsaengnim-ul kidarigo issumnida.* (Lee Sahng-sang-neem-ule kee-dah-ree-goh ee-ssume-nee-dah.) How long have you been waiting? *Olmana kidaryo ssumnikka?* (Ole-mah-nah kee-dah-rio sume-nee-kkah?) I'm sorry to have kept you waiting. *Tangshin-ul kidarigehaeso mianhamnida.* (Tahng-sheen-ule kee-dah-ree-gay-hay-sah mee-ahn-hahm-nee-dah.)

Waiter *Kupsa* **(Kuup-sah);** also *Weita* (Way-tah)

Waiting room *Taehap shil* **(Tay-hahp sheel)**
I'll meet you in the waiting room. *Taehapshileso manna poepgessumnida.* (Tay-hahp-sheel-eh-sah mahn-nah pep-gay-ssume-nee-dah.)

Waitress *Yogup* **(Yoe-guup);** also *weituresu* (Way-tuu-ress)
Please call a waitress. *Yogupul pullo chushipshio.* (Yah-gupe-ule puul-lah chuu-sheep-shee-oh.)

Wake *Kkaeda* **(Kay-da)**
What time shall I wake you? *Myoshie kkaewo durilkkayo?* (Myah-she-eh kay-wah duu-reel-kkah-yoh?) Please wake me at six o'clock. *Yososhie kkaewo chushipshio.* (Yah-sah-shee-eh kay-wah chuu-sheep-she-oh.)

Walk (stroll) *Sanchaek* **(Sahn-chake);** also *Sanpo* (Sahn-poe); Go on foot *kotta* (Kote-tah); Going on foot *Tobo* (Toe-boe)
Let's take a walk after dinner. *Shiksa hue sanchaek hapshida.* (Sheek-sah huu-eh sahn-chake hahp-

shee-dah.)   It is only a five-minute walk. *Goroso o bun gollimnida.* (goh-roh-soe oh-buun goh-leem-nee-dah.)

Wallet (pocketbook)   *Chigap* **(Chee-gahp)**
I can't find my wallet. *Nae chigapul mochage-ssunmnida.* (Nay chee-gah-puul moh-chah-gay-ssume-nee-dah.)

Want   *Piryo* **(Pee-rio);**   Desire   *Parada* (Pah-rah-dah);   Need   *Ul piryoro hada* (Uul pee-rio-roe hah-dah)
What do you want? *Mwoshi piryo hamnikka?* (Mwah-she pee-ryoh hahm-nee-kkah?)   I want to go with you. *Tangshing-wa kachi kago shipssum-nida.* (Tahng-sheen-wah kah-chee kah-goh sheep-ssume-nee-dah.)   Is this what you want? *Igoshi tangshini piryoro hanungoshimnikka?* (Ee-gah-shee tahng-sheen-ee pee-ryoh-roh hah-nune-gah-sheem-nee-kkah?)

Warm   *Ttattutan* **(Taht-tuu-tahn)**
Are you warm enough? *Chungbuni ttattutam-nikka?* (Chuung-buun-ee ttah-ttuu-tahm-nee-kkah?)   It is going to be warm today. *Onurun nalshiga ttattutamnida.* (Oh-nuu-rune nahl-she-gah ttah-ttuu-tahm-nee-dah.)

Wash (cleanse)   *Ssita* **(She-tah);**   also *Setakhada* (Say-tahk-hah-dah); Washable   *Ppal su innun* (Pal suu een-nuun)
I need to wash my hands. *Sonul sshitko shipssum-nida.* (Sohn-ule sheet-koe sheep-ssume-nee-dah.)   Would you like to wash your hands before dinner? *Shiksachone sonul shisushipshio?* (Sheek-sah-chahn-eh sohn-ule she-sue-sheep-shee-oh?)   Is this washable? *Igosun ppalsu issum-nikka?* (Ee-gah-sune ppahl-suu ee-ssume-nee-kkah?)

Washroom (restroom) *Hwajangshil* **(Hwah-jahng-sheel)**
Where is the restroom? *Hwajangshirun odi mnikka?* (Hwah-jahng-she-ruun ah-dee eem-nee-kkah?)

Watch (timepiece) *Shigye* **(She-gay)**
Do you have a watch? *Shigye issumnikka?* (She-gay ee-ssume-nee-kkah?)

Water *Mul* **(Muul)**; Hot water *Toun mul* (Toe-uun muul); Cold water *Naengsu* (Nang-suu)
May I have a glass of water, please? *Mul hanjan chuseyo.* (Muul hahn-jahn chuu-say-yoe.)

Waterfall *Pokpo* **(Poak-poe)**

Watermelon *Subak* **(Suu-bahk)**
Would you like some watermelon? *Subak tushigessumnikka?* (Suu-bahk tuu-she-gay-ssume-nee-kkah?)

Way (direction) *Panghyang* **(Pahng-hyahng)**
Please show me the way to the subway station. *Chihachol yoke kanun panghyangul karuchyo chuship-shio.* (Chee-hah-chahl yah-keh kah-nune pahng-kyahng-ule kah-rue-chah chuu-sheep-shee-oh.)
Is this the right way to Seoul Station? *Igoshi Seoul Yok kanun parun panghyang imnikka?* (Ee-gah-shee Seoul Yahk kah-nune pah-rune pahng-hyahng eem-nee-kkah?)

Wealthy man *Puja* **(Puu-jah)**
Many wealthy men live in this area. *Manun puja-duri ichiyoke salgo issumnida.* (Mah-nune puu-jah-due-ree ee-chee-yahk-eh sahl-goh ee-ssume-nee-dah.)

Weather *Nalssi* **(Nahl-she)**; also *Ilgi* **(Eel-ghee)**;
Fine weather *Choun nalssi* (Choe-uun nahl-she);

Cloudy weather *Hurin nalssi* (Huu-reen nahl-she)
The weather is fine today. *Oneul nalshiga joseum-nida.* (Oh-nay-ule nahl-she-gah joe-say-umm-nee-dah.) What is the weather going to be like tomorrow? *Nail nalssiga ottolkkayo?* (Nah-eel nahl-she-gah aht-tahl-kkah-yoe?)

Wedding *Kyoron* **(Kyoe-yone);** Wedding anniversary *Kyohon kinyomil* (Kyoe-yone keen-yoe-meel)
Are spring weddings popular in Korea? *Hanguk-e-neun bome kyuhoneul mani hamnika?* (Hahn-gook-eh-nay-uun bahm-eh k'yur-hone-ule mah-nee hahm-nee-kkah?)

Week *Chu* **(Chuu);** also *Chugan* (Chuu-gahn); Every week *Mae ju* (May juu); Last week *Chinan ju* (Chee-nahn juu); Next week *Taum chu* (Tah-uum chuu); This week *Ibon chu* (Ee-bone chuu); Weekend *Chumal* (Chuu-mahl)
I will be here for one week. *Hanju tongan yogie momumnida.* (Hahn-chu toe-gahn yoe-ghee-eh moe-muum-nee-dah.) I want to go to Pusan this weekend. *I bun chu-male Pusan-e karyomnida.* (Eee buun chu-mah-lay Puu-sahn-eh kah-ryom-nee-dah.)

Weigh (determine weight) *Mugerul talda* **(Muu-gay-ruul tahl-dah);** Weight *Muge* (Muu-gay)
Please weigh this package. *I sopo mugerul daseyo.* (Ee soe-poe muu-gay-ruul dah-say-yoe.) How much does it weigh? *Mugega ulmana nagamnika?* (Muu-gay-gah ule-mah-nah nah-gahm-nee-kkah?)

Welcome! (greeting) *Oso oshipshio!* **(Oh-soe oh-sheep-she-oh!)**

West *Sotchok* **(Soe-chock)**
It's just five minutes west of here. *Yugiso sotchok-euro obun guri imnida.* (Yuu-ghee-soe soe-chock-uu-roe oh-buun guu-ree eem-nec-dah.)

What *Muot* **(Muu-aht);** also *Musan* (Muu-sahn); *Otton* (aht-tahn)
What is this? *I goshi mout imnikka?* (Ee go-she muu-aht eem-nee-kkah?) What time is it? *Muot-shi imnika?* (Muu-aht-she eem-nee-kkah?) What can I do for you? *Muot-ele dowa deurilkayo?* Muu-aht-ule doe-wah day-reel-kah-yoe?) What would you like? *Muot-eul wonhamnika?* (Muu-aht-ule wahn-hahm-nee-kkah?) What? *Muot?* (Muu-aht?)

When (at what time) *Onje* **(Own-jay)**
When are you going? *Onje gashimnikku?* (Own-jay gah-sheem-nee-kkah?) When will he be back? *Onje dora oshimnika?* (Own-jay doe-rah oh-sheem-nee-kkah?) When can you have it done? *Onje kaji hulsu itseumnika?* (Own-jay kah-jee hahl-suu eet-sume-nee-kkah?)

Where *Odiso* **(Ah-dee-soe);** In what place *Odie* (Ah-dee-eh); To which place *Odiro* (Ah-dee-roe)
Where do you want to go? *Odi kogirul wonham-nikka?* (Ah-dee koe-ghee-ruul wahn-hahm-nee-kkah?) Where are you going? *Odi gashimnikka?* (Ah-dee gah-sheem-nee-kkah?) Where is it? *Odie itseumnikka?* (Ah-dee-eh eet-sume-nee-kkah?)

Which *Onu kot* **(Oh-nuu kote)**
Which do you want? *Onu kot-eul wonhamnikka?* (Oh-nuu kote-ule wahn-hahm-nee-kkah?) Which one is better? *Onu koshi to chosumnikka?* (Oh-nuu koe-she toe choe-sume-nee-kkah?)

While (period of time) *Tongan* **(Tone-gahn);**
Short period *Chamshi* (Chahm-she); A while
ago *Chogum chone* (Choe-guum choe-nay)
I saw him just a little while ago. *Kurul chogum
chone boat seumnida.* (Kuu-ruul choe-guum choe-
nay boe-aht sume-nee-dah.) I am staying only a
little while. *Chamshi tongan-man mumo reumnida.*
(Cham-she tone-gahn-mahn muu-moe ray-uum-
nee-dah.)

Whisky *Wisuki* **(Wees-kee)**
I'll have a whisky and soda, please. *Whisky-wa
soda-rul chuseyo.* (Whisky wah soda-rule chu-say-
yoe.)

White *Hin* **(Heen);** White wine *Paek podoju*
(Pake poe-doe-juu)
A glass of white wine, please. *Paek podoju-ul chu-
seyo.* (Pake poe-doe-juu-ule chu-say-yoe.)

Who *Nugu* **(Nuu-guu);** also *Nuga* (Nuu-gah)
Who is in charge? *Nuga chaekimja imnika?* (Nuu-
gah chake-eem-jah eem-nee-kkah?) Who did
you wish to see? *Nugu-rul poshilkayo?* (Nuu-guu-
ruul poe-sheel kah-yoe?) Who would like to
have a snack? *Nuga ganshik-ul wonhamnikka?*
(Nuu-gah gahn-sheek-ule wahn-hahm-nee
kkah?)

Wholesale *Tomae* **(Toe-may);** also *Tomae-e* (Toe-
may-eh); Wholesaler *Tomae sangin* (Toe-may
sahn-gheen)
Can I buy it at a wholesale price? *Kugosul tomae-
gapse salsu isumnika?* (Kuu-go-sule toe-may gahp-
say sahl-suu ee-sume-nee-kkah?) This is the
wholesale price. *Koshi tomae kapshiminida.* (Ko-she
toe-may kahp-sheem-nee-dah.)

Whose *Nugu-e* **(Nuu-guu-eh)**
Whose coat is this? *Nugu kotu imnikka?* (Nuu-guu

koe-tuu eem-nee-kkah?)   Whose bag is this?
Nugu bag imnikka? (Nuu-guu bag eem-nee-
kkah?)   Whose is this? *Nugu koshimnikku?* (Nuu-
guu koe-sheem-nee-kkah?)

Why   *Wae* (Way)
Why is the train late? *Wae kichaga nujossumnikka?*
(Way kee-chah-gah nuu-joe-sume-nee-kkah?)
Why are we waiting? *Wae wuriga kidarimnika?*
(Way wuu-ree-gah kee-dah-reem-nee-kkah?)
Why don't you try this? *Wae igosul haeboji anseum-
nika?* (Way ee-go-sule hay-boe-jee ahn-say-uum-
nee-kkah?)

Wife   *Anae* (Ah-nay);   also *Cho* (Choe);   My wife
Che anae (Chay-ah-nay);   Your or his wife   *Puin*
(Puu-een)
This is my wife. *Che anae imnida.* (Chay ah-nay
eem-nee-dah)   Please bring your wife with you.
Puin kwa hamkke oshipshiyo. (Puu-een kwah
hahm-kay oh-sheep-she-yoe.)

Wind   *Param* (Pah-rahm);   Windy   *Param punun*
(Pah-rahm puu-nuun)
It is windy today. *Onurun parami semnida.* (Oh-
nuu-ruun pah-rah-mee same-nee-dah.)   The
wind is cold. *Param-i chamnida.* (Pah-rahm-ee
chahm-nee-dah.)

Window   *Chang* (Chahng);   also *Changmun*
(Chahng-muun)
Please close the window. *Changmun-ul toduseyo.*
(Chang-muun-ule toe-duu-say-yoe.)   I would
like a window seat. *Nanun changa-e angoshipsum-
nida.* (Nah-nune chang-gah-eh ahn-go-sheep-
sume-nee-dah.)

Wine (from grapes)   *Podoju* (Poe-doe-juu);   Wine
from rice   *Sul* (Suul);   Red wine   *Ppalgan podoju*

(Ppahl-gahn poe-doe-juu); White wine *Paek podoju*
(Pake poe-doe-juu)
Would you like red or white wine? *Ppalgan po-doju-rul wonhaseyo? Paek podoju-rul wonhaseyo?*
(Ppahl-gahn poe-doe-juu-ruul wahn-hah-say-yoe? Pake poe-doe-juu-ruul wahn-hah-say-yoe?)
A glass of white wine, please. *Paek podoju hanjan chuseyo.* (Pake poe-doe-juu hahn-jahn chu-say-yoe.)

Winter *Kyoul* **(K'yoe-uul);** Winter weather *Kyoul nalssi* (K'yoe-uul nahl-she); Winter season *Kyoul chol* (K'yoe-uul chole)
Is the winter season a good time to visit Seoul? *Kyoul chule Seoul-ul kanun goshi ottosumnikka?* (K'yoe-uul chuu-lay Seoul-ule kah-nune go-she aht-tah-sume-nee-kkah?) It can be very cold in winter. *Kyoul-e-nun maeu chusumnida.* (K'yoe-uul-eh-nune may-uu chu-sume-nee-dah.)

With (together) *Wa hamkke* **(Wah hahm-kay)**
Please come with me. *Na wa hamkke kaseyo.* (Nah wah hahm-kay kah-say-yoe.) Take it with you. *Kugosul kajiseyo.* (Kuu-go-sule kah-jee-say-yoe.)

Woman *Yoja* **(Yoe-jah);** also *Yoin* (Yoe-een); Honorific *Puin* (Puu-een); Businesswoman *Chigop yosong* (Chee-gope yoe-song)
Will all of the women please come this way. *Modun yojadurun irio oseyo.* (Moe-dune yoe-jah-duu-rune ee-ree-oh oh-say-yoe.) She is a well-known woman. *Kunyonun yumyonghan yojaimnida.* (Kune-yoe-nune yume-yong-hahn yoe-jah-eem-nee-dah.)

Wool (sheep) *Yang mo* **(Yahng-moe);** Woolen cloth *Nasa* (Nah-sah); All wool *Sunmo* (Suun-moe)

Is this sweater all wool? *I seta-un sonmo imnika?*
(Ee say-tah-uun soan-moe eem-nee-kkah?)

World (earth) *Segye* **(Say-gay);** Society *Sesang*
(Say-sang)
It really is a small world, isn't it? *Sesang cham
chopseumnida.* (Say-sahng chahm chop-sume-nee-
dah.)

Worry (anxiety) *Kokchong* **(Koke-chong)**
What are you worried about? *Mwal kokchong hashimnika?* (Mwahl koke-chong hah-sheem-nee-
kkah?) Please don't worry. *Kokchong haji maseyo.*
(Koke-chong hah-jee mah-say-yoe.)

Wrapping paper *Pojang ji* **(Poe-jahng jee)**
Please wrap it for shipping overseas. *Haeoero po-
chige pojang haseyo.* (Hay-oh-eh-roe poe-chee-gay
poe-jahng hah-say-yoe.)

Write *Ssuda* **(Suu-dah)**
Please write your name and address here.
Irumkwa chusorul ssuseyo. (Ee-rume-kwah chu-
soe-ruul sue-say-yoe.) Please write down what
you want. *Mwosul wonhanunji ssuseyo.* (Mwah-
sule wahn-hahn-unn-jee sue-say-yoe.)

Writer (author) *Choja* **(Choe-jah);** Novelist
Chakka (Choek-kah); Journalist *Kija* (Kee-jah);
Fiction writer *Chang jakka* (Chalng jahk-kah)
He is a well-known writer. *Kunun yumyonghan
chakka imnida.* (Kuu-nune yume-yohng-hahn
chock-kah eem-nee-dah.) That lady is a popular
novelist. *Kunyonun inkki chakka imnida.* (Kuu-nyo-
nune een-kee chock-kah eem-nee-dah.)

Written application *Shinchong so* **(Sheen-chong-
soe);** Written guarantee *Pojung so* (Poe-juung
soe)

You must fill out a written application. *Shinchong so-rul chaksung haeyaman hamnida.* (Sheen-chong soe-ruul chahk-suung hay-yah-mahn hahm-nee-dah.) This is your written guarantee. *I goshi po-jung so imnida.* (Ee go-she poe-juung soe eem-nee-dah.)

Wrong *Nappun* **(Nahp-poon);** also *Chalmot* (Chahl-moat)
You are wrong. *Tangshin-e chalmoshimnida.* (Tahng-sheen-eh chahl-moe-sheem-nee-dah.) These figures are wrong. *I sujanun chalmoshimnida.* (Ee suu-ja-nunn chahl-moe-sheem-nee-dah.) You are on the wrong train. *Tangshin-un kicha-rul chalmot tatsumnida.* (Tahng-sheen-uun kee-chah-ruul chahl-moat tot-sume-nee-dah.)

X

X-mas **Kurisumasu (Kuu-ree-su-mah-su)**
Do you celebrate Christmas in Korea? *Hanguk-eso Kurisumasu-rul chukha hamnikka?* (Hahn-gook-eh-soe Kuu-ree-su-mah-su-ruul chuuk-hah hahm-nee-kkah?)

X-ray *Aeksusone* **(Ayk-sue-soe-nay);** X-ray examination *Aeksusone komsa* (Ayk-sue-soan kahm-sah)
I would like to have my ankle x-rayed. *Palmoge aeksusone komsarul patko shipssumnida.* (Pahl-moh-geh ayk-sue-soe-nay kahm-sah-ruul paht-koh sheep-ssume-ne-dah.)

Y

Yacht *Yotu* **(Yoe-tuu);** Yacht race *Yotu kyongju* (Yoe-tuu k'yong-juu)
There is going to be a yacht race today. *Onul yotu kyongjuga yolril yejong imnida.* (Oh-nule yoh-tuu kyahng-juu-gah yahl-reel yah-jahng eem-nee-dah.)

Yard (garden) *Madang* **(Mah-dahng);** Yard (measure) *Yadu* (Yah-duu)
How many yards do I need for a suit? *Yangbok hanbore myot yardga pilryo hamnikka?* (Yahng-bohk hahn-bah-ray myaht yah-due-gah peel-ryoh hahm-nee-kkah?)

Year *Hae* **(Hay);** Every year *Mae nyon* (May n'yone); Next year *Nae nyon* (Nay n'yone); Last year *Chinan hae* (Chee-nahn hay)
I am going to Korea next year. *Nae nyone Hanguk-e gal yejong imnida.* (Nay-nyahn-eh Hahn-gook-eh gahl yeh-jahng eem-nee-dah.)

Yellow *Noran* **(Noh-rahn)**
Do you have this in yellow? *Noran goshi issumnikka?* (Noh-rahn-gah-shee eem-ssume-nee-kkah?)

Yesterday *Oje* **(Ah-jay);** Yesterday morning *Oje achim* (Ah-jay ah-cheem)
I arrived yesterday morning. *Oje achime tochak haessumnida.* (Ah-jeh ah-cheem-eh toh-chahk hay-ssume-nee-dah.) Did you go to the Korean Village yesterday? *Oje Hanguk Minsok chone kassumnikka?* (Ah-jeh Hahn-gook Meen-sohk chohn-eh kah-ssume-nee-kkah?)

Yolk (egg) *Norunjawi* **(No-ruun-jah-we)**
Please fry it until the yolk is hard. *Norunjawaiga kudul ttaekkaji twigyo chuseyo.* (Noh-rune-jah-wee-gah kuud-uul tay-kkah-jee twee-gyah chuu-say-yoe.)

You *Tangshin* **(Tahng-sheen);** also *Taek* (Take); Plural *Tangshingdul* (Tahng-sheen-duul)
Are you going? *Tangshinun kamnikka?* (Tahng-sheen-uun kahm-nee-kkah?)

Young *Cholmun* **(Chole-muun)**
She looks like a young woman. *Kunyonun cholmun yoja kachi poimnida.* (Kuu-nyah-nune chole-muun yah-jah kah-chee poh-eem-nee-dah.) You look young for your age. *Tangshin naie pihaeso cholmo poimnida.* (Tahng-sheen nah-ee-eh pee-hay-sah chole-mah poh-eem-nee-dah.)

Your *Tangshin-e* **(Tahng-sheen-eh);** Plural *Tangshindurui* (Tahng-sheen-duur-we)
Is this your magazine? *Igosun tangshin-e chapji imnikka?* (Ee-goh-sune tahng-sheen-eh chahp-jee eem-nee-kkah?) Is this yours? *Igosun tangshin-e goshimnikka?* (Ee-gah-sune tahng-sheen-eh gah-sheem-nee-kkah?)

Yourself *Tangshin chashin* **(Tahng-sheen chah-sheen)**
Are you going by yourself? *Tangshin honja kashimnikka?* (Tahng-sheen hohn-jah kah-sheem-nee-kkah?) Are you by yourself? *Tangshin honja shimnikka?* (Tahng-sheen hohn-jah sheem-nee-kkah?)

Z

Zero *Yong* **(Yong);** also *Chero* (Che-roe)
Did the temperature reach zero last night? *Chinanpam ondoga yongjomkkaji naeryo kassumnikka?* (Chee-nahn-pahn ohn-doh-gah yahng-jahm-kkah-jee nay-ryah kah-ssume-nee-kkah?) It is twenty degrees above zero now. *Chigum yongsang hwashi ishipdo imnida.* (Chee-gume yahng-sahng hwah-she ee-sheep-doh eem-nee-dah.)

Zipper *Chaku* **(Chah-kuu);** also *Chipa* (Chee-pah)
My zipper is stuck. *Nae chaku ga kojong toeossumnida.* (Nay chah-kuu gah koe-johng toe-sume-nee-dah.) Your zipper is open. *Chaku ga yollyo issumnida.* (Chah-kuu gah yahl-lyah ee-sume-nee-dah.)

Zone (region) *Chidae* **(Chee-day);** also *Kuyok* (Kuu-yahk)
This is a restricted zone. *Igosun chehan chidae* [or] *kuyok imnida.* (Ee-goh-suen cheh-hahn-chee-dae [or] kuu-yahk eem-nee-dah.)

Zoo *Tongmurwon* **(Tong-murr-woan)**
Today is a good day to go to the zoo. *Onurun tongmurwon kagie choun nalshi imnida.* (Oh-nuu-rune tohng-muur-won kah-ghee-eh choh-uun nahl-she eem-nee-dah.)

CHANGING FAHRENHEIT TO CENTIGRADE

Fahrenheit		Centigrade
0	=	-18
14	=	-10
23	=	-5
32 (freezing)		0
41	=	5
50	=	10
59	=	15
68	=	20
77	=	25
86	=	30
98.6 (body temp.)		37
104	=	40
122	=	50
212 (boiling)		100

FOREIGN LANGUAGE BOOKS

Multilingual
The Insult Dictionary:
How to Give 'Em Hell in 5 Nasty
Languages
The Lover's Dictionary:
How to be Amorous in 5 Delectable
Languages
Multilingual Phrase Book
Let's Drive Europe Phrasebook
CD-ROM "Languages of the World":
Multilingual Dictionary Database

Spanish
Vox Spanish and English Dictionaries
NTC's Dictionary of Spanish False Cognates
Nice 'n Easy Spanish Grammar
Spanish Verbs and Essentials of Grammar
Getting Started in Spanish
Spanish à la Cartoon
Guide to Spanish Idioms
Guide to Correspondence in Spanish
The Hispanic Way

French
NTC's New College French and English
Dictionary
French Verbs and Essentials of Grammar
Real French
Getting Started in French
Guide to French Idioms
Guide to Correspondence in French
French à la Cartoon
Nice 'n Easy French Grammar
NTC's Dictionary of *Faux Amis*
NTC's Dictionary of Canadian French
Au courant: Expressions for Communicating in
Everyday French

German
Schöffler-Weis German and English Dictionary
Klett German and English Dictionary
Getting Started in German
German Verbs and Essentials of Grammar
Guide to German Idioms
Street-wise German
Nice 'n Easy German Grammar
German à la Cartoon
NTC's Dictionary of German False Cognates

Italian
Zanichelli Super-Mini Italian and English
Dictionary
Zanichelli New College Italian and English
Dictionary
Getting Started in Italian
Italian Verbs and Essentials of Grammar

Greek
NTC's New College Greek and English
Dictionary
Latin
Essentials of Latin Grammar
Hebrew
Everyday Hebrew
Chinese
Easy Chinese Phrasebook and Dictionary
Korean
Korean in Plain English
Polish
The Wiedza Powszechna Compact Polish and
English Dictionary
Swedish
Swedish Verbs and Essentials of Grammar
Russian
Complete Handbook of Russian Verbs
Essentials of Russian Grammar
Business Russian
Basic Structure Practice in Russian

Japanese
Easy Kana Workbook
Easy Hiragana
Easy Katakana
101 Japanese Idioms
Japanese in Plain English
Everyday Japanese
Japanese for Children
Japanese Cultural Encounters
Nissan's Business Japanese

"Just Enough" Phrase Books
Chinese, Dutch, French, German, Greek,
Hebrew, Hungarian, Italian, Japanese,
Portuguese, Russian, Scandinavian,
Serbo-Croat, Spanish
Business French, Business German, Business
Spanish

Audio and Video Language Programs
Just Listen 'n Learn Spanish, French,
German, Italian, Greek, and Arabic
Just Listen 'n Learn...Spanish,
French, German PLUS
Conversational...Spanish, French, German,
Italian, Russian, Greek, Japanese, Thai,
Portuguese in 7 Days
Practice & Improve Your...Spanish, French
Italian, and German
Practice & Improve Your...Spanish, French
Italian, and German PLUS
Improve Your...Spanish, French, Italian, a
German: The P&I Method
VideoPassport French
VideoPassport Spanish
How to Pronounce...Spanish, French,
German, Italian, Russian, Japanese
Correctly

PASSPORT BOOKS
a division of *NTC Publishing Group*
Lincolnwood, Illinois USA